Cornerstones of Catholic Secondary Religious Education

Principles and Practice of the New Evangelization

First published in February 2008

David Barlow Publishing
Telephone 02 4351 8884 | Facsimile 02 4351 8885
PO Box 651, Terrigal, NSW 2260
dbpublishing.net.au
ABN 15 482 647 588

Copyright © Kath Engebretson, Marian de Souza, Richard Rymarz, Michael T. Buchanan

National Library of Australia
Cataloguing in Publication Data

Cornerstones of Catholic Secondary Religious Education:
Principles And Practice of the New Evangelization

ISBN 9781921333019 (pbk.).

1. Religious education - Study and teaching (Secondary).
2. Religious education of teenagers.
3. Catholic Church - Education (Secondary).
I. Engebretson, Kath, 1950- .

268.433

Book design and production by Thymen & Eric
bookbound.com.au

Typeset in Minion Pro, Formata and Frutiger

Printed in Australia by Ligare Pty Ltd
138 Bonds Road, Riverwood, NSW 2210

Cornerstones of Catholic Secondary Religious Education

Principles and Practice of the New Evangelization

Kath Engebretson
Marian de Souza
Richard Rymarz
Michael T. Buchanan

Introduction

This book is written for a wide audience of academics, undergraduate and postgraduate students and teachers. It seeks to bring together in one book the current theory and practical principles of religious education for the Catholic secondary school. In the western world, where new identities of Catholic education are being developed in the face of changing patterns of Church adherence and the pervading ideologies of the twenty-first century, this book is timely. Its essential argument is for the "new evangelization" of which Pope John Paul spoke so often. It both sets out an argument for this new evangelization and develops principles for its practice. New evangelization, John Paul II argued, was the direction of Catholic religious education for this time in the life of the Church.

> In the case of coming generations, the lay faithful must offer the very valuable contribution, more necessary than ever, of a **systematic work in catechesis**. All ought to be aware of the rights that each baptized person has to being instructed, educated and supported in the faith and the Christian life. (John Paul II. *Christifideles Laici*. Post Synodal Apostolic Exhortation. 30/12/88).

John Paul II added that this did not necessarily involve a new programme, but new ways of communicating the riches of Scripture and Tradition. The method is not one of an exclusivist, dogmatic apologetics, but a careful, although passionate and faithful hermeneutic, in which the Catholic Tradition is explained, explored, critiqued and contemplated in light of culture.

The first two sections of this book, therefore, propose the theory and method of the new evangelization for Catholic secondary schools, while the third section covers some of the basic theological topics that religious educators in Catholic schools need to know. These are introductory only and the student or teacher is encouraged to continually deepen their understanding of Catholic theology, exegesis, history, sacramental and moral life through rigorous and continual study.

We, the authors, offer this book in the conviction that it will contribute substantially to the enterprise of the new evangelization in Catholic secondary schools.

Kath Engebretson, Marian de Souza, Richard Rymarz, Michael T. Buchanan.

Table of Contents

Section 3: Foundations of Content for Catholic Religious Educators

CHAPTER 1

Approaches to Catholic Religious Education in Australia: a Brief History

Michael T. Buchanan

Introduction

Throughout the 19th and 20th centuries, approaches to religious education in Catholic schools in Australia have tended to emphasise catechesis. Meaning literally "an echoing of faith", this term refers to helping a person to grow in faith within the tradition of the Catholic Church. The Church is made up of a community of Christian believers and it is within the Christian community that catechesis belongs.

Given this definition of catechesis, can you see any issues that might arise if it is assumed that the Catholic school is a place for catechesis?

Four broad approaches to religious education emphasising catechesis have spanned the last two centuries, and they are commonly referred to as: the Doctrinal Approach (from the establishment of Catholic school until the 1960s); the Kerygmatic Approach (throughout the 1960s); the Life-centred Approach (1970s through to the turn of the 21st century); and Shared Christian Praxis (from the 1980s onwards). These approaches to religious education can be classified as *catechetical* because each approach within the context of Catholic education has been concerned with the sharing of faith and the development of Christian faith. Catechetical approaches to religious education take place within a community of believers who are committed to living out the Catholic Christian heritage (Ryan, 1997). Traditionally, Catholic schools in Australia have been perceived as part of the parish and thus an integral part of the Catholic faith community.

During the second half of the twentieth century and beyond, Australian Catholic schools have also been influenced by educational approaches to religious education that focus on the subject's integrity as an academic discipline. To this end, curriculum development in religious education has been influenced by phenomenological and typological approaches. These approaches have influenced what is referred to in Australian Catholic schools as an educational approach to religious education. With specific reference to Buchanan (2006, 2005, 2003) these approaches to religious education are explored in this chapter. As you work through the chapter you are invited to consider the historical context in which each arose, and to critique their relevance for the contemporary Catholic secondary school.

The doctrinal approach

The doctrinal approach to religious education had an emphasis on learning church doctrine and the vehicle for such learning was a *catechism*. A catechism is a compendium of Catholic belief in book form, and catechisms were originally designed by bishops to assist priests with the instruction of adults who required further understanding of Church teachings. With the introduction of compulsory schooling during the eighteenth century, catechisms were used in schools to instruct children in the Catholic faith.

In Australia as early as 1804, attempts were made in Sydney Cove, New South Wales, to establish a Catholic school and provide religious instruction based on a catechism. However it was not until 1820, with the arrival of Father John Therry in Sydney, that permanent Catholic schools began to be established. Religious education taught from a catechism was a daily event in the school day.

Prior to the mid 1960s and dating back to the establishment of Catholic schooling in Australia, religious education focussed on the rote-learning method of the catechism. It was the method favoured by the Magisterium, that is the leadership body of the Church including the Pope and bishops, and many bishops throughout the various dioceses authorised various versions of catechisms to assist children in learning the doctrines of the Church (Buchanan, 2005). Eventually plans to introduce an Australian version gained momentum. On the 1885 agenda of the First Plenary Council of Australasian Bishops was the issue of producing an Australian Catholic Catechism. The Council directed that all dioceses adopt a catechism based on a style similar to the Irish *Maynooth Catechism*.

A local catechism was produced in Australia and it was commonly referred to as the *Red Catechism* or the *Penny Catechism*. The catechism was considered an authority on Church teachings and it contained 236 teachings of the Church, presented in a series of short questions and answers. The catechism contained everything that was considered necessary to know about the Catholic faith. Below are some questions and answers from the *Catechism* (4th Plenary Council, 1937, p. 15-16).

Chapter 4 – THE INCARNATION AND REDEMPTION

37. What name was given to God the Son when He became man?
God the Son, when He became man, was called Jesus Christ.

38. Is Jesus true God and true man?
Yes: Jesus is true God and true man.

39. Why is Jesus Christ truly God?
Jesus Christ is truly God because He is the Second Person of the Blessed Trinity, and therefore has one and the same nature with God the Father and God the Holy Ghost.

40. Why is Jesus Christ truly man?
Jesus Christ is truly man because, while truly God He has also a human nature, that is a body and a soul like ours.

41. How many persons are there in Jesus Christ?
There is only one person in Jesus Christ, and that person is the Second Divine Person of the Blessed Trinity.

42. Are there two natures in Jesus Christ?
Yes: there are two natures in Jesus Christ, a divine nature and a human nature.

Ultimately this doctrinal approach came under criticism. It emphasised the memorising of set answers to set questions, and it was questionable whether the process of memorising was an effective way of learning about the Catholic faith, since it was possible to memorise and repeat the questions and answers without any real understanding of their content. It was also debatable whether the moral and religious growth of a person could be measured by learning the contents of the catechism. Concern that it was out of step with new understandings relating to stages of faith development gained much attention. The catechism aimed to produce an adult level of faith, which could not possibly be fully appreciated by children (Lovat, 1989; Ryan, 1997). In the twentieth century, the dilemmas of the modern world challenged the way many Catholics would come to terms with God, Church authority, religion and their place in the world. World wars, economic depression and the rise of Communism were some of the factors that challenged the Church's authority and credibility. The dogmatic, authoritarian, pedagogical approach associated with teaching religious education through the catechism began to lose credibility (Jungmann, 1957; Lovat, 1989; Ryan, 1997). Consideration of new methods of religious education began to gain much attention in many countries, including Australia.

Explain the following terms: Catechism, Catechesis, Magisterium, Penny Catechism and Doctrine.

Outline some of the criticisms of the doctrinal approach.

Kerygmatic approach

The kerygmatic approach was strongly focussed on the salvific message of Christianity. Its orientation was towards encouraging students to encounter Jesus as a personal friend and saviour. The "Kerygma" is the Greek word for proclaiming the message (Engebretson, Rymarz & Fleming, 2002). By the 1930s and 1940s some European theologians interested in the liturgy of the Early Christian Church began to explore a kerygmatic approach to catechesis. A German born Austrian Jesuit and theologian named Joseph Jungmann was concerned that too much emphasis had been invested in an intellectual understanding of the Catholic faith (Jungmann, 1957). Jungmann (1957) argued that memorising the catechism was not the most effective pedagogical method for catechesis for young children. He argued that sacramental and liturgical catechesis was more effective in the religious formation of the child than the catechism. Jungmann saw the salvific message contained within the Scriptures as a key to evoking similar experiences of glory and joy commonly associated with the early Christians. The kerygmatic approach challenged the Catholic Church and its religious educators to bring the joyful salvific message into the classroom.

A pupil of Jungmann's and a fellow Jesuit, Johannes Hofinger (1966) believed that Jungmann's kerygmatic approach to catechesis could be developed effectively for children. The kerygmatic approach acknowledged that doctrine must be known but the Kerygma must be proclaimed. Hofinger (1966) argued that catechesis needed to be systematic and that children needed to come to a personal understanding of the joyful message of salvation. Scripture would feature significantly in this spiritual process, and once the child had been inculcated in this process they would be better prepared to learn Church doctrine as presented in the catechism. Hofinger was instrumental in bringing the kerygmatic approach to catechesis to the consciousness of religious educators in Australia. The Australian bishops saw potential in the kerygmatic approach and in 1962 appointed Father John Kelly and a team of catechists to produce a text series titled, *My Way to God*.

The *My Way to God* series was far more interactive for students than the *Penny Catechism*. The series contained colourful pictures, activities, songs, prayers and stories to enable children to come to know Jesus in a personal way (Buchanan, 2006). The Australian Catholic Bishops authorised the *My Way To God* series to be used in all Catholic parishes and schools throughout Australia (Ryan, 1997).

The extract below is from *My Way to God, Book One* (1964, pp. 2-3).

God's care for me

God watches over and cares for
All things
He has made.

He made them all for love of me.
God's special home is in heaven,
But God is really everywhere.

We cannot see God,
But everywhere we go He is there.

Thank you, God, for Your
Loving care of me.

SOMETHING TO DO

1. Draw a gift for which you want to thank God.
2. Draw yourself doing something to please God.

MY OWN PRAYER

Say a prayer thanking God for five things He has given you – one for each finger on your hand.

The kerygmatic approach dates back before the Second Vatican Council (1962-1965) and was concerned with proclaiming the gospel message of salvation. Through this approach God's message of salvation was to be found in a personal way by each Christian and not just in a conceptual way. Such an experience of salvation was to be experienced as joyful and liberating and worthy of celebration. The schema for religious education emanating from the kerygmatic approach was closely identified with catechesis, and assumed that students belonged to families that were active members of the Catholic faith community.

There were educational as well as theological reasons, in the lead up to the Second Vatican Council, which contributed to the short existence of the kerygmatic approach. Teachers in Australia were generally not adequately prepared for the new content and pedagogical focus associated with the kerygmatic approach. They had insufficient preparation in the areas of Scripture and Church history. The kerygmatic approach disengaged many parents and grandparents from their ability to reinforce religious learning. They had come to know their faith through the doctrinal approach and the kerygmatic approach was foreign to their understanding of religious education (Ryan, 1997). Another contributing factor stemmed from a change in Church thinking emanating from the Second Vatican Council. The *Dogmatic Constitution on Divine Revelation* commonly known as *Dei Verbum* challenged traditional understandings about divine revelation. Prior to the Second Vatican Council, Scripture and Church tradition were considered as sources of revelation and, in light of this understanding, it was the teacher's role to hand on the truths of the faith. *Dei Verbum* emphasised that Scripture and Church tradition were not sources of revelation, but rather witnesses to it. The Constitution stressed that God was the only source of divine revelation and that revelation was an ongoing process initiated by God (Abbott, 1966). Ultimately, criticisms of the kerygmatic approach centred on its tendency to repetition, and on the fact that, like the doctrinal approach, it was removed from the life experience of the child.

Explain the following terms: Dei Verbum, Kerygma, Salvation, Salvific message and Revelation.

Describe the Kerygmatic approach.

Outline some of the criticisms of the Kerygmatic approach.

Life-centred approach

The life-centred approach, also referred to as the life-experience approach, gained momentum from the Second Vatican Council, which supported the view that God was not only revealed in past events but also through the present events of ordinary life. The sacred and secular world needed to be understood as integral, rather that separate, in order to understand this enlightened view of revelation. With this perspective at the fore of current thinking, catechesis was seen as much broader than proclaiming the Church's salvation story.

The influence of *Dei Verbum* challenged catechetical theorists to consider new ways of teaching religious education. In the early 1970s, religious educators in Australia were strongly influenced by the Indian Jesuit and theologian Amalorpavadass. He visited Australia in 1973, and his understanding of revelation was a major influence in developing a life-centered pedagogical approach to religious education. He argued that,

> Revelation calls for faith. Faith is a personal and living encounter with the living God, a total acceptance of the revealing and giving person by a loving surrender of one's life according to His word. All this should result in the

sealing of a covenant and the realization of a fellowship in love. Therefore our inter-personal relationship is one of dialogue, covenant and fellowship. Therefore man's response or reaction to God's revelation will be essentially attention and responsibility, expectation and listening, openness and acceptance, and reciprocal self-gift in a total surrender and dedication of oneself. This is what we call faith (Amalorpavadass, 1973, p. 19)

The life-centered approach emphasised the sharing of life experiences between students and teacher, reflection on this life experience, and the linking of this reflection with growth in knowledge and affective understanding of faith content (Engebretson, 2002). This approach to religious education was to become influential in Australian Catholic schools. For example, it was embedded in the Archdiocese of Melbourne since the early 1970s. The 1973, 1984 and 1995 *Guidelines for Religious Education for Students in the Archdiocese of Melbourne, (Guidelines)* have emphasised a pedagogical methodology, which embodied this approach. The *Guidelines* systematised an interactive process consisting of four movements in the act of catechesis. This schema became known by religious educators as the "four-point plan", and consisted of the following teaching and learning process:

- Experience shared (we share our experiences)
- Reflection deepened (we reflect together)
- Faith expressed (we come to know our Catholic faith)
- Insights reinforced (we gain further insights and respond) (Guidelines 1995).

The life-centered approach to catechesis presumed that students were ready and willing to be incorporated into the life of the Church. As such, its starting point was theological and catechetical. The underlying assumption implied that students had an understanding of Church teaching and the person of Christ. The Catholic Education Office of Melbourne produced a series of student resources for use in primary and secondary schools. *Lets Go Together* was produced for use in Catholic primary schools and *Come Alive* was used widely in Catholic secondary schools. The following extract from *Come Alive* (Thomas, 1970, p. 9-10) demonstrates an implied connection to the Catholic faith tradition by the students. Its starting point is Church doctrine followed by a reflection on life-experience in the form of a poem or prayer in relation to that doctrine.

A man may be turned away from good
And driven to do wrong
By his social environment
For the social environment
can be contaminated
by human pride and selfishness.
These are a deeper cause
Of disturbance in the social order
Than economic or political. *Vat II*

LORD, LET US SEE OURSELVES AS WE ARE
GIVE US THE COURAGE TO FACE IN OURSELVES

the selfishness which we hug ourselves in
an embrace so tight that we find it a real
"self denial" to be genuinely interested in others for
their own sakes

the tendency to moodiness that throws a blight
on even our best dedication and hard work

the ambition that wants not so much to get a good work
done well but rather to ensure that it is me
who does it and gets it praised above others for it

the lust for power that wants only partly to work
with others to achieve our goals and partly wants
to work over them, control them and their choices
so that my own ego is boosted and my own submerged
conceit fostered by my enjoyment of power over the
lives and work of other human persons

Give us the courage to recognise and
admit that we are not everything
and that we need God, as God in our lives.

List the types of life experiences students might reflect on as a result of reading this excerpt from *Come Alive*.

What might this excerpt reveal about God to students who read it?

What affect might this excerpt from *Come Alive* have on students who were not familiar with the Catholic faith tradition?

From the 1960s or before, immigration and other sociological factors had diversified the population in Catholic schools, to the extent that there was no longer a homogeneous expression of the Catholic faith. For many people in Australia, the Church was no longer an unquestioned authority. Increasingly students and even their families were not involved in the life of the Church (Ryan, 1997). Many students in Catholic schools were disconnected from faith and parish life, and this made it very difficult to connect their life experiences to religious content in the classroom. The lack of understanding of Church teaching and a personal relationship with Christ made it challenging for students and teachers to always make the link between life experience and faith. Ultimately the life experience approach failed for a number of reasons, some of these being a lack of theological and religious education pedagogy on the part of many teachers, the tendency for religious education lessons to become nothing more than discussions about life, and the growing boredom of students with what was often a very limited intellectual exercise.

Outline some of criticisms of the life-centred approach.

Shared Christian praxis approach

The American religious educator, Thomas Groome has been very influential in Australia. He developed an approach to religious education entitled *Shared Christian Praxis*. Groome (1991) defined shared Christian praxis as,

> ...a participative and dialogical pedagogy in which people reflect critically on their own historical agency in time and place and on their socio-cultural reality, have access together to Christian story/vision, and personally appropriate in community with the creative intent of reviewed praxis in Christian faith towards God's reign for all creation (p.135).

In contrast with the life-centered approach which was based on the theological and catechetical rationale of Amalorpavadass (1971), Shared Christian Praxis was based on critical educational theories (Engebretson, 1999) and was a response to the growing quest for human freedom. This quest was perceived as one of the major contemporary challenges facing the Christian tradition. The response within educational circles was to employ strategies where skills in critical self-reflection could be developed. The goal of religious education was to "create critical participants in the ongoing life of the Christian community" (Lovat, 2002, p. 24-25).

Groome (1980) recommended a five -step religious education program known as the Shared Praxis Model. The five steps were identified as:

- Naming the Present Action: (to reflect on present events and make distinctions between what was really happening and what should be happening)
- The Participants' Stories and Visions: (the beginning of critical reflection on the factors that led to the present situation. It was concerned with the "why" questions, for example: Why do we do as we do?)
- The Christian Community Story and Vision: (aspects of the Christian story were remembered and told. Participants were provided with an opportunity to see their own experience in light of the Christian vision)
- Dialogue between the Inspirational Story and Participants: (in light of remembering the Christian story the participant's experience was examined in light of what *should be* as well as what actually *is*)
- A Decision for Future Action: (Out of an understanding of the way it was and the way it should have been can emerge a decision to close the gap between the lived experience and the Christian vision. At this point praxis was considered to have developed) (Lovat 2002; Engebretson et al, 2002; Ryan 1997).

In relation to general academic standards, Shared Christian Praxis was as academically rigorous and challenging as any other approach (Groome, 1991) in that it emphasised critical self-reflection by initiating groups and individuals to think in a praxis model rather than to learn theories. This could be achieved by providing a model that encouraged participants to reflect on their own feelings and actions, rather than what they should think. The aim of the shared praxis approach was to engage the whole person. It was more than an exercise in learning religious knowledge (Groome, 1991).

Shared Christian Praxis has been very influential in Australia since the late 1980s. The Diocese of Parramatta in New South Wales has used this model in its religious education curriculum, and through particular practitioners it has had similar influence in other dioceses in Victoria, Tasmania, South Australia and the Northern Territory. While Groome did not specifically associate catechesis with his Shared Praxis model, Lovat (2002) has argued that Shared Praxis did take on some of the inaccurate assumptions of catechesis when applied to the classroom. He questioned its ability to meet the requirements and responsibilities of the religious education program offered in Catholic schools, which increasingly had multi-faith populations. Groome (1991) argued that it was inappropriate to separate "education" from "faith formation" in a religious education program. However Rossiter (1988) argued that the separation was necessary in light of the diverse populations in Catholic schools where not all students are willing to participate at a personal faith level. These critiques pointed to the need for a more educational and less overtly catechetical approach to religious education for Australian Catholic schools.

Distinguish between the life-centre approach and shared Christian praxis. What do they have in common and how are they different?

What advantages and disadvantages do you see in this approach for the contemporary Catholic school?

The educational approach to religious education

Introduction

After the Second Vatican Council (1962-1965) the work of Rummery (1975) presented a systematic view of the educational dimensions of religious education. Rummery was concerned with the degree of confusion associated with equating catechesis with religious education. In situations where classroom religious education incorporated many students who were non-believers in the Catholic faith, the effectiveness of approaches emphasising catechesis was seriously questioned (Rossiter, 1988). In some Catholic schooling systems in Australia, an emphasis on the educational dimension of religious education began to influence classroom religious education. There are many approaches to religious education that focus on the educational dimension (Grimmit, 2000). Two approaches which have been significant are Phenomenology and Typology.

Discuss the similarities and differences in teaching religious education in faith based schools to that of non-religious schools.

The phenomenological approach

Smart (1968, 1974, 1978, 1974) was the author of the phenomenological approach as it applied to the study of religion. This approach focussed on the content of what should be taught. It was concerned with the logic of religious education and with the consequences of that logic in a secular or religiously neutral society (Smart, 1968). The approach was founded on the theory that religion can be studied from the "outside". That is, one does not have to belong to the religious tradition or any religious tradition in order to learn about religion. A student taught by this method could gain an educational understanding of religious beliefs and in so doing become literate in the language of religion without being required to accept or approve of those beliefs.

The phenomenological approach to religious education originated in England. The 1944 Education Act in the United Kingdom had mandated the daily act of religious worship and instruction in all schools. Until the 1960s the teaching of religion in British schools was perceived as a confession of Christian faith or an application of Christian faith in the classroom (Hull, 1984). From the 1960s the ethnic, cultural and religious diversity of the British population challenged the effectiveness of compulsory religious education taught from a Christian perspective. A wave of agreed syllabi in religious education appeared in the late 1960s, all with a central focus on Christianity. It was not until 1975 that there was a major breakthrough in teaching religious education from a phenomenological perspective. The *Birmingham Agreed Syllabus* and accompanying *Handbook* were published in that year and were based on Smart's phenomenological approach (Smart, 1968). The *Birmingham Agreed Syllabus* abandoned any intention to foster the faith of any particular religion. It focussed on the critical understanding of religion and it was taught and understood in the context of secular ideologies. Contrasting and comparing various religious traditions and non-religious alternatives such as humanism and communism, was intended to shape a pupil's understanding of religion. The intention of the *Birmingham Agreed Syllabus* was that religious studies be impartial. The teacher was required to teach each religion represented in his or her classroom or school with the same spirit of thoughtful, courteous appreciation and inquiry (Hull, 1984).

The legislation establishing and promoting education in Australia ensured that it remain a secular institution. However, concern about the value of teaching religious education in government schools gained momentum during the 1970s. During the 1970s and 1980s several state government inquiries in Australia were set up to review state education. The study of religion in Australian schools, it was argued, would help to promote tolerance in a population made up of people from diverse religious and cultural backgrounds. The government inquiries resulted in the following reports being tabled in various state parliaments: The Steinle Report (1973) of South Australia, the Nott Report (1977) of Western Australia, the Russell Report (1974) of Victoria, and the Rawlinson Report (1980) of NSW. By the 1980s each of the above mentioned states had commenced the process of implementing the study of religion in state schools. Opportunities for Australia's citizens to develop religious literacy began to be promoted through the state education systems. The philosophy behind most of the reports suggested that there was value in learning about religion in general and about the diverse religions present in Australian society (Lovat, 2002). The development of studies in religion in state schools had to take into consideration the inter-faith and secular composition of the student population. An approach to teaching and learning religion was employed that would respond to the diversity of inter-faith and secular populations present in schools. The phenomenological approach that was favoured in Britain and that had shaped the *Birmingham Agreed Syllabus* had a significant influence on school curricula in religious education in Australia.

The phenomenological approach to religious education had intentions that could clearly be distinguished from the catechetical theory underpinning earlier teaching and learning in religious education in Australian. The phenomenological approach stood clearly in contrast, as its intention was to study religion objectively as a means of gaining insights about a religion from an outsider's perspective. It did not require that a student should have a personal commitment to a particular creed in order to have a deep understanding and appreciation of religion. Acceptance or approval of religious beliefs was not a requirement for understanding such beliefs. Smart (1979) identified a structure for the study of a religion. His work indicated that, from a phenomenological perspective, a religion could be studied through the examination of phenomena such as rites of passage, myths, holy times, holy places, symbols, pilgrimages, scriptures, temples and priests. Studying religion from a phenomenological perspective would make it possible for students to gain insights into the world of religion. In an attempt to fulfil this possibility in the secondary school context, Habel and Moore (1982), applied, tried, tested and adapted Smart's phenomenological theory. Their adaptation has become known as the typological approach.

> What advantages do you see in this more objective approach to the teaching of religion?

The typological approach

Smart (1968) was not concerned with "how" religion should be taught in schools. He was concerned with decisions about "what" should be taught. Habel and Moore (1982), two Australian academics, focused on the "how" question. They developed a theory that identified how Smart's phenomenological approach could be implemented in the religion classroom. Their theory outlined eight "types" or components shared by religious traditions which students could study in order to gain an insight into understanding a particular religion. The study of certain types or components originally identified by Habel and Moore (1982) were: beliefs, texts, stories, ethics, ritual, symbols, social structure and experience. Their work enabled teachers and curriculum writers to apply Smart's phenomenological theory in a practical way in the classroom situation (Ryan, 1997).

The typological approach influenced the construction of public syllabi in religious education throughout various states in Australia (Lovat, 2001). During the 1970s and 1980s state governments responded to the pressure to introduce state accredited courses in religion in schools. State accredited courses in religion were required not to presume a confessional commitment from the students or teacher and to uphold that no one religion would be held in favour over another (Engebretson, 1991). In Australia, the theories of Smart, and Habel and Moore strongly influenced the design of the schema for state accredited courses in religion. These courses relied heavily upon the phenomenological approach and the typological approach developed by Habel and Moore (Ryan, 1997). Phenomenology and typology have not only shaped the state accredited courses in religion, but they have also formed the basis of the learning schema of curricula in religious education impacting on several Catholic schooling systems throughout Australia.

Explain the following terms: phenomenology and typology.

An educational approach to religious education in Australian Catholic schools

Dioceses throughout Australia have also been involved in the development of new curricula in religious education, which have focused more than before on the educational dimension of classroom religious education. A distinguishing feature of the educational approach is that it represents a middle ground between two orientations in religious education theory, these being formation in the Catholic faith tradition and the acquisition of knowledge *about* this and other religious traditions. These orientations are not necessarily in opposition to each other. It is recognised that attention to the educational dimension has the potential to act as a vehicle for spiritual and personal faith formation. Buchanan (2007) drew upon the work of Engebretson, Fleming and Rymarz (2002), Elliot and Rossiter (1982) and Rossiter (1981) to suggest that this educational approach can be viewed as a channel to spiritual development and personal and communal faith, through attention to knowledge, understanding and critical inquiry. The approach is conceptualized in figure 1 as representing a middle ground between catechetical and educational orientations.

Why might the educational approach be more relevant to contemporary Catholic secondary schools than more catechetically oriented approaches?

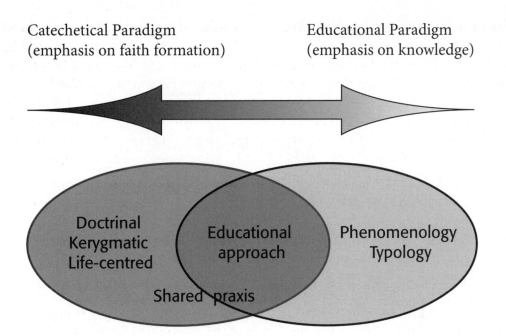

Figure 1: Approaches that informed the orientation of religious education with Catholic schools in the Archdiocese of Melbourne.

Conclusion

Throughout the history of Catholic education in Australia, various approaches to religious education have supported the catechetical mission of the Church. The educational approach to religious education is that which now informs the development of religious education curriculum in most Australian Catholic secondary schools. Religious education curricula in many Catholic schooling systems have incorporated common educational language and goals. Such an inclusion has not diminished the catechetical nature of Catholic schools and the role of religious education. The educational demands made on students and teachers regarding the acquisition of knowledge in religious education are intended to support the catechetical mission of the Church. The distinctive emphasis on the cognitive dimension of learning is integral to the learning process if students are to know the content of the Catholic teaching on faith and morals. A more accountable cognitive based educational approach to learning in religious education remains consistent with previous approaches, which have emphasised a "call to faith" model of catechesis in the context of Catholic education. In the secular culture of Australia, a phenomenon that is discussed in the following chapter, a more objective, cognitively rich approach to religious education is called for.

References and Further Reading

Abbott, W. M. (Ed) (1966). *The Documents of Vatican II.* London: Geoffrey Chapman.

Amalorpavadass, D.S. (1973). *Theology of Catechesis.* Bangalore: National Biblical Catechetical and Liturgical Centre.

Australian Catholic Bishops. (1964). *My Way to God.* Australia: Dwyer.

Buchanan, M. T. (2003). Survey of current writing on trends in religious education. *Journal of Religious Education, 51* (4), 22-30.

Buchanan, M. T. (2005). Pedagogical drift: The evolution of new approaches and paradigms in religious education. *Religious Education, 100* (1), 20-37.

Buchanan, M. T. (2006). A brief history of approaches to RE in Catholic schools. In R. Rymarz, (Ed.). *Leadership in Religious Education* (pp. 11-29). Australia: St Paul's Publications.

Buchanan, M. T. (2007). Management of Curriculum Change: An analysis of religious education coordinators' perspectives on the management of a particular curriculum change in Catholic secondary schools in the Archdiocese of Melbourne. Unpublished doctoral dissertation, Australian Catholic University, Australia.

Catholic Education Office. (1973). *Guidelines for religious education for students in the archdiocese of Melbourne.* Melbourne: Catholic Education Office.

Catholic Education Office. (1984). *Guidelines for religious education for students in the archdiocese of Melbourne.* Melbourne: Catholic Education Office.

Catholic Education Office. (1995). *Guidelines for religious education for students in the archdiocese of Melbourne.* Melbourne: Catholic Education Office.

Thomas, M. (Ed.). (1970). *Come Alive 6.* Australia: Dwyer.

Engebretson, K. (1991). The approach to religious education in the Victorian Certificate of Education. *Journal of Religious Education 39* (2), 9-11.

Engebretson, K. (2002). Writing church-sponsored religious education textbooks. *British Journal of Religious Education 25* (1), 33-45.

Engebretson, K., Fleming, J., Rymarz, R., (2002). *Thriving as an RE Teacher: A handbook for secondary religious educators.* Australia: Social Science Press.

Elliot, R. & Rossiter, G. (Ed.). (1982). *Towards critical dialogue in religious education: A collection of conference papers and case studies which raise issues for religious education in Australian schools.* Australia: Australian Association for Religious Education.

Groome, T. (1980). *Christian religious education: Sharing our story and vision.* New York: Harper & Row.

Grimmitt, M. H. (2000). *Pedagogies of religious education: Case studies in the research and development of good pedagogic practice in RE.* Great Wakening: McCrimmons.

Habel, N. & Moore, B. (1982). *When religion goes to school: Typology of religion for the classroom.* Adelaide, Australia: South Australian College of Advanced Education.

Hofinger, J. (1966). *The art of teaching Christian doctrine.* London: Sands & Co.

Jungman, J. A. (1957). *Handing on the faith.* Germany: Herder.

Hull, J. M. (1984). *Studies in religion and education.* London: Falmer Press.

Lovat, T. (1989). *What is this thing called religious education?* NSW, Australia: Social Science Press.

Lovat, T. (2002). *What is this thing called R. E. A decade On?* (2nd Ed.). Australia: Social Science Press.

Lovat, T. (2001). The ideological challenge of the public syllabus in religious studies. In M. Ryan (Ed.). *Echo and Silence: Contemporary Issues for Australian Religious Education* (pp. 1-13). NSW: Social Science Press.

4th Plenary Council. (1937). *Catechism.* Melbourne: Australian Catholic Truth Society.

New South Wales Government. (1980). *Religion in education in NSW government schools: The Rawlinson report.* Sydney: Govt. Printer.

Rossiter, G. (1981). *Religious education in Australian schools.* Australia: Curriculum development centre Australia.

Rossiter, G. (1988). Perspectives on change in Catholic religious education since the Second Vatican council, *Religious Education 83* (2), 264-276.

Rummery, R. M. (1975). *Catechesis and Religious Education in a Pluralist Society*. Sydney: E. J. Dwyer.

Ryan, M. (1997). *Foundations of religious education in Catholic schools; an Australian perspective*. NSW, Australia: Social Science Press.

Smart, N. (1968). *Secular education and the logic of religion*. London: Faber & Faber.

Smart, N. (1974). *The science of religion and the sociology of knowledge*. New Jersey: Princeton University.

Smart, N. (1978). *The phenomenon of religion*. London: McMillan.

Smart, N. (1979). *The phenomenon of Christianity*. London: William Collins Sons & Co Ltd.

South Australian Government. (1973). *Religious education in state schools: The Steinle report*. Adelaide: Department of Education.

Victorian Government. (1974). *Report on the committee on religious education: The Russell report*. Melbourne: Department of Education.

Western Australian Government. (1977). *Religious education in the government schools of Western Australia: The Nott report*. Perth: Department of Education.

CHAPTER 2

Some Perspectives on Contemporary Culture, Religion and Young People

Richard Rymarz

Which of the statements below do you think best captures the relationship between young people and religion today?

Students today:
* have no faith
* are searching for answers
* have a strong spirituality
* are religious consumers

The rise of individualism and the death of the metanarrative

A detailed analysis of contemporary culture in countries like Australia is a complex task and beyond the scope of this chapter. Some general trends, however, do emerge. These are often more easily distinguished if we contrast society today with that of fifty or so years ago. One of the most frequently commented upon aspects of western society is the emphasis placed on individual autonomy. Individuals today are much more likely to respond to issues on the basis of their own personal interests and preferences. This point is linked with the demise of many strong cohesive social institutions which in the past have influenced behaviour and interests. There are many examples today of institutions who no longer have the authority to make collective decisions for members of that group. The mainstream Churches, groups like the Catholic, Uniting and Anglican communities, for example, no longer speak with one voice on a variety of issues. Just because someone describes themselves as a Catholic or a Labor Party supporter does not mean that they have certain views or behaviours. Bauman (2000) has argued that a rise in personalism is often as a characteristic of the post modern trend in society. This is typified by many factors but one of the most important is the loss of the metanarrative in society – where individuals are no longer bound together by their acceptance of general principles.

Read the following extract.

When God asked Cain where Abel was, Cain replied, angrily, with another question: 'Am l my brother's keeper?' ...from that angry Cain's question all immorality began. Of course I am my brother's keeper; and I am and remain a moral person as long as I do not ask for a special reason to be one...The moment I question that dependence and demand – like Cain did – to be given reasons why I should care, I renounce my responsibility and am no more a moral self. My brother's dependence is what makes me an ethical being. Dependence and ethics stand together and together they fall. (Bauman, 2000, p. 1)

- What happens to a society when people lose the general ethic to care for each other?
- Do you agree that dependence and ethics stand together?
- Do you think we, as a society today, are losing shared values?

The privatisation of religion

In a culture where no compelling metanarrative exists a number of trends begin to emerge. The place of religion in society takes on a new aspect. While some may see society as becoming more and more secular, this new secularity needs some delineation. In the personal sphere individuals are free to believe and practice what they like. Tolerance becomes one of the hallmarks of the culture. Religious views are not contested as long as they remain in the private sphere. Belief in God, for example, in a variety of surveys over a period of time in many western developed nations, has been quite resilient and shows no signs of disappearing. In the public sphere, however, the influence and power of religious groups in society has been diminished. Religious groups, in some ways, have lost their privileged place in society and are now one group among many. The attitude of many to religion is not one of classical Enlightenment hostility but is more often characterised by indifference or a benign vicariousness. To put it another way the attitude is not "religions will die out once people are more educated" but is more like "it is fine to have religious groups around, provided they know their place, but it just does not interest me".

The trend toward greater individuality tends to follow an age gradient. The younger the person the more likely they are to be influenced by the personalist trend in the wider culture. Many teenagers today express a type of religious affiliation that makes their beliefs and behaviours indistinguishable from general cultural norms (Smith and Denton, 2005). This seems to be a significant factor for those teenagers affiliated with some of the more established religious groups, such as Catholics, and less so for newer more evangelical groups.

Passive acceptance of the birth tradition

According to Smith and Denton, whose research was carried out in the United States, most teenagers in economically developed nations have *extraordinarily conventional* religious beliefs and are not alienated from involvement. The vast majority of them are not seekers but are happy to accept the religion in which they have been raised. This, however, for most teenagers should not be read as active involvement, rather a more passive acceptance of the social circumstances in which they find themselves. One illustration of this was the ability of teens to articulate their religious beliefs and values. Most teenagers in countries like Australia have a difficult time explaining what they believe. The reasons for this are varied, but one key factor seems to be a disparity between the religious knowledge of teenagers and what some have termed *other* knowledge. Whereas teenagers are developing a sophisticated language to describe other specialized areas, when it comes to talking about their religious beliefs their articulation is stunted and does not progress past a certain rudimentary level. This can be seen as a failure by many religious groups to educate, nurture and mentor their young people. In contemporary culture the task of the religious community in providing this formation is more even critical because the wider culture, while not overly hostile to religious expression pushes young people away from strong commitment into a nominally religious position.

It is true that after many years at Catholic schools, a large number of students are not able to explain key Catholic beliefs. What factors may contribute to this?

Moralistic therapeutic deism

For many teenagers faith tends to degenerate into *Moralistic Therapeutic Deism (MTD)* a type of default position to which most without strong counter views can easily subscribe. This belief is, in essence, a weak moral system which sees behaviour as being directed to benefit the individual. In this sense it is therapeutic and in accord with general cultural norms, which see the development of the individual and not the general community as a desired goal. MTD is highly personal and naturalistic. God is relegated to a kind of impersonal, distant force that is part of the universe but not in an involved or decisive way. A good analogy for God in this system is presented in the Star Wars movies where a distant, mysterious but controllable *force* inhabits the galaxy.

Religious faith and practice in the lives of teenagers in economically developed nations operate in a social and institutional environment that is highly competitive for time, attention and energy. Religious interests and values in their lives typically compete against those of school, homework, television and paid outside work. In such an environment religion is but one option, and for many young people, it struggles to have an impact on how they live their lives. This is not to say that religion has no influence or has been rejected. Rather it is not a strong or long lasting influence, and is not as important as other factors which appear more prominent in the lives of teenagers and their families. One illustration of this is the ways in which most young people in counties like Australia spend their time. This gives a good indication of which group or interest is winning the battle for the attention and resources of teenagers. Like teenagers in western industrial societies teens spend a large amount of time shopping, spending time with friends, using their computers or other similar activities. Most teenagers do not spend much time in activities that can be described as having a religious focus. For those teenagers who do not regard religion as a high priority, and this would include most teenagers in Catholic schools, their social networks reflect weak religious connections. They are unlikely to have many friends who exhibit strong religious beliefs and do not take part in many activities which could be described as having a religious foundation.

> What is meant by the statement that Australia is a secular country and how may this challenge Catholic religious educators?

Recent Australian research

Australian data, on Generation Y (13 to 29 yrs), gathered by Mason and his colleagues support, in many ways, the findings of Smith and Denton (Mason et al., 2006). There was a strong agreement about the communitarian nature of adolescent and young adult religious affiliation. They found over half the cohort of young people whom they interviewed did not identify with any religious denomination but most believed in God. Generation Y Christians had similar beliefs and practices to those of their parents generation. Approximately one-third of Generation Y are moving away from their Christian origins, but interest in esoteric *New Age* spiritualities by Generation Y has been overstated. The most important contributor to religious commitment is practicing and enthusiastic parents, and religiously observant youth tend to be the most socially committed. To find peace and happiness most Generation Y teenagers turn to friendship, music, work or study. Few turn to religious or spiritual resources, even those have some connection with religious groups.

Mason and his colleagues have developed a typology of Generation Y to describe the major groupings of spiritual and religious expression. Forty three percent have a spirituality linked to the Christian tradition, which is further described as high, medium and low. Thirty one percent can be described as humanists, which is seen as a world view which affirms human experience and reason rather than religious traditions or spiritual paths.

Seventeen percent were classified as eclectic who comprised a collage of themes from disparate sources and nine percent were traditional non-Christian and atheists.

One way of describing Generation Y is to see them as a *tough market*. They like to keep their options open and are unlikely to commit to something if they cannot see some tangible benefits arising. For those in the sample (Mason et al., 2006) who expressed some link with traditional religions a key question arose: *Why should I lead a life of faith when it separates me from most of my peers and I do not seem to be getting anything in return?* At the same time Generation Y will not totally disavow religious associations, as this seems to close down one of their options.

Active Catholic youth

Both the Smith and Denton, and the Mason, Singleton, Webber and Hughes studies investigated large representative samples of youth and young adults. There is also evidence for a developing communitarian expression of religious belief and practice among Australian youth at the middle secondary stage of schooling who can be identified as active or "core" Catholic (Rymarz and Graham, 2006). In this research following Fulton et al (2000), active Catholic was defined as having two of the following three criteria: a) regular Church attendance; b) regular Church attendance and involvement in the parish by parent(s); and c) being involved in something *extra,* as a result of faith commitment, such as being part of a prayer group.

For most active Catholic youth, their links with the Church can be typically described as familial (either strong or weak). It is not something that they themselves see as important but something which arises out of a commitment by their families. They are also not well networked with other active Catholic youth. Most of their friends are reflective of the wider community. Most active Catholic youth are unable to articulate well their religious views, especially those that distinguish them from other groups in the community. There is a strong echo here of the moralistic therapeutic deism discussed earlier. Active Catholic youth find it hard to have their questions answered and to identify suitable religious mentors that will assist them to make the transition to adult models of faith.

There was also clear evidence for a developing communitarian pattern among many active Catholic youth. Many students expressed the view that in the future their level of commitment and involvement will lessen. Some saw this as a result of decreased familial interaction corresponding with moving free of parental expectation and influence. In this way they were repeating the patterns of their older siblings. This was, again, not a disaffiliation but a movement to a more culturally acceptable position where they do not disavow their religious heritage but where it becomes much less important and requires very little of them as individuals.

Two models of religious identity

The communitarian model

From the preceding discussion two models of religious identity can be proposed. One common expression of religious identity is a communitarian pattern. One of the key features of a communitarian pattern is that it places the believer in low conflict with the wider culture. There is not much to distinguish the individual's beliefs or behaviour from most members of the community, certainly once other factors such as socioeconomic background and country of origin are taken into account. Some have described this low conflict idea as a good way of conceptualizing recent changes to Catholic culture, where many of markers of identity such as fasting, processions and a strict Lenten observance have disappeared. In communitarian models of religious identity, boundaries are low. One consequence of low boundaries is that members of the community have a difficult time articulating the core beliefs of the tradition. This is not seen as a high priority as the communitarian orientation is toward the wider culture, or, in other words, the ways you are like others, rather than what makes you special. Another way that this is illustrated is the prominence given to moral descriptors as identifiers of religious allegiance. If what distinguishes a religious person is adherence to say certain values, be they gospel values or otherwise, then it would be surprising if these were exclusive. It all depends, of course, how these values are defined but they are usually seen as strong human virtues such as tolerance and kindness. One would expect that a wide range of people in a community would aspire to respect and internalize values such as these.

Another feature of a communitarian pattern is the emphasis on inclusion. Some have described this as a *big tent* model of Church. There tend to be large numbers involved in communitarian models as the cost of inclusion tends to be minimised. This is a bargain where the believer has effectively managed to reduce the cost of religious affiliation without losing many of the benefits. Think of some of the benefits that accrue to a communitarian member of a religious group. They avoid, perhaps most importantly, an existential void by identifying, albeit loosely, with a historically significant group. They do not need to confront alone major questions about existence and their place in it, this can be done vicariously. There are a range of very practical benefits. They can still be part of a group that may have a strong familial connection, when the family gets together at Christmas, for instance, they can be part of this by visiting a church with other family members. If they want to they can marry in a church, bury their parents in a religious service, send their children to denominational schools and associate with a wide range of people who are very much like them. All of this can be gained for very little cost. You are not required to attend services, hold difficult or challenging beliefs, give up a substantial part of your income or take part in any ritual or process that may stigmatise you. In these circumstances it is not surprising that many young people choose not to formally disaffiliate from Church membership, at least for the time being, when it offers so much.

Communitarian patterns of religious identity are common in groups that have passed their peak in terms of growth and outreach. It is a characteristic of many Protestant groups, which after an initial burst of activity, move from being sects to churches, in the classical sociological sense, and then merge with other like-minded groups and then into the wider culture, waiting for another reformation to reinvigorate the group and provide a rationale for those wishing to join. Churches based on communitarian models tend to decline rapidly in a number of generations. The second generation is the one which displays most of the communitarian patterns mentioned above but it is their children who disaffiliate in large numbers as they find different ways to associate with others and the benefits of religious affiliation become more dispersed.

What factors in Australian society may have led to a wide-spread use of the communitarian model among Catholics?

A commitment model

An alternate way of conceiving of religious identity is to think in terms of a commitment model. This framework is identified by a number of factors. A commitment model often begins with a strong identification with the tradition, typified with a statement such as *being a Catholic is really important to me.* Another crucial descriptor is affective responses such as how much joy being part of the group brings. The affective component is very important in commitment models, it is not just being part of the group but that the believer really enjoys this. The importance of religious affiliation is then demonstrated in a number of ways such as extensive networking with other committed people, and being involved in a range of faith based activities. Committed people have built up a lot of social capital in their religious allegiance and if this suddenly ended they would feel a real sense of loss. By way of analogy, think of a person who was very committed to a local sporting club. Their children play at the club, but their involvement does not stop there. They may be a coach or look after the team on the weekend. They may have meetings with other committed parents and raise money to improve the club facilities. They may join a regional or national group furthering the goals of the sport. They may use the clubs facilities to hold parties on special family occasions. The club means a lot to them because of how involved they are. With enough people like this the club is likely to grow, although at the same time there will be some clashes between the committed and others who do share their passion.

A committed model of religious identity also places high value on ritualised practice. Doing things as part of the group is important. Repeating what those who have gone before have done is vital as these people are owed a debt of gratitude for passing on the faith. The connection with the past is something the committed believer is comfortable with, because it places them in what has been called the "chain of memory". Committed believers therefore tend to place great emphasis on education and they feel they have something of great value to pass on. This is certainly true of religious education.

Another feature of committed religious identity is its strong metaphysical dimension. Here is where the analogy with a highly committed sporting club secretary breaks down. The committed believer exemplifies the exchange with God. They see religion as a communication with the Divine. When they pray, for example, God listens and responds. When they go to Mass they are very much at home in the theological reality of Christ present amongst the congregation. God is alive in their lives and this influenced their behaviour. This is a significant boundary as much of contemporary culture does not recognize an active personal God, and is much more in tune with a deistic concept such as the one envisaged in MTD.

In terms of contemporary culture which template of religious involvement is under most threat? Can anything be done to revive this and is this necessary?

What are the implications of the material in this chapter for thinking about theory in Catholic secondary school religious education?

All of the contemporary cultural and religious phenomena discussed in this chapter need to be considered in developing theory and practice for religious education. The following chapter provides a number of perspectives on the nature and purpose of religious education in Catholic secondary schools that take these into account.

References and Further Reading

Bauman, Z. (2000). Am I my brother's keeper? *European Journal of Social Work*. 3(1), 5-11.

Fulton, J., Abela, A., Borowik, I., Dowling, T., Marler, P and Tomasi, L (2000). *Young Catholics at the new millennium; the religion and morality of young adults in western countries*. Dublin: University College Press.

Mason, M, Webber, R, Singleton, A & Hughes, P. (2006). *The Spirit of Generation Y*. Retrieved March 11, 2007, from http://dlibrary.acu.edu.au/research/ccls/spir/sppub/sppub.htm

Rymarz, R., & Graham, J. (2005). Going to church: Attitudes to church attendance amongst Australian core Catholic youth. *Journal of Beliefs and Values, 26*(1), pp 55–64.

Rymarz, R., & Graham, J. (2006). *Drifting from the mainstream: The religious identity of Australian Core Catholic Youth*. International Journal of Children's Spirituality. *11(3) 371-383*

Smith, C., & Denton, M. (2005). *Soul searching: The religious and spiritual lives of American teenagers*. New York: Oxford University Press.

Cornerstones of Catholic Secondary Religious Education

Some Perspectives on the Nature and Purpose of Religious Education in Catholic Secondary Schools

Marian de Souza

Introduction

The nature and purpose of religious education in Catholic secondary schools has, for many years, been the subject of much interest and discussion. Contributors to the field operate out of varied contexts and concerns which reflect different understandings of the nature and purpose of the subject. The contemporary Australian context has been influenced by the cultural, political and technological changes which have impacted on education. Equally, Australian religious educators have been affected by accelerated changes in educational theory and practices in religious education and by the growing pluralism in theologies in the Catholic Church (Welbourne, 1997). It is not surprising, therefore, to find that there is little agreement concerning the nature and purpose of religious education. This creates a compelling problem for educators trying to find the most appropriate approach for religious education school programs.

The purpose of religious education in Catholic schools

Religious education in Catholic schools has traditionally been seen as an essential part of the mission of the Church. Its nature and purpose were drawn from within the faith community and, as such, was an education from a faith perspective, that is, the objective was to increase knowledge, understanding and practice of the faith tradition with a desire to promote personal faith development. This has been explicitly expressed in Church documents since Vatican II, for instance in *Religious dimension of education in the Catholic school: Guidelines for reflection and renewal* (RDECS), where the school was seen as a "pastoral instrument" of the Church, an instrument that could become "more effective in proclaiming the Gospel and promoting human formation" (1988, #31). The following statement from the RDECS illustrates this thinking:

> The Catholic school is one of these pastoral instruments; its specific pastoral
> service consists in mediating between faith and culture: being faithful to the

newness of the Gospel while at the same time respecting the autonomy and the methods proper to human knowledge (RDECS, 1988, #31).

Consider the above statement. Do you agree/disagree with it? Why?

Using some examples, suggest some ways in which a religious school may mediate between faith and culture in the contemporary context.

A concept of faith

Given that a religious education from a faith perspective has traditionally been the primary purpose of the broad religious education program in Catholic schools, it is important to examine the meaning of "faith" in this context. According to the General Catechetical Directory (GCD), a Church document published by the Sacred Congregation for the Clergy in 1971:

> Faith … can be considered in two ways, either as the total adherence given by man under the influence of grace to God revealing himself, (the Faith *by which* one believes, or as the content of revelation and of the Christian message the Faith *which* one believes). These two aspects are by their very nature inseparable and a normal maturing of the Faith assumes progress of both together (GCD, 1971, #36).

The two elements of faith that have been discussed here refer to both the *act of faith*, that is, the faith response that determines beliefs, values and actions; and to the *content of faith*, that is the knowledge of the content of faith. Dykstra (1990) illustrates this more clearly when he states:

> Faith is deeply related to belief. Faith also connotes profound trust, confidence, and loyalty. It is an affair of the heart as well as of the mind. Commitment and action are also dimensions of faith. Faith has to do with a person's fundamental orientation in life (p. 246).

The values and actions of a person, therefore, are determined by their beliefs and commitments, that is, their faith, and such belief is enhanced by knowledge of the content of that faith. Thus, the mission of the Catholic school is to make the content of the message of faith:

> Intelligible to men (sic) of all times to convert to God through Christ, that they may interpret their whole life in the light of Faith … that they may lead

a life in keeping with the dignity which the message of salvation has brought them and that Faith has revealed to them (GCD, 1971, #37).

Further, in the later *General Directory for Catechesis* (GDC) (1997), there is an explicit recognition that "by deepening the knowledge of the faith, catechesis nourishes not only the life of faith but equips it to explain itself to the world" (1997, #85).

Thus, it is possible to describe three levels of faith: *cognitive* (one's knowledge of the faith tradition), *affective* (feelings associated with one's belief and one's sense of belonging within the community) and *spiritual* (expressions of one's faith commitment – that is, one's values and actions). For instance, participants at a Good Friday liturgy need to have some knowledge of the history and theology of Good Friday, and its place in the liturgical calendar. When they attend a Good Friday service, they may experience certain feelings linked to this knowledge. It could be the feelings generated by the story of Christ's Passion, the knowledge of Christ's role in their salvation, or their sense of their Catholic identity – that is, being Catholic and being part of a community with a shared story and a rich tradition. It is the depth of the knowledge and the feelings they experience that is likely to generate further expressions of their faith that is, values and actions that demonstrate their commitment. Therefore, it is important that these three levels of faith are acknowledged and addressed in religious education classrooms.

Examine the notion that faith has three dimensions – cognitive (knowledge), affective (feelings) and spiritual (expressed values and action). Select a religious activity, for instance, a baptism ceremony or a religious procession/festival. Analyse the activity in relation to the knowledge, feelings and expressions (values and actions) that may be evident or implied amongst the participants.

Catechesis and evangelization – Religious Education from a faith perspective

Traditionally, there have been two aspects of religious education from a faith perspective. These are evangelization and catechetics. *The Renewal of the Education of Faith* (REF) (1970) was used as a reference point to establish the principles of catechesis in Australia. The document used the terms "evangelization" (#25) and "catechesis" (#30), as well as the terms "pre-evangelization" (#26) and "pre-catechesis" (#31) quite specifically when discussing the appropriate catechetical process for different stages of readiness. Thus, the REF recognised that it was necessary to have a variety of educational approaches in order to take into account the needs of different age groups and their different life-situations:

The point of reference which will determine the value of the whole process of educating in faith is the reality of life here and now: The daily situation of the

Christian, his vocation, his mentality of faith, his communion with Christ in the Church, his place in the world, and his eternal destiny (REF, 1970, #162).

Evangelization is "that first announcement of salvation to someone who, for various reasons, has no knowledge of it, or does not yet believe it" (REF, 1970, #25). Catechesis, however:

> is intended for those who have made, even implicitly, the fundamental choice of Christ and His Church. It is at the service of men (sic). It takes into consideration their actual stages of Christian growth, their crises and their spiritual progress. It meets them as they are by a variety of means and methods suggested by the competent pastoral authority or the experience of those who are adults in the faith (REF, 1970, #31).

Therefore, the main focus of the catechetical process is to help a person to continue to grow in faith. The catechetical process originally referred to adults who were preparing for baptism, and it was the specific process they undertook as went through this preparation. Therefore it assumed an initial choice for Christian faith. It took place within a community of believers.

The General Catechetical Directory (GCD) also recognised that there was an interdependence between evangelization and catechesis that arose from both their nature and practice. Responding to the pluralistic values of contemporary society, it suggested that:

> In times past, the cultural tradition favoured the transmission of the Faith to a greater extent than it does today; in our times, however, the cultural tradition has undergone considerable change, with the result that less and less can one depend on continued transmission by means of it … some renewal in evangelization is needed for transmitting the same Faith to new generations … Christian faith requires explanations and new forms of expression so that it may take root in all successive cultures (GCD, 1971, #2).

Nichols (1978) believed that the catechetical process, "assuming a faith, however, dormant or troubled", should be part of religious education (p. 26). He argued that catechesis should "aim at a Christian vision of human life as it is and could be" instead of focusing on specific "Church" topics or events (p. 26). However, Nichols acknowledged that the dual purposes of evangelization and catechesis overlap and, consequently, the terms "pre-evangelization" or "pre-catechesis" could be used. Speaking of religious education in the pluralist classrooms of Britain in the 1970s he said:

> Some of the powerful forces which influence children as they grow up today smother the idealism, the sense of mystery and humanity's needs for

salvation which usually motivate the response of faith. Often it is necessary to prepare the ground by trying to develop these human qualities. Especially in difficult social areas this may prove to be a long and arduous task. This pre-evangelization is, in the secularised world of today, an important part of religious education (1978, p. 16).

Another perspective offered by Ryan and Malone (1996), described two distinct functions provided by catechesis and evangelization in religious education. The catechetical process places emphasis on the sharing and the ongoing development of faith and it assumes that the context consists of a community of believers who are attempting to live their lives according to the Catholic faith tradition. With the evangelical process, on the other hand, the emphasis or goal is to proclaim the Christian Gospel in such a way that students are invited to believe in it as the Word of God and accept it in their lives. Gascoigne (1995) elucidated his understanding of the evangelization process when he described its primary task as being one that leads to an understanding of the Gospel as "an ultimate and saving word about human existence" (p. 279). He argued that for this to happen the life-situation of the human person, including their values and experiences, must be taken into account. Thus, we need "to foster a Christian identity that will give pre-eminence to the saving and liberating power of the Gospel by interpreting its words in and for the diversity of human contexts" (Gascoigne, 1995, p. 279).

Catechesis, then, generally provided the basis for religious education that was developed in Catholic schools over the past century. However, given the compulsory nature of religious education in Catholic schools, it cannot always be assumed that classrooms today are filled with groups of students who believe in and are committed to the Catholic faith tradition. This has been a concern which was discussed by theorists in the seventies and eighties, such as Moran (1970), Rummery (1975) and Crawford and Rossiter (1988). Certainly, in today's classrooms, there are large numbers of students who are disassociated from the Church, and whose parents' experience of religious education took place after the Second Vatican Council (1962-1965) where, too often, there was little focus on cognitive learning. As a result, there are many students in Catholic religious education classrooms today who know little about their faith tradition. This is a huge challenge for teachers in this subject. It also points to the fact that the catechetical process would have limited application in these multi-faith and multicultural classrooms. In recognition of this feature, Macdonald (1988) stated:

> In a particular Catholic secondary school situation, where teachers decide that catechesis is not appropriate or possible, education in faith may be expressed as evangelization so as to enable youth:
> • to consider the human quest for meaning in life;
> • to reflect on human experience in the light of various meaning and values systems;

- to develop a seriousness about human values;
- to become aware of the different belief systems within the community;
- to explore the different dimensions of religion;
- to develop a sensitive understanding of the religious systems by which people live, including Christian, non-Christian and traditionally non-religious systems, and
- to develop a critical understanding and appreciation of Christianity and of the Catholic faith tradition in particular (p. 36).

From the above discussion, it can be seen that in contemporary Catholic secondary classrooms, the two aspects of religious education from a faith perspective, evangelization and catechesis, both have a role. Through the evangelization process, those students who have not yet heard the Word of God, could be offered opportunities to hear it and invited to interpret its relevance to their daily lives. Thus, students may make an initial response, whether this be in a shifting of attitude, belief or action. However, if within the classroom, there are students who make up a "believing community" in that they share their religious beliefs and practices, the catechetical approach will help such students to further develop their faith.

What do you understand by the terms "catechesis" and "evangelization"?

Write 300 words discussing the role of catechesis and evangelization in contemporary religious education classrooms.

To sum up, the main intention of approaches to religious education that is drawn from a faith perspective is to offer students opportunities to develop knowledge about the faith tradition and to include opportunities for reflection on personal and faith issues (See Figure 2).

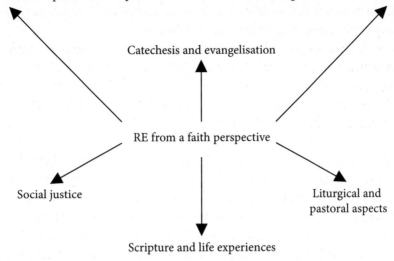

Figure 2: Features of Religious Education from a faith perspective

However, while this traditional orientation remained the central feature of religious education in Catholic schools, an educational perspective in religious education has evolved over the past forty years, where more attention has been given to the cognitive dimension of the study. Initially, such approaches were developed in state schools and did not have, as their primary aim, the education of believers in their own particular faith tradition. Instead, they focused on the general education of the student and incorporated a study of religion as a subject in its own right. Nonetheless, in Catholic and other religious schools, the educational perspective was seen as a complementary factor to the faith perspective which continued to be an important consideration in the programs.

Faith and educational perspectives in religious education

Much of the discussion about the different perspectives in religious education evolved from the term "religious education" and the differences pertaining to the two fields of study - Religion and Education. Moran (1970), whose early writings had a significant influence on many Australian religious educators, argued that the traditional religious education programs or catechetics in Catholic schools were a "cross-breed" that did not emerge from two distinct schools but rather "from the aim of confessional groups to indoctrinate" (p. 14). He suggested that, in order for religious education to gain any credibility in its own right, it would need to move away from this intent. Instead it should focus on the development of a new area of study which drew on theology and sound educational theory, the former providing the method and the latter providing the content (p. 21). Thus, Moran was interested in putting catechesis into an educational framework rather than a faith-oriented one.

Moran (1970) argued that the crisis in the catechetical movement at that time, which derived from the fact that, in practical terms, the role of the Church had little meaning in modern society, created a demand for courses in religions other than Christianity. He proposed an ecumenical and inter- religious aspect for religious education which, he believed, had links to past approaches (catechetical) but completely transformed them in that it did not necessarily afford Christianity a normative position. He asserted that the aim of ecumenical education was the same as education, that is, "the lived truth of the humanised world" (p. 85) and that his approach would lead to "experience-centred" religious education that should be taught in an intellectually challenging framework which was free from a proselytizing approach. He said that, of its nature, religion should "bring the emotional and the rational into an intelligent union but a study of religion that would accomplish this feat presupposes that much else has been studied" (p. 85). He claimed that his approach did not "prescribe that people must accept a religious belief and ritual but that this issue ought to be intelligently dealt with in education" (p. 85). Such a program should aim to extend the understanding of students so that if they make their choice to live by a particular religion or not to live by it, the choice would be an informed and intelligent one.

Write a paragraph that identifies the main thrust of Moran's argument for religious education from an educational perspective.

Drawing on Moran's writings, Rummery (1975) presented a detailed analysis of a range of approaches in catechesis, including the traditional approach, the kerygmatic approach and the life-centred approach and followed this by exploring their relevance to the teaching of religion in the pluralistic society of the 1970s. He suggested that the purpose of catechesis was to create dialogue and action between believers, and this group-sharing of their faith should lead to an enhancement of their personal faith. However, the difficulty of using this approach in a today's classroom which contains a diversity of beliefs is, at once, obvious. Rummery's contribution to the literature was significant in that it extended Moran's discussion on the relationship between the traditional approach of an education in faith and the broader concept of religious education as contained in a phenomenological approach (see Chapter 1 for a discussion on the phenomenological approach). Rummery compared the catechetical approach with four other methods of approaching a study to religious education, that is, "teaching that, education in, teaching how and teaching about" (p. 157).

According to Rummery's descriptions, the first approach, the "teaching that", was closest to the catechetical approach. This involved teaching fundamental Christian truths to people who shared the same beliefs. The second approach referred to "education in religion" where the intent was to transmit a distinct form of knowledge (religion) without bias, so that no particular faith tradition was given more emphasis than another but there was enough depth to avoid superficiality. The third approach, "teaching how", was based on the phenomenological approach as devised by Smart (1966, see Chapter 1) which recognized religion as a form of knowledge and emphasized understanding so that individuals could make informed choices. The final approach, "teaching about", was similar to the third one but was problematic because it lacked the emotional and experiential aspect of religion, that is, it denied aspects that related to the actual nature of the subject. It focused on the cognitive component and could be reduced to a mere factual study.

Identify the differences in the four approaches that Rummery discusses.

Rummery made it clear that the aims of the traditional catechetical approach and the others were separate, in that the latter incorporated a cognitive and intellectual approach which was quite distinct from the indoctrination or conditioning approach of the former. While the former depended on teaching and sharing activities amongst believers, the others did not necessarily require a commitment or a sharing of beliefs from either the teacher or the students. The strength of the phenomenological approach lay in its intent which was to attempt to teach religion more openly without expecting any allegiance to a particular faith tradition. While this is a more appropriate approach for an adolescent whose developmental stage is still at the point of exploration and experimentation rather than commitment, it raises the question of its suitability in a confessional school. A further question is whether catechesis, which is confessional in its approach, has any compatibility with the phenomenological approach which is non-confessional. Rummery suggested that there could be a point of convergence between the two, the latter stressing understanding, empathy and experience of religion viewed in multi-dimensional fashion and the former, at some stage, perhaps culminating in a dialogue of believers. He presented the theory that "catechesis may logically crown the phenomenological approach which, by its nature, prepares for and remains open to faith" (p. 181) which is a real strength in a multi-faith society. This was an aspect of the phenomenological approach that was recognized as having some value for religious education in Catholic schools.

What do you think Rummery meant when he said: catechesis may logically crown the phenomenological approach which, by its nature, prepares for and remains open to faith.

Both Moran's (1970) and Rummery's (1975) studies were written in the 1970s but they have had a significant impact on the way in which religious education programs have evolved in today's classrooms. Moran's (1970) theory questioned the "readiness" of secondary students for a course that focused on a comparative study of religions. He based his argument on the fact that students must be adequately prepared in earlier years and this cannot be assumed. He also acknowledged the pluralistic nature of contemporary American youth, and the need for a religious education program that took this factor into consideration. Both these factors are relevant to Australian religious education today. Rummery (1975) described religious education that combined elements of catechesis with an approach that had a broader educational focus, which gave greater emphasis to the cognitive aspects of the subject. The former viewed the subject from a faith standpoint and the latter from an educational standpoint. These two dimensions, religious education from a faith perspective and religious education from an educational perspective, which had an intellectual base, are essential aspects of current programs in Catholic schools.

Rossiter (1981, 1983) also described a faith and an educational perspective to religious education. While the primary purpose of religious education from a faith perspective was directed towards "better understanding of, and deeper personal faith in," a particular faith tradition (1981, p. 4), he described this as a "hope" rather than a finally achievable goal. While the classroom programme was a "channel" to faith through knowledge, the whole religious education curriculum included liturgical and pastoral activities which were shared by the school community, and there was an implicit religious influence of the school's social life in which, ideally, the teacher was a committed believer. This approach was most common in religious or church schools and assumed that the recipients formed a community of believers (1981, p. 4). Thus, the formal classroom religious education curriculum was just a part of the broader, informal curriculum of the Catholic school which contributed to the religious education of students.

Following on from this, Rossiter suggested that the educational perspective, provided a basis for an approach that was more concerned with "knowledge, understanding and affective appreciation of religion than with "faith development" and "faith responses" of pupils (Rossiter, 1981, pp. 4-5; Crawford & Rossiter, 1985, p.45). The general framework in which this approach resided arose from the educational process and it made no assumptions about the religious beliefs of either the teacher or the student. It recognised religion as a distinct field of study that would make its own contribution to the general education of the student and, as such, it would take on historical (history of religions), sociological (the role and influence of religion in society) and psychological (an understanding of human behaviour and its links to religious motivation) aspects. As well, it focused on activities contained within the formal curriculum and it was characterised by its intellectual approach to the study. It did not grow out of the concerns of a community of faith but was seen as a subject that could make a valid contribution to the secular curriculum, in its own right, just as any other subject would. Such an approach grew out of the developments in secular schools in Australia which wished to incorporate some studies of religion into their programs in the seventies (See Figure 3).

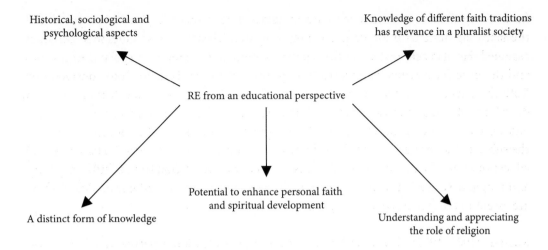

Figure 3: Features of religious education from an educational perspective

To sum up, faith and educational perspectives have determined the different approaches to religious education in Catholic schools in the past four decades. The knowledge component of the first included a study of the religious tradition but gave greater emphasis to the personal and faith aspects of religious education, that is, learning in the affective domain. The second focused more on the cognitive aspect of the subject but recognized that increased knowledge could enhance the students' personal faith.

Religious education and personal development

Yet another aspect of religious education that became more influential in the 1970s was the greater attention given to the personal dimension in religious education. This emphasis emerged in education, at the wider level, but it also affected religious education classes both in Australia and overseas. Crawford and Rossiter (1988) argued that interest in education for affective/personal development was stimulated by the growth in the area of humanistic psychology which suggested that small group discussions about personal matters could bring about personal change. "It implied that feelings, attitudes and convictions are revealed and developed in an intimate personal setting" (Crawford & Rossiter, 1988, p. 52). Terms, such as "personalism" or "education for personal change" had also been introduced into discussions on religious education (Crawford & Rossiter, 1985, pp. 9-10, p. 60). The approach to education for personal change, "stressed the empowerment of young people" (Crawford & Rossiter, 1985, p. 9). It sought to encourage them to take a more informed, responsible, active role in their own development, while recognising that external factors continued to play a part in shaping their lives.

In religious education, in particular, affective aims were seen as having priority over cognitive aims since one of the prime foci was the enhancement of a personal faith and spirituality (Crawford & Rossiter, 1988). Indeed, at a time when Catholics, drawing on their new understanding of Revelation, were seeking to discover a more personal and reflective approach to their own faith and spiritual development, religious education teachers welcomed the views of humanistic psychologists such as Rogers (1961, 1969), Erikson (1968, 1980) and Maslow (1968). Humanistic psychologists focused on the potential that all individuals have to develop as unique people who are self-directed and capable of setting goals, making choices and initiating action. Both Erikson and Maslow also described various stages of growth and maturity through which individuals develop, each stage being identified by specific characteristics which have implications for the development of learning programs. Therefore, the particular emphasis of the humanistic approach was the growth and development of the individual. (See Chapter four for further discussion of these theories of human development).

The relationship between personal development, religious education and lifelong learning was also acknowledged in *The Renewal of the Education of Faith* where reference was made to the fact that catechesis could have relevance for a person as he/she progressed through the different stages of life:

> Each successive stage of human growth has its own special significance. It also plays a part in a person's progress towards maturity ... Errors or inadequate truths taught at a certain age, may have serious consequences for a person's human and Christian development ... At every stage of their development, Christians should have access to the whole of the revealed message, in a form and in terms that they can understand (REF, 1970, #134).

Nichols (1978) asserted that religious education for young people should contribute to the process of emotional growth and should concern itself with improving the quality of personal relationships. He argued that adolescents were in search of their inner selves, one that "depends on values, convictions and meanings" (1978, p. 39). As such:

> catechesis must contribute to personal security, confidence and a sense of personal worthwhileness during the important years of adolescence. It must also offer or strengthen a conviction of personal destiny and vocation: that we are on earth to "build an immortal soul". In this way... it should provide the dynamism and the unity of moral life (Nichols 1978, p. 39)

Drawing on the above discussion, it can be seen that approaches to religious education from a faith perspective which focused on the experiences of the student, did address some aspects of personal development.

With the advent of the new millennium, personal aspects of education and adolescent development have received more recognition at the broader curriculum level (for instance, the Victorian Essential Learning Standards curriculum documents introduced in 2005 (see: www.eduweb.vic.gov.au/edulibrary/public/curricman/support/3-3.pdf) incorporates the personal and social domain of learning; and there is evidence, explicitly and implicitly that other State curriculum documents also have incorporated a focus on personal and social learning. As well, the Australian Federal Government has initiated Values Education for all Australian schools (see: www.valueseducation.edu.au/values/) and these, potentially, have some implications for learning and teaching in religious education. Many Catholic schools which have implemented Values Education have found that addressing the nine core values that have been identified by the Australian Government fits in well with the culture of Catholic schools since most of the core values do coincide with values implied in commitment to a Christian vision of life.

Choose one topic in religious education and suggest the content and teaching activities that can be used which will have links to personal and social learning and values education.

Select one of the nine core values and plan a religious education lesson around it, making sure that you find an appropriate Scripture passage or other aspect of Catholic life such as Catholic ethics or doctrine that teaches and/or reflects the same value.

One of the early theorists who offered some insights into the personal dimensions of learning in religious education was Grimmitt (1987). He drew on his experiences from teaching religion in secular British government schools with their pluralistic environment, and suggested that both religion and education contribute to the process of "humanisation" (p. 195). He proceeded to argue that religious education should address social, moral and spiritual aspects of personal growth. Grimmitt theorized that education in religion should have a humanising approach, rather than a theological one since all "religious" educators are essentially "secular" educators who engaged in education as their prime activity even if theological insights have been used (p. 258). Their main commitment was to the achievement of educational goals by way of a process which conformed to general educational principles. Grimmitt sought to establish a relationship between education and religion and found this problematic. He argued that neither could support a theory of a value-free method of study. Both were value-laden and, therefore, attempted to impose their own values on each other. However, he believed that human beings could not be value-free in their thinking:

> Human beings have no alternative but to formulate beliefs about their nature and the nature of their human experience and to commit themselves to particular beliefs about themselves and their world by an act of faith. Holding beliefs or believing is therefore an essential constituent not only of meaning-making but of humanization itself … the only alternative to belief for the human being is not unbelief but another belief (p. 195).

> Explore the statement: Human beings are not able to be value-free? Think of some examples that support or negate this statement.

Expanding on this, Grimmitt suggested that, both religion and education recognised this trait in the human person since both contributed to the human person's ability to interpret their everyday experiences, that is, both contributed to the process of "humanisation". Thus, it is precisely because religion and education were both "interpretative" and "humanising" that they could enter into a relationship with one another (p. 195).

> Discuss how religion and education may contribute to the process of humanization.

Grimmitt (1987) proposed a curriculum framework for religious education which derived from an application of the theory that "reality and human consciousness were socially constructed to an understanding of the process of humanization and the contribution beliefs and believing made to that process" (p. 257). Human persons were shaped by their interactions with and experiences of others and by their internalization of facts, values, beliefs and attitudes, all of which were determined by their social, cultural and ideological inheritance. Thus, they were moulded in the image of that reality, or that view of the human which was the norm for their times. However, humans needed to discover and embrace new visions which lay outside their cultural and personal histories.

Following on from this, Grimmitt (1987) described the special characteristics of religious education as its contribution to the development of human spirituality and spiritual development. He defined the former as "a human capacity for a certain type of awareness – often called "spiritual awareness" - which may be stimulated by religious consciousness but which is not contingent upon it" (p. 125). Spiritual development was the "activation of the human capacity for self-transcendence and movement towards a state of consciousness in which the limitations of human finite identity are challenged by the exercise of the creative imagination" (p. 125). As well, he made clear distinctions between spiritual development and religious development, in that the latter provided a means by which human spirituality may be nurtured, moulded and given direction.

In the end, according to Grimmitt, this is what religious education should be about, helping young people to transcend whatever factors are limiting their growth towards human maturity. Students should begin by exploring their own "life-worlds" as the first step towards "critical consciousness" and "self-awareness". Next, they should move on to a study of religions which should juxtapose the new content, that is, other religions, with the familiar content, that is, the content of the student's "life-world". By learning about different beliefs and values, students could use them as instruments to evaluate critically their own beliefs and values. By learning "*about* religion" they also learn "*from* religion" about themselves (Grimmitt, p. 141). Continued growth and understanding of a religious tradition is linked to greater self-knowledge and self-awareness. This, in turn, increases students' capacity to reflect on, evaluate and interpret their experiences which leads to personal growth and the development of religious, spiritual and moral awareness. Religious education, then, may contribute to personal growth and human maturity by developing in students' growing self-awareness and self-knowledge.

> Identify three ideas that provided the basis for Grimmitt's proposal for a religious education framework that you found interesting. Give reasons for your choice.

Another idea about the links between religious education and personal development was offered by Crawford and Rossiter (1988) who suggested that the aim of personal education was to "educate young people to consciously choose a path to personal growth in which they value right actions for their own intrinsic sake rather than for fear of the consequences of a contrary choice" (p. 55) and argued that there should be a cognitive basis for affective/personal learning in the classroom because:

> an open, informative, critical inquiring study of religion will do more to develop faith and the other aspects of personal development, than any approaches which try to deal with these personal areas more exclusively and explicitly (p. 58).

> Do you agree/disagree with the above argument? Why?

Crawford & Rossiter (1993) were critical of those educators who tried to "de-school" (p. 491) the religious education classroom in an attempt to make it more productive in the area of faith and personal development, and they argued that the error lay in not recognising the connection between the personal and the academic aspects of religion:

> It is relevant to note that there should never have been that artificial dichotomy that some like to think exists between the academic and the personal dimensions of religious education – this faulty thinking is evident where academic study is linked just with "knowledge", while more personal activities (even though hard to gauge) are said to promote "faith development" (1993, p. 491).

One inference that could be drawn from the discussion on religious education which emphasizes personal development, is that if a greater emphasis was given to personal development across the curriculum, there is much that can be learnt from programs that focus on the personal dimension in religious education. Accordingly, learning in religious education may, potentially contribute to learning in other areas of the curriculum, particularly with the new State curriculum approaches referred to earlier.. Such integration between religious education and the broader curriculum would give rise to the need for improved communication between subjects and across the curriculum. For instance, some religious education classes have included topics like drug education, sex education, life skills education, which have enabled new links to be forged between Religious Education and other subjects in the curriculum, and which sometimes have resulted in a team approach to the curriculum. Most of these programs have focused on values education and aimed at promoting a healthy lifestyle which would assist students' development. However, there is a distinct contribution that religious education makes to the education of the student and, therefore, it is important that it should be allowed to retain its identity and not become lost in a range of other personal development courses. Instead, recognition should be given to the nature of religious education and its ability to complement learning in other subjects.

To sum up, a focus on personal development in contemporary classrooms may be seen as an important consideration in secondary religious education programs. It could be particularly beneficial and meaningful to students in today's world where the influence of traditional social institutions and religions has declined. As well, many young people today, do not have the extended family and community links that were so much part of previous generations. Instead, the extended exposure to a variety of beliefs, behaviours and lifestyles that young people witness or experience through the media and the World Wide Web may create a level of confusion about their own beliefs and practices. Thus, if religious education incorporated an element of personal learning, the interactions and experiences with others students within the religious education classroom may help individual students to internalize Christian values, beliefs and attitudes which should ultimately influence their behaviour (see Figure 4).

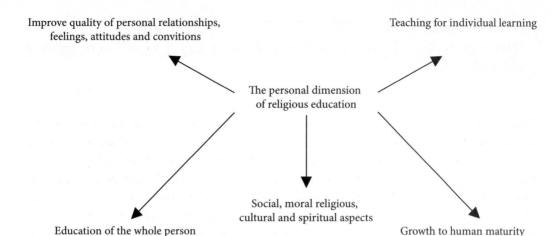

Figure 4: Features of the personal dimension of religious education

Conclusion

In this chapter, the nature and purpose of religious education in Catholic schools has been examined. Since the Catholic school has a role in the faith community as part of the vision of the Catholic Church, religious education should be drawn from a faith perspective. However, in contemporary classrooms an education perspective is essential since it provides the subject with a broader knowledge base and recognizes that religious education has a place within the broader curriculum because it provides a particular form of knowledge. Further, by including a study of different religions, its content had more potential to be relevant for students who live in the multi-faith and multicultural context of today's society. Finally, there is the personal aspect of religious education which needs to be incorporated into classroom programs which, potentially, may make religious education more meaningful and relevant for students, and it may have some significance for establishing links to other subject areas where personal and social learning has been identified as a dominant strand for learning across the curriculum. All of these perspectives, of course, need to be considered in the context of the physical, psychological, emotional, social and spiritual development of the adolescent and that is the focus of the following chapter.

Write 500 words discussing the important elements of contemporary religious education.

What questions about the nature and purpose of religious education have been raised for you by this chapter?

References and Further Reading

Australian Episcopal Conference. (1970). *The renewal of the education of faith*. Sydney: E.J. Dwyer.

The Congregation for Catholic Education. (1988). *Religious dimension of education in the Catholic school: Guidelines for reflection and renewal*. Homebush, NSW: St. Paul's Publications.

Congregation for the Clergy. (1997). *General directory for catechesis*. Strathfield, NSW: St. Paul's Publications.

Crawford, M. & Rossiter, G. (1985*). Teaching religion in the secondary school: Theory and practice*. Strathfield, NSW: Christian Brothers Resource Group.

Crawford, M. & Rossiter, G. (1988). *Missionaries to a teenage culture*. Strathfield, NSW: Christian Brothers Resource Group.

de Souza, M. (2006). Rediscovering the spiritual dimension in education: promoting a sense of self and place, meaning and purpose in learning. In M. de Souza, K. Engebretson, G. Durka, R. Jackson, A. McGrady, (Eds). *International Handbook of the Religious, Moral and Spiritual Dimensions of Education*. 2 volumes. Dordrecht, The Netherlands: Springer Academic Publishers.

de Souza, M. (2005). Engaging the mind, heart and soul of the student in religious education: Teaching for meaning and connection. In *Journal of Religious Education*. 53:4, pp. 40-47.

de Souza, M., (2004). Teaching for effective learning in religious education: A discussion of the perceiving, thinking, feeling and intuiting elements in the learning process. *Journal of Religious* Education.52:3, pp 22-30.

Dykstra, C.R. (1990). Faith. In *Harper's encyclopedia of religious education*. (Eds. I.V. Cully, & K.B. Cully) pp. 245-7. San Francisco: Harper.

Erikson, E. (1968). Norton, New York: *Identity: Youth and crisis*.

Gascoigne, R. (1995).'Evangelization and Catholic identity'. *The Australasian Catholic Record*, *72*(3) pp. 269-279.

Grimmitt, M. (1987). *Religious education and human development*. Great Wakering: McCrimmon.

Macdonald, M. (1988) *Assessment in religious education in Catholic secondary schools.* Unpublished thesis, D. Theol. Melbourne: Melbourne College of Divinity.

Maslov, A. (1968). *Towards a psychology of being.* New Jersey: Princeton University Press.

Moran, G. (1970). *Design for religion: Towards ecumenical education.* NY: Herder & Herder, Inc.

Nichols, K. (1978). *Cornerstone.* Slough: St Paul's Publications.

Rossiter, G. (1981). The gap between aims and practice in religious education. *Word in Life 29* (1), pp. 24-28.

Rossiter, G. (1983). The place of commitment in classroom religious education. In Castles & G. Rossiter (Eds.) *Curriculum Theory and Religious Education.* Strathfield, NSW: The Australian Association for Religious Education.

Rogers, C. (1969). *Freedom to learn.* Columbus, Ohio: Charles E. Merrill Publishing Company.

Rummery, R. (1975). *Teaching religious education and catechesis in a pluralist society.* Sydney: Dwyer.

Ryan, M. & Malone, P. (1996). *Exploring the religion classroom: A guidebook for Catholic schools.* Wentworth Falls, NSW: Social Science Press.

Smart, N. (1968). *Secular education and the logic of religion.* London: Faber.

Welbourne, L. (1997). Editorial. *Word in Life 45* (1) p. 1.

Cornerstones of Catholic Secondary Religious Education

CHAPTER 4

Adolescent Development:
Implications for Learning and Teaching

Marian de Souza

Many of the changes in teaching and learning that occurred through the 1970s and 1980's were influenced by theories about the way the human person grows and develops (Rogers, 1969; Erikson, 1968; Maslow, 1968, and others) which led to a greater focus on the individual. Rogers described "significant, meaningful and experiential learning" (1969, p. 4) which had "a quality of personal involvement, ...was self-initiated, ... was pervasive, ... was evaluated by the learner, ... and had meaning as its essence" (1969, p. 5). Roger's writings had some influence on the development of educational programs, including religious education, where the learning became child-centred and recognition was given to the experiential factor being an important part of the learning process.

Reflect on some of the learning and teaching experiences you had when you were in school and consider whether they were teacher-directed or student-centred. Identify the elements of these experiences that indicate which category they would belong to. Share your thinking with a small group of students and, as a group, decide which experiences were most conducive to effective learning.

With the focus on the child, humanistic psychologists in the sixties and seventies began to investigate the growth patterns of an individual and the effect this may have had on the learning process. One basic assumption was that there were a number of developmental stages that individuals move through in their growth to maturity, and that each stage could be identified by certain characteristics. Two schools of thought dominated the field of developmental psychology – cognitive development and psycho-social development. The former focused on how individuals interpreted and made sense of the outer world according to their mental skills and abilities. Thus, their intellectual processes transformed their experiences into a form that they were able to draw on when they were confronted with a new situation or problem. Changes in these processes were linked to physical maturity which suggested that significant types of behaviour would be apparent at successive age levels. Psycho-social theories, such as those offered by Erikson, were based on the understanding that the individual's ego progressed through a series of inter-related stages. Educators became interested in these developmental theories and the implications they had for the individual's learning process. However, there has been much criticism about aspects of developmental theories, for instance, the stages are not necessarily sequential, nor do they necessarily relate to specific age brackets. Further, issues related to the impact of gender and culture on an individual's growth and development have also been examined (for instance, Gilligan, 1982).

Despite the critics, developmental theorists have triggered much discussion related to the effectiveness of teaching and learning strategies. They also had a significant impact on curriculum documents since the 1980s. *Frameworks* (Ministry of Education - School's Division 1988), and the *Curriculum and Standards Frameworks* (Victorian Board of Studies 1995) all had a strong emphasis on the need to cater for individual abilities and differences. This feature was also considered in the revised *Guidelines for Religious Education for Students in the Diocese of Melbourne* (CEO, Melbourne 1995) which refers to the "many ways of knowing" and the need for the teacher to draw on the students' individual experiences to create relevant experiences for the individual student (1995, p. 30). Finally, in some of the most recent Religious Education curriculum documents, there are clear directions about learning that address the developmental stages of students. For instance, in the Ballarat Religious Education curriculum document, *Awakenings* (2005), Chapter three focuses on "The world of the student" with a detailed section on "Growth and Development" which opens with the following statement:

> Students differ from each other in temperament, abilities, achievements, maturity, styles of learning and in many other ways. However, they share a common journey towards maturity, passing through recognizable levels of growth. The developmental levels from early childhood to late adolescence approximately coincide with the six levels around which the general curriculum is organized in Victoria.
>
> At each level, individual development results from the interplay of maturation and experience, occurring in the context of a particular family, society and culture (2005, p. 82).

While the new Melbourne Religious Education curriculum documents do not specifically mention the developmental aspects of students' lives, they do refer to the students' life experiences in the planning of the proposed units of work.

Think back to your years as a Year 7 student, a Year 10 student and a Year 12 student. Write a few lines about your particular interests and needs at each of those year levels. Share these thoughts with a group to discover similarities and differences between the different year levels. Discuss what implications this may have for learning and teaching at those levels.

The following sections will present a brief overview of some theories that have relevance for the developmental aspect of adolescents.

The psycho-social theories of Erikson

Erikson (1968) was one theorist who identified stages in human development which resulted from the interaction between the individual's growth and maturity, intellectual and emotional development, and the succession of social roles that the individual experienced. These stages were recognized by educators as having some relevance for the design of strategies to enhance learning, for instance, how children think or how to cater for the different learning styles. Erikson formulated a theory of personality development drawn from psychoanalysis, but took into account the social and cultural influences. His descriptions of personality development were based on the *epigenetic* principle (1968 p. 92) where he hypothesized that, similar to the way foetus development takes place at particular periods of time, personality forms as the ego progresses through a series of interrelated stages. In his view, personality development was a series of turning points or psychological crises, which he described in terms of dichotomies of desirable qualities and behaviours. He argued that people need to possess both the positive and the negative qualities of each stage, but in order to adapt successfully to their social environment, it is necessary that the positive qualities are stronger.

Erikson focused on psychosocial stages of ego development, in which a person has to develop new skills and relationships in order to function within different social contexts. More importantly, he believed that personality development was a life-long process which he referred to as the eight stages of the life-cycle. These were:

1. *Trust v mistrust:* In the early years, if an infant was not nurtured or properly cared for, they could become mistrustful and wary and this could be transferred into later stages in their dealings with others.
2. *Autonomy v doubt:* This was when toddlers became adventurous and wanted to experience the world. They needed support and guidance. Over-restriction, criticism and not allowing them to do things for themselves could lead to self doubt.
3. *Initiative v guilt:* This occurred in early to middle childhood, a period when children tested their cognitive and motor skills. Their initiative and endless curiosity needed

patience, support and some freedom. By allowing them to show some initiative their self-assurance could increase. Once again, too much restriction, impatience and control could lead to guilt when they did show some initiative. These feelings could also affect them in later life, for instance, different expectations that were gender based could lead to guilt if children wished to cross the gender barrier. An example of this would be when girls played football or boys played with dolls.

4. *Industry v inferiority:* This was a period from late childhood when there was a lot happening and children were extremely active, making and doing things. They asked more questions, sometimes quite sophisticated ones. Peer groups became more influential and they could reinforce feelings of confidence and security.

5. *Identity v role confusion:* This was the period of adolescence where the social world expanded and provided more exposure to different social contexts. Children had already developed a sense of identity from their previous experiences within the extended family network and they began to test it out in new situations. Their interests grew to include what was happening in the wider world, for instance, their interest in political, religious and social issues developed. Social networks beyond the family became increasingly important as the adolescent attempted to find a place within them. When they had difficulty fitting in, role confusion could result. This could be a result of inadequate opportunities to develop social skills earlier or unresolved conflicts from earlier stages. For instance, if they had not learnt how to trust people, they may be unable to develop relationships which could lead to isolation or to further feelings of inferiority, and even guilt. Thus, their personal growth continued to be hindered. Sometimes, this could lead to excessive behaviour as the individual made an extreme effort to fit into the group, or it could result in anti-social behaviour, that is, misbehaviour or delinquency, or anti-personal behaviour, that is, drug and alcohol abuse.

6. *Intimacy v isolation:* This was the period of early adulthood where there was a need to establish a close and committed relationship with another person. Failure to do so could, once again, lead to a sense of isolation.

7. *Generativity v Stagnation:* This was the period of middle age when a person was usually concerned with establishing and guiding the next generation, that is, having children and raising them. Adults could attempt to do this in productive and creative ways, for instance, through teaching, research, working towards securing the future for the next generation and so on.

8. *Integrity v Despair:* Integrity was being able to accept one's life as something that had to be. Despair occurred when a person was disillusioned with his/her life and felt that time was too short to begin again in an effort to gain integrity (adapted from Erikson 1968, p. 94).

Erikson's fourth and fifth stages would appear to be most relevant to adolescents, who are at a stage where they are beginning to develop their own sense of identity and becoming interested in the outer world in terms of political and social issues. Marcia (1980) who extended Erikson's work, also argued that adolescents needed to undergo an identity crisis in order to further their own psychological maturity. He suggested that this may involve them in rejecting their parent's beliefs and values and moving towards an articulation of their own.

Why do you think Erickson and Marcia assume the need for an "Identity crisis" before a person may progress to the next stage of development. Do you agree with this assumption? Give reasons for your answer.

Maslow's theory of motivation

Maslow (1968; 1970), a humanist psychologist also offered a theory relating to human growth based on need gratification which

> is the most important single principle underlying all healthy human development. The single holistic principle that binds together the multiplicity of human motives is the tendency for a new and higher need to emerge as the lower need fulfils itself by being sufficiently gratified. The child who is fortunate enough to grow normally and well gets satiated and *bored* with the delights that he has savoured sufficiently, and *eagerly* (without pushing) goes on to higher more complex, delights as they become available to him/her without danger or threat (Maslow, 1968, p. 55)

Maslow suggested a hierarchy of human needs which, he believed, corresponded to the growth and maturity of the human person, and that when basic needs, such as physical needs, were satisfied to some degree, other "higher needs emerged" (Maslow, 1970, p. 38). Maslow proposed the following five-level hierarchy of needs:

- physiological needs: hunger, thirst;
- safety needs: need to be safe, free of pain, danger, anxiety;
- belongingness and love: need for affection, to value and be valued as part of a group;
- esteem: need for recognition by one's peers, and
- self-actualization: need to develop one's potential, need to place long-term benefits to self and society before short-term pleasures, develops a sense of priorities among needs, need to know "who am I?" (adapted from Maslow, 1970, Chapter 4, pp. 35-58).

The esteem needs, as identified by Maslow, appear to correspond to features of Erikson's fifth stage where individuals are beginning to expand their horizons. Thus, peer groups can become instrumental in contributing to an adolescent's sense of identity. If the process of searching for one's identity does lead to role confusion, and if this becomes a pre-occupation of late adolescence, educational programs, such as religious education which can include aspects of personal development, may address this. Further, if religious educators wish to increase the interest levels generated by their programs, they may need to recognize and articulate the needs of their students so that they can include content that is relevant and meaningful to their particular stage of development. Equally, they may need to incorporate strategies that can utilize the influence of their peers which could have the potential of enhancing their learning. Finally, they may also need to recognize that, to enhance the personal development aspects which include a religious and spiritual dimension, the teaching strategies should link cognitive, affective and spiritual learning, thereby increasing the potential for the program to be both intellectually challenging and meaningful.

> Do you think that Maslow's theory of a hierarchy of needs has some implications for planning and practice in religious education?

Other developmental theorists who have had relevance for religious education provided a "stage-theory" framework drawn from their respective research studies in the United States. These theories were drawn from the cognitive developmental school of thought so that a stage was seen not so much as a predetermined set of life issues as a particular way of organizing experiences. The first was Kohlberg (1969, 1981) with his stages of moral development and the second was Fowler (1981) with his stages of faith development. While both theorists have had their share of critics, the fact remains that they have offered religious educators an "unparalleled opportunity" to draw on their theoretical framework, thus providing educators with a "basis and structure for clarifying goals and pursuing realistic objectives in their programs" (DiGiacomo 1993, p. 66).

Moral development: Kohlberg

Kohlberg's (1969, 1981) cognitive-developmental theory, which focused on the general structures of moral judgement, has had some influence on approaches to religious education. He found that people matured in their moral reasoning by passing through several levels. Each of these levels is identified by the reasons that are given for choosing between right and wrong. Thus, a level of reasoning is not decided by the action that is considered to be wrong but by the reasons given that determine whether the action is wrong. Kohlberg described three levels of moral development, each of which had two stages.

Pre-conventional level
1. Orientation towards punishment – where one is deterred from doing something wrong because of the consequences that might occur, for example, punishment of some sort.
2. Reciprocity – where right action is when one seeks to satisfy one's own needs, and occasionally the needs of others.

Conventional level
3. Good girl-good boy orientation – where one seeks the approval of others for good behaviour.
4. Orientation towards authority – where doing one's duty, showing respect for authority and maintenance of the social order determines the right behaviour.
Post-conventional level
5. Social contract orientation – where the right action is determined by standards that have been accepted and agreed upon by the whole community.
6. Universal ethical principle orientation – where there is an orientation toward the decisions of conscience and toward self-chosen ethical principles that relate to justice, equality of human rights and individual human dignity (adapted from Kohlberg 1969, p. 376 and 1981, pp. 17-22)

Kohlberg's framework for moral development had some consequences for the teaching of Christian morality, and provided a basis for the development of teaching programs in moral and ethical issues and social justice. It assisted educators to understand the reasoning structures which influence people as they arrive at solutions to moral dilemmas. Kohlberg found that most adolescents reasoned at the third stage, the conventional level, and tended to solve their moral problems with reference to something outside themselves.

However, Gilligan (1977, 1982) pointed out that Kohlberg's data was gathered from an all-male sample and that the post-conventional levels for female moral development were simply not examined. Gilligan argued that differences arise in a social context where factors of social status and power combine with reproductive biology to shape the experience of males and females and the relations between the sexes.

Gilligan (1982) found that there were contrasts between male and female moral-decision making and that girls generally, were consistent in their knowledge and interest in human relationships. In her study, adolescent girls were more concerned with trying to find solutions to moral problems that leave both parties satisfied (pp. 417-518). However, boys from the same age group were more objective in applying logic and justice to provide a satisfying outcome. Certainly, these two levels of reasoning, that is, girls trying to find a solution without hurting anyone in the process and boys retaining a level of detachment in their process of moral reasoning, should not lead to the conclusion that adolescent boys are more advanced in their moral reasoning than their female counter-parts. Rather, recognition should be given to the fact that their gender differences possibly determine their responses.

Drawing on a number of research studies, Moylan (1993) discussed findings that supported Gilligan's research, which showed differences between the way male and female adolescents use their reasoning abilities (pp. 14-15). These suggested that most girls tend to be more personal in their reasoning, that is, they were at Kohlberg's third stage, whereas, boys may be more impersonal in their reasoning and so tended to move into the fourth stage earlier. Further, the findings indicated that it was unlikely that the decision-making of these adolescents would operate at an earlier or later stage. Generally, the third and fourth stages are the relevant ones when dealing with adolescents and the "de-structuring and reconstructing" (Moylan 1993, p. 15) of the process can cause confusion and distress for them and for those significant others who are interacting with them, such as parents and teachers:

> The kind of "vacuum of moral reasoning" which occurs can manifest itself by the adolescent's appearing sceptical, negative, relativistic and by his or her appearing to revert to an earlier stage of self-centredness. By prodding adolescents beyond their predominant level of moral reasoning, parents and teachers may precipitate this condition (Moylan, 1993, p. 15).

A criticism of Kohlberg's theory raised by Pell (1982) argued that Kohlberg was overly optimistic when he claimed a relationship between stages of thinking and action (1982, p. 9). Pell examined Kohlberg's early and later writings to discuss some contradictions that related to this factor and concluded that for a 'variety of theoretical and empirical reasons' the relationship remains "obscure" (1982, p. 9). Pell claimed that stage progress, particularly in the first four stages, does not always ensure better moral performance and referred to Kohlberg's experiment in cheating where 80% of the principled subjects in the last level refused to cheat. Pell believed that Kohlberg put great emphasis on the intellectual process but failed to recognise the role of human emotions in moral reasoning and action and, as such, the theory was "seriously incomplete and possibly misleading" (1982, p. 9). He said:

> there is no adequate explanation of the emotions as an essential constituent of human nature, or as a vital element in moral development, or as a potent force for disturbing the "proper" relationship between particular judgement and particular action (Pell 1982, p. 9).

Another aspect related to the stages of moral development as discussed by Biggs and Telfer (1987, pp. 324-25) claimed that moral levels are affected by levels of conformity.

Thus, students who successfully resist conforming to peer group pressure or to authority pressure to inflict punishment on someone else usually operate at a higher level, according to Kohlberg, than those who did conform. They also argued that cognitive developmental theory does not provide all the answers, for instance, people do not consistently arrive at the same judgements across a variety of situations. They often are influenced by the circumstances governing the action or event. They also insist that judgement is only one of many determinants of behaviour. However, the cognitive structure is useful in classifying the different kinds of judgement that people make.

Closely related to the above discussion is the claim that Kohlberg's theory has universal application. Certainly, there would be some behaviours that would be considered wrong regardless of the laws and practices of different countries. However, moral values, such as equality, freedom, the preservation of human life and so on, are not universally applied across cultural boundaries. Freedom of speech, for example, might reflect a particular perspective that is culturally specific. Equally, when birth control, abortion and homosexuality are contentious issues within a single country such as Australia, they would be even more difficult to resolve at a global level when a diversity of beliefs are involved. Given the pluralistic nature of Australian classrooms, religious educators need to be aware of these implications when they develop aspects of moral education in their programs. This is particularly the case at senior secondary levels where students, inundated with mass media, have a heightened awareness of social, cultural, moral and ethical issues. Furthermore, the students are at an age where they are inclined to seek solutions to them.

The findings discussed above need to be considered by religious educators when interacting with their students. Kohlberg's theory does provide a useful structure for programs in moral development. In particular, his use of the moral dilemma as a strategy in moral education can be a most effective tool for teachers. However, any attempt to encourage students in their passage to moral maturity needs much patience, careful handling and attention to language ability and cultural diversity. This is particularly important for religious educators when they include values education and an attention to the personal dimension in their religious education programs.

The following is an excerpt from a research study (de Souza, 1999) which applied Kohlberg's stage theory to analyse the responses of Year 12 students to a particular scenario given to them during individual interviews:

Scenario: The class is having a test. You were at sport training/practice the night before and did not have time to study. Your friend says that you can copy from him/her as the marks are going to be counted towards your assessment. You know there are a few students doing this as your teacher does not keep a strict watch. What do you do?

Of the eight students who responded in the negative, six gave reasons which ranged from moral values to fear of getting caught. These are presented below:

Student 1: *None of my friends would let me and even if they did, I still wouldn't do it.*

Student 2: *I wouldn't copy, I'd talk to the teacher or something.*

Student 3: *I wouldn't do it, mainly because it's cheating myself. I think my marks should be my mark. I take pride in knowing I do the best I can do whatever that might be, so really, it's not only because I would be cheating the teacher and other people, I just wouldn't do that to myself.*

Student 4: *I would not copy, I think it is wrong.*

Student 5: *I would just hand up my paper with what I could do but I would go and see the teacher and explain what had happened and I would ask if I could make it up or something.*

Student 6: *I don't think I'd cheat but that's not based on moral grounds. It would be more a fear of getting caught.*

Of the two students who answered in the affirmative, one attributed her actions to her shifting faith:

Student 7: *Yeah, I'd copy, this is it, my faith isn't that strong.*

The other was the student who had previously claimed to have no faith or belief in God, the implications being that he set his own code of conduct:

Student 8: *I'd cheat, what does it matter, I'd find out the answers anyway.*

Using Kolhberg's stage theory, at which level of moral development do you think each of these students were? Give reasons for your answers.

Faith development: Fowler and Flynn

Fowler's (1981) research sought to identify different stages of faith development. He and his associates conducted 359 interviews between 1972 and 1981 with people whose ages ranged from three and a half years to eighty-four years. While there was an equal representation of males and females among the subjects, they were heavily dominated by white Americans

(97.8%) and Christians (81.5%) respectively. Other religions which were represented were Judaism (11.2%), Orthodox Christians (3.6%) and others not specified (3.6%) (Fowler 1981, p. 315).

Fowler (1981) concluded that there were six stages of faith development which followed a pre-stage he called "Undifferentiated" (p. 121) which he linked to infancy. The six stages were:

1. Intuitive-Projective Faith (Experienced faith): Young children copied the language and actions of adults close to them.
2. Mythic-Literal Faith (Affiliative faith): At this point older children began to express beliefs that they had heard and began to act upon them.
3. Synthetic-Conventional Faith (Conventional faith): Children in their pre-teen years began to be influenced by a wider network including their peers.
4. Individuative-Reflexive Faith (Personal faith): Teenagers experienced the tension of choosing to stay with the known and familiar or developing their individuality and exploring unknown territory. Fowler claimed that this latter step was necessary for faith to continue to develop.
5. Paradoxical-Consolidative Faith (Community faith): Young adults choose to live according to their own beliefs and commitments.
6. Universalising Faith (Universal faith): This was the approach to mid-life and beyond when people focused on truths and what it means to be human. At this stage people were comfortable with their beliefs and could develop a commitment to change the world (adapted from Fowler 1981, pp. 119-211 and Fowler et al 1991, pp. 24-25).

Fowler did attempt to link specific age brackets with the six stages but conceded that stage attainment would vary from person to person. More importantly, he asserted that only a few individuals would reach the sixth and final stage, for instance, people like Mother Theresa or Gandhi.

From the descriptions given above it would appear that the third and fourth stages have relevance to teaching at secondary levels, and that there is similarity between these stages and the ones described by Erikson and Maslow in relation to adolescence. Fowler's third stage should occur towards the end of childhood and, while it may only last to the late teens, it is quite possible that it might continue to a later age. DiGiacomo suggested that this stage was close to Kohlberg's third stage, the "conventionally moral" person, and was an accurate picture of the "kind of Catholic who dominated the pre-Vatican II church" (DiGiacomo, 1993, p. 68). He followed this by observing that the "new" Catholics that emerged in the wake of the Second Vatican Council (1962-1965) had the characteristics of Fowler's fourth stage, the "independent-reflexive" (1993, p. 68). The transition to this latter stage may begin in the late teens and is indicated by "a newly autonomous perspective as the individual becomes less dependent on others to construct and maintain his world of meaning" (1993, p. 68).

Given these observations, it would seem that the third stage has the most interest for religious educators since it is the most appropriate time, according to Fowler, that an informed and in-depth presentation of the faith tradition can take place. Francis (1988) claimed that it is also at this stage that Fowler encouraged the religious educator to "recognise the importance of promoting growth in the capacity and quality of believing" rather than maintaining the lesson at the level of imparting information (p. 6). He says:

> Christians would claim that knowledge does not equal faith, nor ... does psychological maturity equal spiritual formation. They are not opposed to each other ... but can work as partners in the quest for meaning, purpose and deliverance (Francis, 1988, p. 6).

Thus, teachers should be sensitive to the needs of their students, most particularly at this stage, and create a setting where students have the personal freedom and opportunity to taken a stance somewhere on a commitment/non-commitment continuum as the case may be.

However, Francis also highlighted a problem with Fowler's sample in respect of it being truly representative, since it contained people who were "overwhelmingly white and largely Christian" (1988, p. 6). Ninety-six per cent of the sample were not only religious but of the Judaeo-Christian tradition. Since religious faith is not a exclusive to Christians and Jews, it follows that in the multicultural and multi-faith environment of late twentieth-century American, British and Australian society, a truly representative sample would need to include people from different faith traditions. Only then could the results guarantee some degree of generalizability of the stages of faith development. However, despite these concerns, Fowler has provided educators with a framework upon which they can base further explorations into faith development.

Flynn (1985, 1986), a religious educator in Australia, explored the faith journeys of 2,041 Year 12 students from twenty-five Catholic schools in New South Wales and the Australian Capital Territory during 1982 to 1984. Should this be 1994? The study attempted to determine whether characteristic patterns were associated with the faith of these young people and whether these were the result of drift or conscious decision.

Flynn found that there were six clearly defined patterns of faith amongst late-adolescents. These were:

i) experienced faith: the highly imitative faith of the young which is based on the observation and experience of significant others;

ii) conventional faith: where adolescents were beginning to make a transition from their early faith patterns, which were dependant on external factors, to a more personalised faith;

iii) searching faith: a time when the childhood forms of faith no longer provide meaning in the lives of adolescents and they begin a journey of searching faith;

iv) rejection of faith: a rejection of the Church as an institution rather than as a community of faith and a period of rejecting authoritative figures such as parents, home, teachers and other significant people;

v) owned faith: where adolescents were beginning to develop their own way of relating to God, thus, they were in the process of forming a "personally owned faith"; and

vi) personal faith in Jesus: where adolescents indicated that they had a growing personal faith in Jesus and felt that their lives needed a "transcendent dimension" and to be "centred on God" in order for them to have meaning (1986, pp. 12-14).

Thus, Flynn found evidence that adolescents could be at any of the above stages but the stages themselves did not necessarily represent a progression, that is, movement from one to the next. The movement from childhood faith that was influenced by parents and home background, to the owning of a more personalised faith has some parallels with Fowler's stage theory and other developmental theories that mark the progress of an individual's search for their own value system. These theories provide useful insights for religious educators who need to acknowledge that faith is not a static thing, it is a developmental process that requires a nurturing environment amidst other believers who can and will share their faith experiences. Thus, opportunities that provide students with a level of freedom, flexibility, exposure and affirmation in their religious education classes have the potential to enhance their personal faith maturation and development.

> Write a reflective passage about how your image of and belief in God may have changed over the years. What factors may have contributed to the changes?

The spirituality of young people in the contemporary world

Every now and again, the dwindling congregations in Christian churches and the role of the Church in contemporary Australian society becomes the focus of the media, a topic to be kicked around on a playing field with movable goal posts. One by-product of such discussions often leads to conclusions being drawn about the irreligiousness of contemporary youth. Rarely do these discussions speak positively about the wealth of spirituality that may be evident in youth culture, if only it is looked for.

Speaking of Generation X who would be the parents of today's students, Beaudoin (1998), argued that if we seriously explore the cultural symbols and practices of Generation X we would find a people who are engaged in a serious search for a religion in which they can believe:

> Catholic Xers can continue to claim their own faith and not just passively accept what their Church teaches them. We witness again and again that although the Church may ideally be sacramental – a living sign of God's presence – faith in God and faith in the Church are not the same thing... Catholic Xers can make sure that their criticism are as direct as possible by immersing themselves in the history and tradition of the Church... By using knowledge of this history and tradition as a resource to criticize current Church arrangements creatively, Catholic Xers make their criticism even more pointed...

> If the Church as an institution can hear this harsh criticism, it can learn from Gen X. At a fundamental level, it needs to bring its practices and preaching back to its origins and its center – Jesus – in order to appeal to Christian Xers (1998, pp. 64-65).

Di Giacomo (1993) echoed this when he argued that young people saw Jesus "not as Creator, Lord and Judge but as Friend, Lover and Companion" (p. 16). He advised that:

> Catholic schools and youth programs must help turn out a new kind of Catholic for the 21st century: Christian humanists who have been effectively evangelized, who know their faith and are open to Gospel values. A new style of catechesis must evolve, if the next generation of Catholics is to be committed to church renewal and the transformation of society. It must be at once faithful to authentic Christian tradition, and attuned to the religious mentality of the young (1993, p. 12).

Lyon (2000), a Canadian sociologist, in his discussion of religion in post-modern times uses the metaphor of Jesus in Disneyland and says:

> Religion or, rather, spirituality has undoubtedly become a consumer item. New sources of meaning are sought that include prominently the figure or at least the name of Jesus. In Canada ... Jesus has become an icon of choice on T-shirts and tote-bags and appears in rap music lyrics and in best-

selling books. But this is equally and undoubtedly a post-modern Jesus. As theologian Henry Maier comments, while a personal relationship with God is sought, "people want an easier, faster, no-fuss, microwavable God." The cross remains a major stumbling block for many – as it always will – but in Maier's estimation, Jesus is popular because "he's a pluralist, he welcomes outsiders, he welcomes women, he is against organized religion, he's for economic justice. Jesus comes dressed up in the clothes of our own culture" (pp. 136-137).

These views highlight the fact that in contemporary society, while religion may be an aspect of spirituality, spirituality incorporates a much broader facet of human life. Additionally, while many young people appear to have become alienated and have distanced themselves from organized religion, they remain a deeply spiritual people who are engaged in a serious search for the purpose in life. One expression of young people's spirituality is their involvement, passion and insightfulness in issues that concern themselves and their peers and should not be underestimated or overlooked. In her discussion of spirituality in contemporary society, Maria Harris (Harris & Moran, 1998) pointed out that the spirituality of young people today is alive and well and she asserted that the vital element in the spirituality of young people:

> is its connectedness, its relational and communal character, which is in contrast to a privatized and individualistic spirituality. The impulse towards connectedness places the practice of justice in a special and privileged place, with justice understood as "fidelity to the demands of all our relations". Such justice includes not only our relations to other human beings; it includes our relations to the nonhuman universe as well: to the other animals, the trees, the ocean, the earth, and the ozone layer (p. 46).

The sense of connectedness as being at the core of youth spirituality today is also highlighted by British researchers Hay and Nye (1998) who used the term "relational consciousness" to describe the situation when children were aware of being in relationship with something or someone, that is, I-Others, I-Self, I-World and I-God. Drawing on their research findings, they argued that the feeling of connectedness added a special value to children's ordinary or everyday perspective.

One outcome of this feeling of connectedness is the trend of young people towards community. In 1997, Richard Eckersley's research into young Australian's perceptions of the future found that "their dreams for Australia were of a society that placed less emphasis on the individual, competition, material wealth and enjoying "the good life", and more on community and family, cooperation and the environment. Some expressed their wishes in terms of a greater recognition of the "natural", "human" or "spiritual" aspects of life." (p. 247).

Hugh Mackay (2001) commented on "Why our young pine for life in the tribe?" in *The Age*, Saturday, March 10th, 2001, and concluded that "their tribal identity often means more to them than their personal identity". He added "when their families are fragmented and traditional sources of identity are lost or blurred, this generation doesn't retreat into isolation; it connects." Mackay then discussed the findings from his own research among school leavers where the dominant theme that was woven into reflections on school life was emotional security, a place where they felt that they belonged. Mackay (2001) also spoke about the trend set by young people with older people following them, that is, the search for a new framework to help them make sense of life in an uncertain world:

> For some the new framework is spiritual. For others, it is based on the desire to reconnect with "the herd", so that individuals obtain a stronger sense of identity and of emotional security from re-creating communal connections that simulate the "village life" to which so many Australians aspire (p. 5).

From the discussion given above, identify some expressions/actions of young people in today's society that you believe indicate that they are/are not a spiritual people.

Conclusion

Drawing on the theories discussed in this chapter, there is a clear case for religious educators to recognize the different developmental stages of their students in terms of their faith, moral and spiritual development. As well, they should understand and address the associated needs of individual students in their learning requirements. In particular, students in contemporary Catholic classrooms need to be provided with a support and a solid grounding in their faith tradition which could enhance personal faith, moral and spiritual development and challenge their thinking.

Finally, while humanistic and developmental psychology by itself does not provide all the answers for religious educators, the theorists discussed in this chapter have made a valid contribution to the understanding of human development. Their work should assist religious education teachers to develop learning programs that acknowledge the varying stages of development that their students may be experiencing. This has implications for the choice of content and strategies that are appropriate for these individual differences so that learning in the subject can be accessed at various levels.

References and Further Reading

Biggs, J. & Telfer, R. (1987). *The process of learning*, 2nd edition. Sydney: Prentice Hall Australia.

Beaudoin, T. (1998). *Virtual Faith: The irreverent spiritual quest of Gen X*. California: Jossey-Bass Inc. Publishers.

Catholic Diocese of Ballarat (2005). *Awakenings. Core document: religious education P-12 curriculum*. Ballarat: The Catholic Diocese of Ballarat.

Catholic Education Office, Melbourne (1995). *Guidelines for the religious education of students in the Archdiocese of Melbourne-senior secondary*. Melbourne: Catholic Education Office.

de Souza, M. (1999). *Students' and teachers' perceptions of Year 12 religious education programs: Implications for curriculum*, unpublished PhD thesis. Melbourne: Australian Catholic University.

DiGiacomo, J. (1993). *Morality and youth: fostering Christian identity*. Kansas: Sheed and Ward.

Eckersley, R. (1997). 'Portraits of youth: Understanding young people's relationship with the future', *Futures*, 29 (3) pp. 243-249.

Erikson, E. (1968). *Identity: Youth and crisis*. New York: Norton.

Flynn, M. (1984). 'Religious education in Catholic schools: Which direction should we take?', *Word in Life, 32* (4) pp. 20-26.

Flynn, M. (1986). 'The journey of youth in faith: Drift or decision?', *Word in Life, 34* (2) pp. 12-16.

Fowler, J. (1981). *Stages of faith: The psychology of human development and the quest for meaning*. Blackburn: Dove.

Francis, S., 1988, 'Fowler's faith development theory and the teaching of religion in the voluntary context: How applicable is it?', *Religious Education of Australia, 4* (1) pp. 4-7.

Gilligan, C. (1977). 'In a different voice: Women's conceptions of self and of morality', *Harvard Educational Review*, 47 (4), pp. 481-517.

Gilligan, C. (1982). *In a different voice. A feminist critique of a well-researched area: moral development.* Cambridge, MA: Harvard University Press.

Harris, M. & Moran, G. (1998). *Reshaping religious education.* Louiseville, Kentucky: Westminster John Knox Press.

Hay, D. & Nye, R. (1998). *The spirit of the child.* London: Fount Paperbacks.

Kohlberg, L. (1969). 'Stage and sequence: The cognitive-developmental approach to socialization', in D.A. Goslin (ed.), *Handbook of socialization theory and research.* Chicago: Rand McNally.

Kohlberg, L. (1981). *The philosophy of moral development.* San Francisco: Harper and Row.

Mackay, H. (2001). 'Why our young pine for life in the tribe?' in *The Age*, Saturday, March 10, 2001.

Maslov, A. (1968). *Towards a psychology of being.* New Jersey: Princeton University Press.

Ministry of Education, Victoria (1988). *The school curriculum and organisation framework*, Ministry of Education, Victoria.

Moylan, J. (1993). 'Adolescents and their growth as moral persons', *Word in Life, 41* (3) pp. 14-17.

Pell, G. (1982.) 'Knowing the good and doing otherwise: Kohlberg on judgement and action', *Journal of the Institute of Catholic Education*, 3. November, pp. 1-12.

Rogers, C. (1969). *Freedom to learn.* Columbus, Ohio: Charles E. Merrill Publishing Company.

CHAPTER 5

The Whole Religious Education Curriculum

Michael T. Buchanan

Introduction

In partnership with parents and parishes the Catholic school contributes to the formation of the next generation of Catholics. The importance placed on the formation of children in faith or the life of the Church is rooted in the history of the Catholic Church in Australia. One outcome of the first Plenary Council of Australasian Bishops in 1985 was a mandate by the bishops directing parish priests to prioritise the building of a parish schools followed by the building of a parish church (Ryan & Malone, 1996). The Second Vatican Council (1962-1965) continued to emphasise the important contribution the Catholic school makes towards the formation of children in the Catholic tradition. The Congregation for Catholic Education declared that "In the light of her mission of salvation, the Church considers that the Catholic school provides a privileged environment for the complete formation of her members" (1977). This chapter explores some of the ways in which a Catholic school's whole religious education curriculum assists in the formation of the human person. The whole religious education curriculum extends well beyond the formal classroom program.

Discuss the contributions the formal classroom religious education curriculum might make to the formation of a student in faith and in the life of the Church.

List as many activities and programmes that might be offered at a Catholic secondary school and comment on how they might contribute to the formation of a student in faith and in the life of the Church.

Classroom religious education

From the 1970s on, Australian academics considered the formal religious education classroom as an appropriate place for the intellectual study of religious education. As early as 1975 Rummery called for a systematic approach to teaching the educational dimensions of religious education and in the following years Rossiter (1988) also emphasised that the intellectual study of religion was the most appropriate approach to use when teaching religious education in the formal religious education classroom. Rossiter (1981) emphasised that the study of religious education as an academic discipline has the potential to act as a channel to personal and communal formation in faith.

Under the leadership of the bishops, each diocese takes responsibility for the direction of classroom religious education programs taught in their schools. It is common and appropriate for curriculum documents to situate religious education within the context of the mission of the Catholic Church. Drawing on an apostolic exhortation of Pope Paul VI, *Evangeli Nuntiandi* (1975), the Melbourne archdiocese religious education curriculum framework makes this specific point. "In essence the religious education program is assisting the Church in its fundamental work: The Church exists to preach the Gospel." Many dioceses organise their curriculum documents according to content strands which are underpinned by the doctrines of the Church. The following example indicates the organisation of the content strands of Hobart's curriculum document, *Good News for Living* (Catholic Education Office, Hobart, 2005).

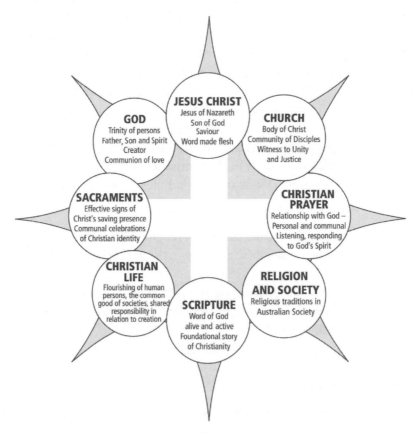

The Catholic Education Office, Melbourne organises its content stands according to five categories which are designed to support the goals of classroom religious education and aims to support the development of each student's understanding and appreciation of the following:

1 Scripture and Jesus	2 Church and Community	3 God, Religion and Life	4 Prayer, Liturgy and Sacraments	5 Morality and Justice
The Scriptures and the message of Jesus Christ and openness to their significance for living	The living tradition of the Catholic Church and a willingness to participate in its mission	God creation, awareness if the existence of good and evil, and a capacity to search effectively for meaning in life	God in prayer, liturgy and the sacraments and a willingness to participate in both personal and communal prayer	Catholic moral teaching and an ability to work for justice in the world

The strands and contents depicted above are drawn from the curriculum framework document *Coming to Know Worship and Love* (Catholic Education Office, Melbourne, 2005, pp. 8-9).

Choose another diocese within Australia and compare and contrast the way in which it has organised its content areas with Hobart and/or Melbourne.

You may wish to consider some of the following web sites:
CEO, Ballarat: http://ceo.balrt.catholic.edu.au/
CEO, Brisbane: http://www.bne.catholic.edu.au/asp/index.asp
CEO, Bathurst: http://www.ceo.bathurst.catholic.edu.au/links_cath_edu.html
CEO, Darwin:
	http://www.darwin.catholic.org.au/CatholicEducation/catholiceducation.html
CEO, Parramatta: http://www.ceo.parra.catholic.edu.au/
CEO, Perth: http://www.archdiocese-perth.org.au
CEO, Sandhurst: http://www.ceo.sand.catholic.edu.au/
CEO, Sale: http://web.ceo.sale.catholic.edu.au/
CEO, Sydney: http://ceo.syd.catholic.edu.au/

State accredited classroom religious education

Many Catholic schools offer state accredited courses in religious education as part of their classroom religious education program. For example in Victoria schools can choose to offer combinations of Religion and Society units 1-4, and Texts and Traditions units 1-4 as part of their senior classroom curriculum. The theoretical approach underpinning these programs is strongly influenced by phenomenology and typology and does not assume a particular faith orientation from the student or teacher. However if we accept Rossiter's (1981) assertion that the intellectual study of religion has the potential to act as a channel to personal and communal faith, then this possibility should also exist in the study of state accredited religious education.

Explore the following web sites and discuss whether the content portrayed in one or both of the state accredited course has the potential to form a person in terms of personal or communal faith.

Religion and Society:
http://www.vcaa.vic.edu.au/vce/studies/religion/religionsocietysd.pdf

Texts and Traditions:
http://www.vcaa.vic.edu.au/vce/studies/txtraditn/txtstradssd.pdf

or any of the accredited courses in religious studies from any other Australian state education system.

What kind of education and qualifications are needed by a classroom teacher of religious education in the Catholic secondary school?

Religious education beyond the classroom

In the context of the Catholic school the formation of children within the Catholic faith is not the sole responsibility of the classroom religious education program. There are many other aspects of the religious education curriculum which extend well beyond the formal religious education classroom. It is possible for all staff members to become involved in these aspects or components of the religious education curriculum. These components may include activities such as: social justice groups, Retreats, Liturgy and Prayer, and the celebration of religious feasts.

Many Catholic schools have social justice groups or social justice activities for students to participate in. A Christian person's involvement and concern for social justice exemplifies Christ-like behaviour. Central to Jesus' mission was his concern for the poor and oppressed in the world (Luke 4: 18-19).

Involvement in social justice activities provides an opportunity for students to be formed in a very important aspect of Church ministry. There are many social justice activities that students and teachers can be involved in. Some activities can be linked to organisations within the broader Catholic community.

Many Catholic schools organise fund raising initiatives and donate profits to charities and organisations committed to promoting the dignity of all people and especially the poor and oppressed. Fund raising initiative are ways in which all teachers and students can be involved in the religious education curriculum beyond the classroom curriculum. Some examples of ways to raise funds are: walkathons, casual clothes days, confectionary drives etc. Student engagement in community service programs may provide an opportunity for learning Christian ministry through participation in the local community. In some schools, community service programs are linked to the activities of a particular year level and students volunteer to help in organisations such as aged care, soup kitchens, and dining halls that provide a meal for people in need.

Liturgy and prayer also provide a significant opportunity for all members of the school community to participate in the religious education program. The liturgical life of a Catholic school enables individuals to express faith as a community and also contributes to a person's attention to their own personal faith. Every person can contribute in some way in the planning and preparation of liturgical and prayer celebrations. Some curriculum documents, for example *Coming to Know Worship and Love* (Catholic Education Office, Melbourne, 2005) have encouraged participation in prayer and liturgical experiences by suggesting possible prayer activities at the conclusion of each unit of work. Religious feast days are often celebrated in Catholic schools. . Many schools are named after saints and the feast day of the saint is an important day of celebration within the school community.

How might a teacher who is not a religious education teacher assist in the school's Liturgy programme?

Schools often organise opportunities for students to participate in retreats or reflection days. These opportunities provide a context for individuals and groups to pay specific attention to the development of spirituality and personal and communal faith (Engebretson et al, 2002). It is important to consider the specific reasons for holding a retreat weekend or day. The purpose of the experience might be:

- To build or deepen community within the school
- To deepen a sense of identity and belonging
- To develop a sense of involvement within the Church
- To enable people to explore specific faith or moral issues

- To prepare a particular group of students for life in the secondary school or for graduation into the world

It is always important to re-examine the goals of a youth retreat even in situations where the school has a long-standing history of retreat programs. This is because school communities, like the rest of society, are subject to demographic shifts, changing times and diversity in groups and leaders (Pastua, 1984). It is probable that what worked one year with a particular group may not work in the following year with another group. It is beneficial to hold preliminary planning meetings and consider the reasons for holding a retreat or reflection day with a particular group. Consideration should be given to the composition of staff members to be involved in the retreat and the roles staff are expected to fulfil. In general the roles of the staff will be oriented towards:

- Clarifying the goals of the retreat
- Setting the direction of the retreat
- Developing the format and content of the retreat
- Organising the time schedule of the retreat and activities within the program
- Determining the location of the retreat
- Developing the job descriptions and responsibilities of each individual staff member
- Securing the hiring of outside resources such as venues and in some cases specialised retreat leaders.

Pastua (1984) has suggested that the following issues be addressed in an initial meeting in order to make the retreat happen:

Making the retreat happen

Suggested meeting agenda for the first meeting

[ ] (before the first meeting) The authorised person notifies the staff of a planning meeting

[ ] Appoint a temporary/permanent coordinator to run the meeting

WHY

[ ] Set the goals for the retreat

WHO

[ ] Discuss the character and needs of the retreat participants

[ ] Clarify staff responsibilities

[ ] Decide whether an outside retreat team is needed or whether to build one from school personnel

WHAT

[ ] Decide the format of the prayer experience (one-day, weekend, evening)

WHEN

[ ] Choose tentative dates

WHERE

[ ] Make plans to find a location for the retreat and secure availability of facilities

WHY

[ ] Review the meeting and assign responsibilities

[ ] Set date for next meeting

How might a teacher who is not a religious education teacher assist in a school's retreat programme?

School life and the whole religious education curriculum

There are other aspects of school life and culture which reflect the religious education curriculum beyond the formal religious education classroom. To assist students and other members of a school community in the formation of the whole person in Christ, the religious life of the Catholic school should underlie everything that happens in a Catholic

---

school. The mission statement of each Catholic school can encourage this by making specific reference to the teaching of Christ and various Church teachings or doctrine. If a school's mission statement ignores the Christian message, then it gives permission for members of the community to do likewise.

Religious signs and symbols enable opportunities for members of the community to connect with the traditions of the Church. Religious pictures and statues and art around the school are tangible signs of the faith tradition being expressed within the community. Schools should constantly consider the number and location of religious art around the school. Some consideration should be given to the relevance of religious art in areas such as: the school reception area, board room, staff work areas, classrooms, chapels, halls, libraries, the school grounds and classrooms. The number and location of religious pictures, statues and art within a school may suggest something about the religious identity of a particular school.

Take a tour of a Catholic school make a list of the various religious signs and symbols around the school.

Identify their location and discuss the appropriateness of the location each.

Consider whether or not it would be appropriate to place religious symbols in other important locations within the school.

A school's discipline policy provides another opportunity for members of the school community to be inculcated in the Catholic faith tradition. Discipline that focuses on restoring people to right relationships by enabling room for forgiveness and reconciliation, provides an opportunity for individuals and the community to experience the mercy of Christ (Harris, 1996). Many schools have adopted restorative practices as part of their discipline policy. Restorative practices in school are inspired by the philosophy and practices of restorative justice, which puts repairing harm done to relationships and people over and above the need for assigning blame and dispensing punishment. A restorative approach to conflict or wrong doing consists of asking four questions:

1. What has happened?
2. Who has been affected?
3. How can we involve everyone who has been affected in finding a way forward?
4. How can everyone do things differently in the future?

Further information on restorative practices can be explored at:
http://www.transformingconflict.org/Restorative_Approaches_and_Practices.htm

Go to the restorative practices web site and identify some of the skills teacher may need to acquire or exercise in resolving conflict using this approach.

Restorative practices web site:
http://www.transformingconflict.org/Restorative_Approaches_and_Practices.htm

Pastoral care is another important aspect of school life that should reflect the religious dimension of the whole school curriculum both within and beyond the classroom. If a school is committed to the value and dignity of every person in the sight of God, then it stands to reason that pastoral care should be encouraged and provided in Catholic schools with the intention, and in the hope, that it conveys a reminder of God's love and grace. Pastoral care has a commitment to caring for the whole person. When schools orient their attention to a person's spiritual needs, as well as physical, social, intellectual and emotional needs, then pastoral care can be viewed as "holistic". Concern for the whole person enables an individual to feel valued and welcomed in the Christian community. When pastoral care permeates all the structures and process oriented towards helping a "holistic" approach to education, people have the opportunity to grow in personal and communal faith. Some Catholic schools appoint pastoral care coordinators and teachers and develop programs which are timetabled into the school calendar. These programs are oriented towards promoting pastoral care for all members of the school community.

Teachers who work in Catholic schools are able to participate in helping to form human persons (Sacred Congregation for Catholic Education, 1982) and in this context they share in the responsibility for promoting the mission of the Church. To this extent it will depend on teachers whether or not the Catholic school will achieve its purpose (Congregation for Catholic Education, 1997). Every teacher in a Catholic school is able to make a contribution to a religious education program that is oriented towards the personal and communal formation of human persons in the faith. Pope John VI (1975) emphasised this point in *Evangeli Nuntiandi*: "Modern man listens more willingly to witnesses than to teachers, and if he does listen to teachers, it is because they are witnesses." Pope John Paul II (2001) further stressed that "young Catholics are called to follow Jesus: not just in the future as adults, but now as maturing disciples and in partnership with parents and families, teachers play and significant role in nurturing a religious education curriculum oriented towards the formation of the whole person in the faith life of the Church.

The whole religious education curriculum contributes to the formation of the human person at a communal and personal faith level. The table below indicate aspects of the of school life which are oriented toward the delivery of religious education.

Classroom religious education	Activities beyond the formal classroom	Implied contribution to religious education
• School-based religious education curriculum guided by curriculum documents from Catholic Education Offices. • State accredited courses in religious education • Qualified teachers of religious education	• Social justice groups and activities • Community service • Liturgy • Prayer • Retreats • Reflection days	• Mission Statement • Religious signs and symbols • Discipline Policy • Restorative Practices • Pastoral Care • Teachers as witnesses

Peruse the contents depicted in the table and make a list of any other aspects of school life that contribute to the whole religious education curriculum.

References and Further Reading

Catholic Education Office, Hobart. (2005). *Good new for living.* Hobart: Catholic Education Office, Hobart.

Catholic Education Office, Melbourne. (2005). *Coming to know worship and love.* Melbourne: James Goold House.

Congregation for Catholic Education. (1977). *The Catholic school.* NSW: St Paul's Publications.

Congregation for Catholic Education. (1997). *The Catholic school on the threshold of the third millennium.* Australia: St Paul's Publications.

Engebretson, K., Fleming, J., Rymarz, R., (2002). *Thriving as an RE Teacher: A handbook for secondary religious educators.* Australia: Social Science Press.

Harris, M. (1996). Proclaim jubilee: *A spirituality for the twenty-first century.* Louisville, Ky: Westminster John Knox Press.

John Paul II (2001). *Ecclesia in oceania.* http://www.vatican.va/holy_father/john_paul_ii/apost_exhortations/documents/hf_jp-ii_exh_20011122_ecclesia-in-oceania_en.html

Pastua, M. L. (1984). *The Catholic retreat book: Everything you need to plan prayer experiences for a day, an evening, a weekend.* Cincinnati: St Anthony Messenger Press.

Paul VI. (1975). *Evangeli nuntiandi. http://www.vatican.va/holy_father/paul_vi/apost_exhortations/documents/hf vi_exh_19751208_evangelii-nuntiandi_en.html*

Ryan, M. & Malone, P. (1996). *Exploring the religion classroom: A guidebook for Catholic schools.* Australia: Social Science Press.

Rossiter, G. (1981). *Religious education in Australian schools.* Australia: Curriculum Development Centre Australia.

Rossiter, G. (1988). Perspectives on change in Catholic religious education since the second Vatican council, *Religious Education 83* (2), 264-276.

Rummery, R. M. (1975). *Catechesis and Religious Education in a Pluralist Society.* Sydney: E. J. Dwyer.

Sacred Congregation For Catholic Education. (1982). *Lay Catholics in schools: Witnesses to faith.* Australia: St Paul's Publications.

Cornerstones of Catholic Secondary Religious Education

CHAPTER 6:

Cognitive and Affective Dimensions of Religious Education

Michael T. Buchanan and Kath Engebretson

Introduction

An educational approach to religious education is concerned with both cognitive and affective dimensions of learning. These dimensions have been associated with outcomes based religious education. This chapter explores an educational approach to religious education which is based on cognitive and affective learning outcomes

Towards outcomes based religious education

The development of an outcomes based model of religious education was not the result of one particular factor. There were various influences contributing towards this shift. Among these influences were a changing population in Catholic schools, the introduction of state accredited courses in religious education, and the fact that various state governments had developed curricula founded on outcomes based learning and teaching. For example in Victoria, until the introduction the *Victorian Essential Learning Standards* the government emphasised outcomes based learning across the curriculum as part of the curriculum standards framework (Victorian Curriculum Assessment Authority, 2001). Within the context of school-based religious education in Catholic schools these factors contributed to the development of outcomes based religious education.

Migration had a significant impact upon the changing population of Catholic schools. Resulting from immigration trends from the 1950s and well beyond, the students in Catholic schools were no longer a homogeneous group of Catholics inculcated in the ministerial and ecclesial life of the Church. Since the Second Vatican Council (1962-65) the populations that make up most Catholic schools in Australia have come from diverse religious and secular backgrounds (Engebretson, 2002; Liddy; 2002; Lovat, 2002; Rossiter; 1988). The life-centred approach was situated within a catechetical context and assumed that students belonged to and practised the Catholic faith tradition (Catholic Education Office, Melbourne, 1973; 1984; 1995). This approach received much criticism for this assumption as well as its emphasis on the lived experiences of students (Ryan, 1998). Some considered that this over emphasis was counter productive to students understanding the traditions and teachings of the Church (Constable, 1992). Another criticism of the life –centred approach with its emphasis on catechesis, was that it excluded students who were not Catholic and not inculcated into the faith life of the Catholic Church (Engebretson, 2002; Liddy; 2002; Lovat, 2002; Rossiter, 1988).

Confidence in the ability of the religious education programs in Catholic schools to be made relevant all students began to decline (Engebretson, 2002). For many educators catechetical approaches to religious education were perceived as ineffective in enabling students who were not committed to Catholic belief and practice, to see the relevance of religious education. The desire of many educators to enable religious education to be relevant to all students generated much thought about outcomes based learning.

Another factor which led to an interest in outcomes based religious education was the state accredited religious education courses. Many Catholic schools included these courses in their senior school curricula, and like other stated accredited subjects, the learning schema was outcomes based. Comparatively large numbers of students in Catholic school were enrolled in state accredited religious education courses, and through them many teachers perceived that students were more engaged in the cognitively rich outcomes based approach to learning in religious education. The state accredited courses appeared more academically demanding (Engebretson, 2002) than school based courses that were often underpinned by the life-centred catechetical model. However these courses exposed gaps in students' knowledge about the Catholic faith. Parents and teachers were concerned that the life-centred approach had not effectively enabled students to learn much about religion, their own tradition or others. Discussions about an education in religious education with an emphasis on learning religious knowledge and skills through the achievement of learning outcomes gained momentum (Crotty & Crotty, 2000; Rossiter, 2000; Thomas; 2000).

> Briefly summarise the factors which have contributed to an emphasis on outcomes based learning in religious education in many Catholic schools.

Two dimensions of religious education

A learning outcomes approach in religious education assumes that the discipline has two inter-locked and inter-dependent processes, the cognitive and the affective. The cognitive dimension refers to learning about the world of religion it its many dimensions. This is an objective study, which is focused on growth in knowledge and skills. Its content may be the beliefs, ritual practices, social structure, history, ethical positions, symbols, stories or texts of a particular religious tradition, (or more than one tradition). All students, regardless of their personal religious beliefs are able to engage with this cognitive (learning about) dimension of classroom religious education. Over a lesson, unit of work, year's programme or school curriculum, the cognitive dimension is presented systematically and coherently so that students explore the world of religion broadly but also at some depth. The cognitive is the main focus and starting point of classroom religious education.

Intertwined with the cognitive aspect is the affective process of making sense of the cognitive at a personal level. In all education, the student learns not only at an intellectual level but inevitably seeks to appropriate the content and to extract its meaning. This is the affective dimension of education. In religious education, the student will not only engage at an intellectual objective level, but will also inevitably begin to consider the implications of the content in his or her own life, or will link it to previous or present life experience. Some students will do this much more consciously than others. This affective process consists of reflecting on the implications of the content, integrating the content with life experience, being challenged by the content to deeper awareness or sensitivity, responding in a personal and creative way to the content. For some students the affective process will lead to reflection on personal values and/or faith, and may contribute to development in values and faith. The affective dimension is implicit in the learning process, but the teacher will often make it explicit by providing opportunities for reflection and response. In another context, Grimmitt has referred to these dimensions as "Type A and Type B" knowledge, and he sees them working together in a constructivist view of education.

> In a society such as ours, everyone has to cope with multiple realities, and reality is not adequately defined only by reference to forms of knowledge or disciplines. The Reality as a Social Construct thesis places Type A knowledge (received, fixed, objectively existing knowledge) *within* the framework of Type B knowledge (personally and socially constructed knowledge) where it exists alongside other realities, especially *personal and interpersonal realities* … Bringing the forms of knowledge within a framework of reality which is socially constructed does not rule out that such knowledge is objective, as compared with inter-personal or intra-personal knowledge which is subjective. It does however deny that such knowledge is absolute, and not subject or relative to the social processes that create it. (Grimmitt, 1983, p. 23).

Summarise the different emphases in the cognitive and affective dimensions of religious education and show how they are interlocked.

Cognitive learning outcomes in religious education

The first step in religious education unit or lesson planning is to set cognitive and affective learning outcomes. In the case of cognitive learning outcomes, these are brief statements that set out the knowledge and skills that will be achieved by the students by the end of the unit or lesson. Therefore they draw on a range of content and a range of thinking and learning processes. The thinking and learning processes that can be incorporated into cognitive learning outcomes are shown in this table:

Remembering
Recognising; Recalling; Retrieving knowledge from memory; Identifying; Naming.

Understanding
Interpreting; Exemplifying: Finding a specific example or illustration of a concept or principle; Classifying; Summarising; Inferring; Comparing; Explaining; Paraphrasing; Translating; Representing; Clarifying; Illustrating; Categorising; Abstracting; Generalising; Extrapolating; Interpolating; Predicting; Concluding; Contrasting; Matching; Mapping; Constructing models.

Applying
Executing; Implementing; Carrying out; Using.

Analysing
Differentiating; Distinguishing; Organising; Discriminating; Selecting; Focusing; Outlining; Structuring; Integrating.

Evaluating
Checking; Critiquing; Detecting; Testing; Monitoring; Coordinating; Judging.

Creating
Generating; Planning; Producing; Hypothesising; Designing; Constructing.

The six categories of thinking shown in the table represent a development from quite simple to more complex skills. It is important that in setting cognitive learning outcomes that the teacher goes beyond the recalling and understanding dimensions, to engage the students in more demanding processes such as analysing, evaluating and creating. A good way to make sure that cognitive learning outcomes are realistic and achievable in the unit or lesson for which they are set, is to concentrate on the verbs that designate the particular skill being used.

The following table shows some cognitive learning outcomes that may be developed for a lesson based on the parable of the sheep and the goats from the Gospel of Matthew. First read the parable in Matthew 25: 31-46.

Possible cognitive learning outcomes that may be used to help Year 9 students to understand this gospel text may be as follows:

By the end of this lesson students will be able to:
- **Identify** the characteristics literary form of a parable in this extract.
- **Comprehend** and discuss thee meaning of terms nations, sheep, goats, Kingdom within the context of the parable.
- **Explain** the meaning of the parable for the Christian reader.
- **Use** the message of the parable to explore the work of the St. Vincent de Paul Society today.
- **Judge** the extent to which the work of the St. Vincent de Paul Society is true to the message of this parable.

You can see from the learning outcomes suggested above that once you have decided your cognitive learning outcomes you almost have your lesson planned. In the case of the cognitive learning outcomes provided above, the content of the lesson would consist of an analysis of the parable in terms of the characteristics of a parable, an exploration of the work of the St. Vincent de Paul Society through a speaker, film or written description, then class analytical discussion where the links between the message of the parable and the work of the Society would be drawn and students would have the opportunity to evaluate the extent to which these cohere.

In summary, cognitive outcomes are concerned with measuring the achievement of knowledge and skill centred learning. As shown above, cognitive learning outcomes are generally set out in clear statements that indicate the knowledge and skills intended for the students to achieve by the end of the lesson. They are generally drawn from a range of thinking and learning processes (Anderson and Krathwohl 2001). Identifying and outlining the cognitive learning outcomes for each lesson, unit of work, year's programme or school curriculum assists in the development of cumulative sequential curriculum planning. The documentation of learning outcomes helps to indicate and reinforce how the lesson objectives can be achieved. Identifying and documenting cognitive learning outcomes allows for students and teachers to clearly interpret the required level of achievement. Through the articulation of cognitive learning outcomes the teacher or curriculum planner is able to indicate whether a topic is to be explored broadly or in some depth.

Practising developing cognitive learning outcomes.

- List some alternative cognitive learning outcomes and content that may be put into this lesson on the parable of the sheep and the goats.
- Develop four cognitive learning outcomes, based on the table of cognitive processes shown above, for a Year 8 lesson on the story of the conversion of St. Paul.
- Develop three or more cognitive learning outcomes for a Year 10 lesson on the Sacrament of the Sick. Make sure that the outcomes you set are achievable in one lesson.
- List four possible cognitive learning outcomes for a Year 9 lesson on the biblical prophet Amos.

Make sure that in your cognitive learning outcomes you employ a range of thinking and learning processes. It is helpful to use the stem: *by the end of this lesson students will be able to*, because it helps you to concentrate on the particular skills you intend students to use.

A cognitive outcome should clearly articulate the knowledge and/or skill that will be achieved from engaging in the lesson or learning process. A teacher should be able to assess or judge the extent to which the outcome has been achieved. Detailed below are cognitive outcome statements based on some units from the Victorian and Sydney religious education textbook series: *To Know, Worship and Love*. Read each statement and comment on whether or not it is a cognitive outcome of a teaching strategy.

By the end of this lesson / unit students will be able to:
1. Illustrate signs and actions associated with each of the sacraments.
2. Share information that they have researched about St Pius X.
3. Identify in order the steps in the Rite of Confirmation.
4. Identify the similarities between Bar Mitzvah and Confirmation.
5. Record some of the hardships that St Paul endured during his lifetime.
6. Design a symbol representing the Kingdom of God.
7. Contribute to a debate on the issue "Is Australia a classless society?"
8. Map the spread of the Reformation through the world.
9. Summarise the outcomes of the Council of Trent.
10. Explain the difference between "vocation" and "commitment"
11. Recall the number of religious orders in Australia, and describe the Christian service provided by some of these orders.

Critique each of the cognitive outcomes listed above. Consider whether or not each cognitive outcome needs to be rewritten in order to clearly articulate what specific knowledge and/or skill a student is expected to gain. Also consider whether or not the language means that the students' learning of knowledge or skills can be demonstrated and assessed.

Affective learning outcomes

The cognitive learning dimension allows for the development of rational intelligence. However, students seldom only learn at the intellectual level. It is common for learners to seek ways to explore the knowledge content in a manner that offers meaning to them. This can be achieved through the affective dimension of education. The affective process consists of contemplating the implications of the content, integrating the content with life experience, being challenged by the content to deeper awareness or sensitivity, responding in a personal and creative way to the content (Engebretson, Fleming and Rymarz 2002). The affective dimension is implied in the cognitive learning process and naturally leads to it. The affective domain invites the student to internalise the knowledge content and has the potential to touch an array of feelings and reflective capacities.

Based on an understanding that the affective dimension can caters for the development of feelings, reflection, values, attitudes and faith, it is difficult determine whether or not affective learning outcomes can be achieved within a particular lesson or at all. A teacher will have little control over whether or not an affective outcome has been achieved by each student. However religious education in Catholic school is not simply concerned with the acquisition of knowledge for its own sake (Buchanan, 2005). The emphasis on cognitive outcomes is viewed as one of several important vehicles able to contribute to an individual's formation within the Catholic faith tradition. Attention to the affective dimension assists this possibility.

Entering into the affective dimension may involve an experience of inner transformation and not all students are always ready to do this at a particular or given time. Regardless it is important that an opportunity for students to enter into the affective domain is planned into the lesson or unit of work. Whether the student takes up that opportunity in the way it is intended is beyond the control of the teacher. When planning a lesson or unit of work a teacher should consider the complementarity between the cognitive and affective dimensions of learning. In particular, consideration could be given to the opportunities that provide for students to interact with the content focus articulated in the cognitive outcome.

In summary, unlike cognitive learning outcomes, affective learning outcomes are less able to be achieved fully in one lesson. This is because they cater for the development of attitudes, values, emotional, spiritual, and /or faith response which is more complex and longer term than the mastery of particular knowledge and skills. Therefore, the achievement of cognitive learning outcomes may be the subject of formal assessment but it would be impossible to fairly assess the extent to which affective learning outcomes have been achieved, because they represent very individual and long-term development. Therefore it is useful to use the word "hope" when deciding on affective learning outcomes. In the classroom we can provide opportunities for affective learning outcomes to be attended to, but we cannot ensure that these are achieved because they are closely linked with the personal development and freedom of the student. To illustrate a range of affective learning outcomes, let us return to the parable of the sheep and the goats from the gospel of Matthew.

By the end of this lesson it is hoped that students will have:
- Contemplated the challenge presented to the individual in the parable.
- Remembered and prayed for someone who cared for them when in need.
- Become more aware of the needs of individuals and groups within Australian society
- Grown in sensitivity to the needs of the poor
- Developed greater respect for the work of Christian individuals and groups in social justice.

When setting affective learning outcomes the terms we can use include:
- Show awareness of
- Show sensitivity to
- Accept
- Participate
- Demonstrate an attitude of
- Appreciate
- Respond to
- Demonstrate commitment to
- Accept responsibility for
- Reflect on …

We can only ever **provide opportunity for** the achievement of affective learning outcomes, but that fact does not denigrate their importance and the necessity of building opportunity for them into lessons and units of work.

Develop some affective learning outcomes for a lesson on:

- The *Our Father* prayer to Year 7s
- The role of conscience in decision making to Year 10s
- The ethical issues of euthanasia to Year 11s
- Muslims in Australia to Year 10s
- The Catholic Church and the Reformation to Year 9s

Attention to the affective dimension should provide opportunities for the student to interact with the cognitive dimension. In some way attention to the affective should enable the student to make sense of the cognitive knowledge in a personal way.

Detailed below are affective outcomes statements based on some chapters in the Melbourne and Sydney *To Know Worship and Love series.* Read each statement and comment on whether or not it provides an opportunity for the student to interact with knowledge in a personal way.

By the end of this lesson / unit students will have the opportunity to have:
1. Developed an appreciation for parables as a key means of understanding the teachings of Jesus.
2. Appreciated the importance of peace makers to our world.
3. Considered the importance and role of godparents.
4. Appreciated the symbolism and differences in various ways of conducting the Rite of Baptism.
5. Contemplated the importance of their own baptism.
6. Learned to value the quality of humility.
7. Thought about the lonely people within society and tried to understand what it would be like to be in their position.
8. Contemplated their views on marriage or the single vocation.
9. Grown in understanding and belief about the birth, death and resurrection of Jesus.
10. Grown in awareness of society's treatment of people in relation to gender

Critique each opportunity to interact within the affective dimension listed above. Consider whether or not each affective opportunity needs to be rewritten in order to clearly indicate the opportunity given to students to interact within the affective domain.

Putting it all together

Imagine that you want to use the content provided in the following extract for a lesson on *Cathedrals* with a Year 10 class. Draw up a list of cognitive and affective learning outcomes, being sure to use a range of skills. Then list how you might go about presenting the lesson so that the learning outcomes might be achieved.

Cathedral

A Cathedral is the main church of a bishop's diocese or archdiocese. It is the Church where people gather to pray and worship under the leadership of their bishop. The word "Cathedral" comes from "Cathedra", the Latin word for "Chair". Therefore, the Cathedral is where we find the Bishop's Chair, a sign of his office and a sign of unity in the diocese. The floor plan of a cathedral is in the shape of a cross and the entrance faces west. The nave is the longest part of the cross and this is the assembly area for the congregation. The two arms of the cross called the transepts form right angles to the nave and meet at the crossing. Ideally a Cathedral points to the east, but when it doesn't the sanctuary, which contains the main altar, is said to be at the ecclesiastical or liturgical east, the entrance is said to be at the ecclesiastical or liturgical west, and the aisles to the ecclesiastical or liturgical north and south.

Labelling activity
The following are some architectural terms associated with Cathedrals. Label a typical floor plan with as many of these as you can.

Ambulatory: This is the walkway around the curve of the apse, and behind the altar, which provides space for processions and for visiting small chapels.
Apse: This is a semicircular or multi-angled area, projecting from the east or ecclesiastical east of the Cathedral and which contains a number of small chapels.
Baptistry: An area where baptisms are performed, centred on the baptismal font, and traditionally located at the west end of the Cathedral, just inside the entry.
Belfry: The chamber or tower in which bells are hung.
Buttress: A support built against the wall and designed to strengthen it.
Carillon: A collection of bells, which may be rung in rapid succession to play a tune.
Cathedral glass: Glass which is translucent, but not transparent, usually of a whitish colour.
Chancel: The extended area of the ecclesiastical east end of the Cathedral. Usually narrower than the nave, and traditionally containing the altar.
Chevet: The curved east end of the Cathedral where it includes radiating chapels.

Choir: The section of the ecclesiastical east end of the Cathedral reserved for singers.

Crossing: The intersection of the nave, chancel and transepts in a cathedral.

Dado: The lower section of an interior wall.

East end. The part of the Cathedral extending east of the transept, comprising the sanctuary.

Font: A container of water used for baptisms.

Gargoyle: a projecting stone spout often carved in the form of a grotesque creature, designed to take water from a roof.

Gothic: Gothic is the late medieval style of European architecture, from about 1200 to 1600.

Hammer Beam: A horizontal timber bracket with a curved brace below it.

Narthex: A space running across the ecclesiastical west end of a Cathedral and opening to the back of the nave.

Nave The long west arm of the cathedral that holds the congregation.

Pillar: A slender upright structure used to support and arch, cornice e or other weight.

Sacristy: A chamber, often to one side of the chancel, in which are kept vessels, sacred vessels and valuables.

Sanctuary: Part of the chancel, between the altar rails and the east window, which contains the high altar.

Spire: A steep pointed roof, in the shape of a cone or pyramid, rising from a Church tower.

Transept: The arm of the cathedral that cuts across between the nave and the chancel.

Vault: An arched ceiling or roof of stone or brick sometimes imitates in wood or plaster.

West End: That part of the Cathedral extending west of the transepts, comprising the nave, and narthex.

Research

Find out about the history of the Cathedral in your own diocese.

Visit the Cathedral and sketch some of its features.

What special features does the Cathedral in your diocese have?

Use the Internet to find out about some of the great Cathedrals of the world.

Adapted from the Catholic Education Office Melbourne publication, "All Who Gather".

A kit prepared for secondary schools on the occasion of the centenary of St. Patrick's Cathedral.

References and Further Reading

Anderson, L. and Krathwohl, D. (2001). *A Taxonomy for Learning, Teaching and Assessing: A Revision of Bloom's Taxonomy of Educational Objectives.* New York: Longman.

Buchanan, M. T. (2005). Pedagogical drift: The evolution of new approaches and paradigms in religious education. *Religious Education, 100* (1), 20-37.

Catholic Education Office, Archdiocese of Melbourne. (1973). *Guidelines for religious education of students in the archdiocese of Melbourne.* Melbourne: Catholic Education Office.

Catholic Education Office, Archdiocese of Melbourne. (1984). *Guidelines for religious education of students in the archdiocese of Melbourne.* Melbourne: Catholic Education Office, Archdiocese of Melbourne.

Catholic Education Office, Archdiocese of Melbourne. (1995). *Guidelines for religious education of students in the archdiocese of Melbourne.* Melbourne: Catholic Education Office, Archdiocese of Melbourne.

Congregation for Catholic Education. (1977). *The Catholic school.* Australia: Society of Saint Paul.

Congregation for the Clergy. (1998). *General directory for catechesis.* Australia: St Paul's.

Constable, C. (1992). A parent reflects. *Word in Life, 40* (4), 1-14.

Crotty, M. & Crotty, R. (2000). Assessing the role of the RE textbook. *Journal of Religious Education, 48* (2), 23 – 27.

de Souza, M. (2001). Addressing the Spiritual Dimensions in Education: Teaching Affectively to Promote Cognition. *Journal of Religious Education 49* (3) 31-41.

de Souza, M. (2005). Engaging the mind, heart and soul of the student in religious education: Teaching for meaning and connection. *Journal of Religious Education, 53* (4), 40-47.

Elliott, T P. (Ed.). (2001a). *To know worship and love Years 7 teacher companion.* Melbourne, Australia: James Goold House.

Elliott, T P. (Ed.). (2001b). *To know worship and love Years 9 teacher companion.* Melbourne, Australia: James Goold House.

Elliott, P. (Ed.). (2002a). *To know worship and love teacher companion year 8.* Melbourne, Australia: James Goold House.

Elliott, P. (Ed.). (2002a). *To know worship and love teacher companion year 10.* Melbourne, Australia: James Goold House.

Engebretson, K. (2002). Writing church-sponsored religious education textbooks. *British Journal of Religious Education 25* (1), 33-45.

Engebretson, K, Fleming, J and Rymarz, R. (2002). *Thriving as an R.E. Teacher: A Handbook for Secondary Religious Educators.* Australia: Social Science Press.

Grimmitt, M. (2000). Contemporary pedagogies of religious education: What are they? In. M. Grimmitt (Ed.). *Pedagogies of religious education: Case studies in the research and development of good pedagogic practice in RE* (pp. 24-52). Great Wakering, England: McCrimmon.

Habel, N & Moore, B. (1982). *When religion goes to school: A typology of religion for the classroom.* South Australia: South Australian College of Advanced Education.

Liddy, S. (2002). Children's spirituality, *Journal of Religious Education, 50* (1), 13-19.

Lovat, T. (2002). *What is this thing called R. E. A decade On?* (2nd Ed.). Australia: Social Science Press.

McInerney, P. (2004). *Making hope practical: School reform for social justice.* Australia: Post Pressed.

Pell, G. (2001). From the Archbishop. In Elliot, Peter (ed.) *To Know Worship and Love Teaching Companion Year7 & 9.* Melbourne: James Goold House.

Rossiter, G. (1988). Perspectives on change in Catholic religious education since the second Vatican council. *Religious Education, 83* (2), 264-276.

Rossiter, G. (2000). The qualities of an excellent student text in religious education. *Journal of Religious Education, 48 (2),* 13-16.

Ryan, M. (1998). An evaluation of outcomes based approaches in religious education curriculum guidelines. *Word in Life: Journal of Religious Education, 46* (1), 14-19.

Thomas, J. (2000). Survival without texts. *Journal of Religious Education, 48 (2),* 54 – 57.

Victorian Curriculum and Assessment Authority. (2001). *Curriculum Standards Framework II.* Melbourne: Victorian Curriculum and Assessment Authority.

CHAPTER 7

The Spiritual Dimension in Religious Education: a Complementary Factor in the Learning Process

Marian de Souza

Throughout the past century, education programs have been generated by a particular concept of intelligence (IQ) that is rational intelligence. To be sure, an understanding of intelligence has particular relevance to the development and application of learning programs across the curriculum and, as such, a brief overview is presented here.

In the early 1900s, tests were devised to measure processes such as memory, attention, comprehension and discrimination which were considered elements of rational intelligence (Binet, 1904, revised by Terman at Stanford University, 1916). Terman used the tests to indicate a child's level of performance in logic and reasoning, and he linked them to the age of the child. Thus, they yielded a global figure called an intelligence quotient (IQ). Learning and assessment in western education, then, were based on this concept of intelligence, so that performance in particular areas such as language and logic, particular skills such as verbal and mathematical, and processes such as comprehension, reasoning and memory were measured to determine a person's intelligence. Accordingly, cognitive learning became the dominant factor of educational programs and this also influenced religious education, where there was some assumption that the transmission of knowledge of the faith tradition would, somehow, promote commitment to it. Anecdotal evidence would suggest that, for many, this may have been a false assumption. It could be argued that such programs did not address the whole child since they were confined to particular human traits and abilities and this did raise some problems in subjects like Religious Education where the affective and spiritual dimensions are also important features,

Gardner's Multiple Intelligence theory

It was in the late twentieth century that some new research led to significant changes in the way educators began to think about and practice their profession. To begin with, Howard Gardner (1983, 1993) rejected a unitary view of intelligence and the concept of IQ. He proposed a theory of multiple intelligences (MI Theory) and argued that, for most people, these intelligences worked together to help them solve problems and engage competently with their cultural environment, that is, an intelligence was "an ability to solve problems or fashion products that were of consequence in a particular cultural setting or community" (Gardner, 1993, p. 15). Thus, a person identified a particular goal they wished to achieve, and they were able to develop strategies within and relevant to their cultural setting, to help them obtain that goal. In view of his argument, Gardner, at first, identified seven intelligences, and later, he added the eighth. These were: verbal/linguistic; logical/mathematical; visual/spatial; bodily/kinaesthetic; musical/rhythmical; interpersonal; intrapersonal; naturalist. Gardner argued that while each individual had all or most of these intelligences, they existed in different strengths and intensities in each individual. Accordingly, it was important for teachers to incorporate these eight ways of knowing into their classroom practice, since it gave students a better opportunity to be successful in their learning.

Although there were several suggestions that Gardner should identify a spiritual intelligence, he avoided this. Instead, in a videoed interview with Peter Salovey (1999) he jokingly made a reference to a "half intelligence": existential intelligence – that is the ability which enables people to ask questions about the meaning of life, death and ultimate realities. However, Gardner was hesitant about describing this as a spiritual intelligence and suggested that more research was needed.

Using Gardner's MI Theory, suggest activities to teach the Scripture passage: Mt 5:1-12 – the Beatitudes. Remember that the activities should allow the student to access the content and express their learning in different ways, using the eight intelligences that Gardner identified.

Emotional intelligence and learning in the affect

Other research that has examined different concepts of intelligence and which, therefore, have relevance for teaching and learning, was carried out in the nineties. Salovey and Mayer (1990) psychologists from Yale and New Hampshire Universities respectively, proposed a theory of emotional intelligence which was the individual's ability to process emotional information, particularly as it involves perception, assimilation, understanding and management of emotion. Their model of emotional intelligence identified four branches of mental ability which moved from a basic process (perceiving and expressing emotions) to more advanced psychological processes (conscious, reflective regulation of emotion):

- Emotional identification, perception and expression of emotion (identifying emotion in faces, music, stories and so on).
- Assimilating emotion in thought (for instance, relating emotions to other mental sensations such as taste, or colour as in art) and using emotion in reasoning and problem solving (integrating emotion in thought).
- Understanding and analysing emotion (solving emotional problems such as knowing which emotions are similar, or opposites, and what relations they convey).

- Reflective regulation of emotion (understanding the implications of social acts on the emotions, and the regulation of emotion in self and others) (Mayer et. al., 2000, pp. 396-420).

Certainly, it is useful for educators to have some knowledge and understanding about these different aspects of emotional intelligence to assist them in their classroom management strategies.

Another theorist, Daniel Goleman (1996), suggested that the emotional mind responds to a situation much more quickly than the rational mind. This is an important consideration in the teaching and learning process that needs to be acknowledged and utilized. Immediate emotional responses are something the rational mind cannot control and Goleman suggests that they are a response of the *heart* not the *head*. However, he contends that the mind can trigger an emotional response through its thoughts, and such a response can be controlled – that is, thinking precedes feeling and these take longer (by seconds or minutes) to unfold (p. 293). Further, Goleman claimed that the rational mind makes logical connections between causes and effects, but the emotional mind is indiscriminate, connecting things that merely have similar striking features. The logic of the emotional mind is associative; it takes elements that symbolize a reality, or trigger a memory of it, to be the same as that reality so that similes, metaphors and images speak directly to the emotional mind, as do the arts – novels, film, poetry, song, theatre, opera. Great spiritual teachers, like Buddha and Jesus, touched their disciples' hearts by speaking in the language of emotion, teaching in parables, fables, and stories. "Indeed, religious symbol and ritual makes little sense from the rational point of view; it is couched in the vernacular of the heart" (Goleman, 1996, p. 294).

Ultimately, Goleman pointed out that emotional intelligence is a basic requirement for an effective use of our rational intelligence – that is, our feelings play an important role in our thought processes.

Think of a time when your emotions may have affected your ability to learn. Consider how your emotional state may have had an impact on the learning process. This could have led to a positive or a negative result.

Goleman claims that great spiritual teachers taught their followers by using the language of emotion. Can you find a parable, fable or story that Jesus used which is an example of this and discuss how it may speak to the heart before the mind.

Watch some scenes in the film *Jesus Christ Superstar* and read relevant parts of one of the gospel passages, for instance, Mt 26:1-75 or Mt 27:1-66. Reflect on your response to both experiences. Did one resource involve your thoughts and feelings and, perhaps, produce insights or reflections to a greater degree than the other?

Write 300 words explaining your responses and discuss them in light of the theories of emotional intelligence.

Spiritual intelligence

Finally, there have been some theorists who have argued for the possibility of a spiritual intelligence, and have drawn on neuro-scientific and psychological research to provide a rationale to support this concept. Zohar and Marshall (2000) are perhaps, the better known advocates of this theory. They have drawn on various neuro-scientific studies based on the workings of the brain to propose that there is a third intelligence which they label spiritual intelligence (Spiritual Quotient or SQ). They claim (pp. 3-4) that the human person uses this intelligence to address and solve problems of meaning and value, and to place their lives and actions in a wider, richer, meaning-giving context. It is the intelligence that allows them to assess that one course of action or one life-path is more meaningful than another. They argue that SQ is essential for the effective functioning of the Intelligence Quotient (IQ) and Emotional Quotient (EQ).

Neither IQ nor EQ, separately or in combination, is enough to explain the full complexity of human intelligence nor the vast richness of the human soul and imagination. SQ allows human beings to be creative, to change the rules and to alter situations. It allows us to play with the boundaries, playing an "infinite game". SQ gives us our ability to discriminate. It gives us our moral sense, an ability to temper rigid rules with understanding and compassion and an equal ability to see when compassion and understanding have their limits. We use SQ to wrestle with questions of good and evil and to envision unrealized possibilities – to dream, to aspire, to raise ourselves out of the mud (p. 5). This process "unifies, integrates and has the potential to transform material arising from the other two processes. It facilitates a dialogue between reason and emotion, between mind and body. It provides a fulcrum for growth and transformation. It provides the self with an active, unifying, meaning-giving centre" (p. 7).

Zohar & Marshall offer the following characteristics of SQ:

- the capacity to be flexible (actively and spontaneously adaptive)
- a high degree of self-awareness

- a capacity to face and use suffering
- a capacity to face and transcend pain
- the quality of being inspired by vision and values
- a reluctance to cause unnecessary harm
- a tendency to see the connections between diverse things (being "holistic")
- a marked tendency to ask "Why?" or "What if?" questions and to seek "fundamental" answers
- being what psychologists call "field-independent" – possessing a facility for working against convention
- a capacity to be a "servant leader" – being able to bring a higher vision and value to others and showing them how to use it, in other words, a person who inspires others (pp. 15-16)

Other research that has examined the spirituality of young children came from Hay and Nye (1998) who described an unusual level of consciousness or perceptiveness, relative to other passages of conversation spoken by that child. These conversations were expressed in a context of how the child related to other people, self, the world and God. They coined the term "relational consciousness" which reflected two patterns that drew all the data together:

> Thus, children's spirituality was recognized by a distinctive property of mental activity, profound and intricate enough to be termed "consciousness", and remarkable for its confinement to a broadly relational, inter- and intra-personal domain (Hay & Nye, 1998, p. 113).

> "Consciousness" was used here as something more than being alert. Rather, it suggested a reflective consciousness, as in a meta-cognitive process. Children's awareness of being in an "I-Others," "I-Self, "I-World and "I-God' relationship was indicated from what they said and there was a special sense of this relationship adding value to their ordinary or everyday perspective. … In this 'relational consciousness' seems to lie the rudimentary core of children's spirituality, out of which can arise meaningful aesthetic experience, religious experience, personal and traditional responses to mystery and being, and mystical and moral insight (Hay & Nye, 1998, p.114).

> Spiritual intelligence represents a dynamic wholeness of self in which the self is at one with itself and with the whole of creation and in this "relational consciousness" seems to lie the rudimentary core of children's spirituality, out of which can arise meaningful aesthetic experience, religious experience, personal and traditional responses to mystery and being, and mystical and moral insight. (Hay & Nye, 1998, p.114).

Another perspective came from Newberg, D'Aquili & Rause (2001) who claimed that there was nothing magical about mystical experience, that it was "nothing more or less than an uplifting sense of genuine spiritual union with something larger than the self" (2001, p. 101). They concluded that "humans are natural mystics blessed with an inborn genius for effortless self-transcendence" (p. 113) and that like all experiences, moods, and perceptions, these unitary states are made possible by neurological function. More specifically, they are "the result of the softening of the sense of self and the absorption of the self into some larger sense of reality that we believe occurs when the brain's orientation area is deafferented, or deprived of neural input" (pp. 113-4). Thus, these writings from the field of neuroscience also point to relationality as being part of spirituality.

A research study into the spirituality of young people (de Souza, Cartwright & McGilp, 2004) supported the notion that individuals experience different levels of connectedness beginning with their relationships within their immediate family and community and which sometimes extend to include the unfamiliar and unknown "Other". Thus, human spirituality could be described as expressions of connectedness to Other. At one level, this may be reflected in relationships to families and friends, in other words, to those who are close and similar to the individual. At a wider circle, this may be expressed in the feelings of empathy and compassion that the individual may experience to people who are different. It could be argued that when a person's growth reaches the wider circle, they enter another level of spiritual maturity, and their connectedness to the Other at this level helps them to understand another part of themselves, that is, they may recognize a part of the Other as something that is a part of themselves. Thereby, the widening circle of connectedness to Other brings a deepening knowledge of the inner Self; a deeper connectedness to Self. This reflects Thomas Merton's assertion that he searched for his identity not only in God but in others where "the process of inner transformation that leads to self-discovery is simultaneously a process of discovering our deep relatedness to others" (as cited in Del Prete, 2002, p. 165).

These findings led de Souza (2003, 2004) to conclude that the path to spiritual maturity may be described as a journey towards Ultimate Unity. The journey may spiral through different circles of connectedness to Self and Other which, for some, may have the potential to lead to the deepest level of connectedness where an individual experiences becoming one with Other – Ultimate Unity. In this, de Souza's conclusions supported Newberg's (2001) contention that the neurology of transcendence is a movement towards Absolute Unitary Being, that is when the self blends into other and mind and matter become one and the same (p. 156). Newberg proposed a "unitary continuum" where, at one point, a person may interact with others and the world but experience it as something from which s/he is apart. However, as s/he moves up the unitary continuum, that separateness becomes less distinct (p. 145).

To be sure, there is a considerable body of literature that examines and discusses spirituality as pertaining to the relational dimension of being. It is expressions of connectedness that an individual experiences to Self and to a Social and Communal Other, to Other in the physical world and ultimately, to a Transcendent Other. Certainly, there are different levels and depths of the connectedness that the individual may have but, in the end, these lead to a sense of self-esteem and self knowledge which assists the individual to find a place in their respective networks and communities which, in turn, brings a sense of meaning and purpose to their daily lives.

Revisit the characteristics of spiritual intelligence and discuss whether you believe that SQ may have had a role in your own learning experiences? For instance, can you describe a time when your spiritual intelligence may have provided you with an intuition or some wisdom that you may not have gained through your rational thinking?

To sum up, the concepts of these three intelligences do provide a useful framework for learning and teaching in religious education (indeed, it could be useful to apply it to the wider curriculum) and they may be linked to the processes of the cognitive, affective and spiritual dimensions of learning, that is, perceiving (consciously and non-consciously), thinking, feeling and intuiting. New theories about intuition argue that they are a result of non-conscious learning (for instance, Breen, 2000; Eraut, 2000; Hillman, 1996; Hogarth, 2001; Myers, 2002) and this kind of learning needs to be factored into the development and practice of educational programs.

In addition, given the unique nature of religious education, these three areas do have some significance. Apart from the knowledge and skills that need to be learnt (cognitive learning), there is also the need to stir the emotions which may result in a display of interest, some kind of response and participation (affective learning). However, religious education, as with some other subjects (for instance, the arts and humanities) needs to look beyond merely promoting an interest in the subject and eliciting initial responses from students. It needs to address the personal, moral and spiritual growth of students within their social and cultural contexts.

In addition, the learning strategies and resources need to engage the thinking and the feelings of the students in their personal search for meaning and decision-making. Arguably, this has the potential of contributing to their religious development, involvement and/or commitment to their faith tradition. However, it is essential to recognize that these latter outcomes are desirable rather than intended, thus, removing any sense of indoctrination, and retaining, instead, an atmosphere of hope, trust and individual freedom. The next section offers an approach to learning and teaching that attempts to do this.

A learning approach that incorporates the spiritual dimension in religious education

The learning approach that is offered here recognizes that while students' learning is based on what they consciously and non-consciously perceive through their senses, their initial response may be at the intellectual level (thinking - knowledge based) or the emotional level (feelings based). These responses will then lead to an integration of the two so that the intellect and the emotions work together to produce a deeper level of knowledge and engagement. However, if the learning is to go beyond the surface, it must touch the "soul" of the student. It must reach that core where the learning becomes transformed by an inner response which may and should lead to outward expressions of changed thinking and behaviour. It is at this level that intuiting becomes the fourth aspect of an integrated learning process so that the learner's response becomes transformed without her/him consciously knowing exactly how or why the change has occurred. The motion then is generative, moving from initial perceptions at the surface or the conscious mind which generates thoughts and feelings that merge with previous learning and instincts at the depth non-conscious level before returning to the surface/conscious mine in transformed expressions. (See Figure 5 - de Souza, 2004, p. 27)

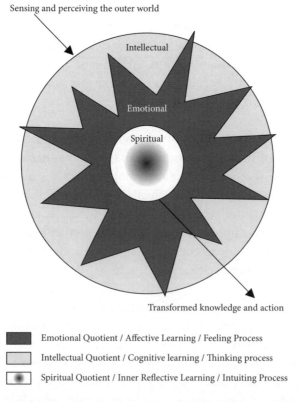

Figure 5: A Curriculum model for learning, thinking, feeling, intuiting.

According to Jung, intuition is the function that tells us of future possibilities. It is the proverbial hunch and the function that informs us about the atmosphere that surrounds an experience or event. It is sometimes seen as unconscious perception as opposed to sensation, which can be seen as conscious perception (O'Connor 1985, 1988, 1990).

In general, then, intuitive learning would appear to operate at a non-conscious level where new thoughts and feelings, which have been provoked by new perceptions or sensations, become absorbed through a "rumination" process (Claxton, 2000, p. 40) into the learning that an individual has accumulated non-consciously that is, through non-conscious perceptions, and which are stored at a depth level, at the core of his/her being. Subsequently, new learnings evolve from this merging which may translate into changed attitudes and/or behaviour. Thus, learning that is transformational is an integration of these four elements, perceiving, thinking, feeling and intuiting. Without integration it is possible that learning may remain superficial or "surface" learning.

These four elements enable us to become familiar with both our inner and outer worlds, and this is essential if learning is to become meaningful to and address the whole person. Therefore, it may raise the potential for learning to address the relational aspects of a student's life, that is, the spiritual dimension. This is something that has not always been clearly articulated. Indeed, an integration of these elements is vital if education, ultimately, seeks to be transformational. An illustration of this process is offered here:

> I would like to identify a topic for a lesson and explore various responses to it. For instance, if the topic is "bullying", one student may promptly think about what they know of bullying: what the word means, what previous information may have come their way, have they ever bullied someone or seen someone bullied. These last two thoughts are likely to prompt some feelings so that thoughts and feelings merge. Another student who has been bullied is more likely to respond initially with feeling so that subsequent thinking will be coloured by the feelings. If the teaching of the content is to be effective, the learning activities will be designed to move the thoughts and feelings through to a deeper level At this level, the individual may have previous relevant knowledge which has been gained unconsciously through the senses, such as having unconsciously noticed the expression, body language or subsequent behaviour of a person who has been bullied and knowing at a depth level that the person has been affected, hurt, traumatized and so on. The merging of the new knowledge and the previous knowledge now raises the potential for the individual to recognize what it means to bully or to be bullied, the rights and the wrongs of the situation, and to feel some empathy with the person who has been bullied. If the learning has reached a depth level, it should prompt some future action and/or response to the practice of bullying or to bullies themselves – the transformation (de Souza, 2003, pp. 27-28).

Many teachers in RE classrooms do, in fact, address the spiritual dimension of learning but this may be incidental rather than planned and, consequently, it is possible that it may not happen at all. If the learning approach described here is used there needs to be a conscious element in the planning of any lesson or unit of work that factors in the cognitive, affective and spiritual dimension of the learning process. In other words, attention must be given to the conscious and non-conscious learning that takes place through the senses leading to thoughts, feelings and intuitions.

One problem that may arise is the question of writing learning outcomes in the planning since learning outcomes statements imply that specific learning will take place. However, what is offered here is a way around this problem. Cognitive learning outcomes are measurable and therefore are stated accordingly:

By the end of the lesson students will define, OR describe, OR recall, OR recognize, OR illustrate and so on.

On the other hand, affective and spiritual learning outcomes are expressed as a desired outcome so the statement indicates that the opportunity will be provided for this learning to happen. At no time is there a statement that says it will happen and no attempt is made to measure such learning. Affective and spiritual learning outcomes are stated accordingly:

By the end of the lesson opportunities will be provided for students to show awareness of, OR experience, OR accept, OR appreciate, OR display interest and so on.

And

By the end of the lesson opportunities will be provided for students to develop a sensitivity to, OR empathize with, OR develop compassion, OR reflect inwardly, OR accept responsibility, OR contemplate and so on.

The reasons for including statements about affective and spiritual learning despite the fact that they may not be demonstrable or, indeed, measurable, are to ensure that the teacher will keep these aspects of the learning in mind as they plan and teach the lesson. This reduces the chance that the learning may remain at the cognitive level, surface learning, with an emphasis on tasks that keep students busy and assist with classroom control.

Such an approach also challenges the teacher to find new ways of communicating the content in ways to seriously engage their students for instance, using an arts approach, to teach topics that may be perceived as "boring" by many students. The arts promote learning through different senses leading to a variation of perceptions, thereby increasing the possibilities of developing students' creativity and imagination. This is equally the case with the use of other visually and aurally stimulating resources and activities which connect and resonate with students' stories and lives, so that they become more relevant and meaningful. Anecdotal evidence from my postgraduate students when they plan a unit of work using this kind of approach in their own classrooms indicates that their own students' learning has been effective, meaningful and enjoyable. Words to the effect that this was the best RE lesson for both teacher and students are commonly used to describe the experience.

Choose a topic from one of the diocesan RE curriculum documents and write up three learning outcomes – cognitive, affective and spiritual. Then select some learning activities that you can use to teach the learning outcomes. Remember, the spiritual learning outcome should lead to transformation in thinking and action.

To conclude, addressing the perceiving, thinking, feeling and intuiting processes in the learning situation are vital for a healthy classroom environment where opportunities exist for students to connect and find meaning. This is particularly necessary in the contemporary context when so many students and their parents are unchurched. Many of the parents with school-going children today belong to Generation X and only have a superficial knowledge about their faith tradition (Lynch, 2002; Rymarz, 1999). In such instances, religious education may be likened to the teaching of a foreign subject where connections must first be established if it is at all to become meaningful. In addition, strategies that nurture and give expression to the inner life should be included in the daily program. These may be drawn from early Christian practices and would include time for silence, solitude and contemplation. More attention needs to be given to activities that promote, positively, the relational aspects of young people's lives rather than those that continue to propagate the highly charged competitive climate that encourages the individual to work against their co-students, thereby generating a de-humanizing effect. Further, children should be encouraged to recognize that their individual gifts are God given for the use and benefit of all, thereby deepening their sense of connectedness to the Other.

Most importantly, teachers need to become more reflective and intuitive practitioners themselves so that they can bring "soul" into their educational practice. This is an essential factor in the educational process if the spiritual dimension is to be recognized and addressed appropriately. Only then, may religious education programs offer students increased opportunities to develop meaningful knowledge about their faith tradition, and help them become faith-filled and hope-filled people.

(Much of this material has been drawn from articles appearing in the *Journal of Religious Education*, *49* (3) 2001, *52*(3) 2004 and *53* (4) 2005).

Consider what you have learnt about the three dimensions in learning. Write 500 words discussing whether or not you think this learning approach would be useful in religious education classrooms and support your stance.

References and Further Reading

Breen, B. (2000). What's your intuition? In *Fast Company*, Issue 38, September 2000, p. 290. Retrieved 12 May, 2004, from www.fastcompany.com/online/38/klein.html.

Claxton, G. (2000). The anatomy of intuition. In T. Atkinson & G. Claxton (Eds) *The intuitive practitioner, On the value of not always knowing what one is doing*. Buckingham, Philadelphia: Open University Press.

de Souza, M. (2005). Engaging the mind, heart and soul of the student in religious education: Teaching for meaning and connection. In *Journal of Religious Education*. 53:4, pp. 40-47.

de Souza, M., (2004). Teaching for effective learning in religious education: A discussion of the perceiving, thinking, feeling and intuiting elements in the learning process. *Journal of Religious* Education.52:3, pp 22-30.

de Souza, M. (2001). Addressing the spiritual dimension in education: Teaching affectively to promote cognition. *Journal of Religious Education*, Australian Catholic University, 49:3, pp. 31-41.

de Souza, M., Cartwright, P. & McGilp, E.J. (2002) *An Investigation into the Perceptions of their Spiritual Wellbeing of 16-20 year-old Young People in a Regional Centre in Victoria*, unpublished report. Ballarat: Australian Catholic University.

Del Prete, T. (2002). Being what we are: Thomas Merton's spirituality in education, in J. Miller, & Y. Nakagawa (Eds.) *Nurturing our Wholeness*. Rutland, VT USA: Foundation for Educational Renewal.

Eraut, M. (2000). The intuitive practitioner: A critical overview. In T. Atkinson & G. Claxton (Eds.) *The intuitive practitioner, On the value of not always knowing what one is doing*. pp 255-268. Buckingham, Philadelphia: Open University Press.

Gardner, H. & Hatch, T. (1990) 'Multiple Intelligences go to schools: Educational

Gardner, H. (1983) *Frames of mind*, Basic Books, New York.

Goleman, D. (1995) *Emotional Intelligence: Why it can matter more than IQ*. London: Bloomsbury Publisher Inc.

Hay, D. & Nye, R. (1998). *The spirit of the child*. London: Fount Paperbacks

Hillman, J. (1996). *The soul's code: In search of character and calling*. Australia: Random House.

Hogarth, R.M. (2001). *Educating Intuition*. Chicago and London: The University of Chicago Press.

Lynch, G. (2002). After religion: 'Generation X' and the search for meaning. London: Darton, Longman & Todd Inc.

Mayer,J.D., Salovey, P. & Caruso, D. (2000) 'Models of emotional intelligence' in Sternberg, R., (ed.) *Handbook of intelligence*.UK, Cambridge University Press.

Myers, D.G. (2002). *Intuition. Its powers and perils*. New Haven and London: Yale University Press.

Newberg, A., D'Aquili, E., & Rause, V. (2001) *Why God won't go away: Brain science and the biology of belief*. NewYork: Ballantine Books.

O'Connor, P. (1985, 1988, 1990). *Understanding Jung*. Port Melbourne: Mandarin.

Rymarz. R (1999). Constructing the future: A reflection on the post-conciliar generations. *The Australasian Catholic Record*. 76(1) 24-33.

Salovey, P., & Mayer, J.D. (1990) 'Emotional intelligence' in *Imagination, Cognition and Personality*, 9, pp.185 – 211.

Salovey, P. (1998). *Optimizing intelligences: Thinking, emotion and creativity*, video, National Professional Resources, Inc. N.Y.

Zohar, D., & Marshall, I. (2000) *SQ: Spiritual intelligence, The ultimate intelligence*, Bloomsbury publishing, US.

CHAPTER 8

Shared Christian Praxis

Marian de Souza

What is Shared Christian Praxis?

Shared Christian Praxis was introduced by Groome (1980) in the United States and was further developed through the 1980s. (see Groome, 1991). It was quite well received in Australia and has been influential in the development of religious education guidelines in some dioceses through the 1980s and into the 1990s, for example, the Parramatta Guidelines, *Sharing our story: Religious education curriculum* (CEO, Parramatta, 1992). More recently other dioceses have based their Religious Education Curriculum upon an adaptation of the Praxis model (for instance, the Canberra-Goldburn diocese: *Treasures new and old*, and the collaboration between some of the Victorian dioceses and Hobart – Ballarat: *Awakenings*; Sandhurst and Sale: *Journeying together in hope*; Hobart: *Good news for living*).

Shared Praxis referred to a process that was practised by groups of people who came together, voluntarily, to share their Christian faith, and to reflect critically on, and apply their faith tradition to, their everyday lives. Groome linked his praxis approach to the educational theories of critical theorists such as Habermas and Freire (Groome, 1980, pp. 172 - 177) and made reference to the faith developmental theories of Fowler (1980, pp. 66 - 73). By placing his approach to religious education in the framework of both contemporary educational theory and theological understandings, Groome raised the credibility of religious education as a subject in the general curriculum. He offered a religious education model which combined the intention to educate in faith with sound educational and theological links. As such, it provided a useful basis for the development of programs in Catholic schools.

One of Groome's arguments was that religious education should aim to empower people in their search for transcendence. Thus, it should raise their spiritual awareness, develop a consciousness that rises beyond their physical world, and enable them to give expression to it. It should be "a deliberate attending to the transcendent dimension of life by which a conscious relationship to an ultimate ground of being is promoted and enabled to come to expression" (Groome, 1980, p. 22). As well, he asserted that his approach derived from his own Christian background and he described it as "a group of Christians sharing in dialogue their critical reflection on present action in light of the Christian story and its Vision toward the end of lived Christian faith" (Groome, 1980, p. 184). In his later writings, Groome alternately referred to praxis as a "meta-approach" (1991, p. 280); a "framework" and "style of ministry" (1991, p. 296).

There were five stages in the learning process of the shared-praxis model which were:

- Naming present action,
- Critical reflection,
- Dialogue,
- Accessing the Story
- Vision (lived response) (Groome, 1980).

Translating this into practice meant that first a topic was chosen and studied in terms of what it meant to students in their present lives. This was followed by a critical reflection on the situation, the questions "why", "what" and "how" were asked. The third stage encouraged participants to learn more about the origins of the situation through learning and dialogue, The fourth stage examined what the scriptures and Christian tradition said about the topic, and considering the gap between present reality and the Christian vision, and finally the fifth stage aimed at planning for future action to live as Christians, that is, faithful to the teachings of Jesus.

Later developments and applications

Groome's praxis approach has continued to be developed during the intervening ten years to the stage where a pre-step, a "focusing activity", was incorporated into the process (Groome, 1991, p. 155) which emphasized its link to the life-centred approach (see chapter 1) . The intention of the focusing activity was to focus students' attention on their own lives, their immediate environment and the world in which they live. They were encouraged to reflect on their relationships with their families, peers and their local and international communities. This served as an introduction to the "generative theme" (Groome, 1991, p. 156) or topic of the learning experience or unit of work, and provided opportunities for introductory activities that prepared for and led into the first two steps of the process, that is the naming of and critical reflection upon present praxis:

Speaking from their experience in Parramatta, Bezzina, Gahan, McLenaghan & Wilson (1996) suggested that, with its emphasis on active partnership and dialogue between teachers and students, Groome's approach to teaching and learning in the praxis model appeared to be very appropriate for contemporary classrooms. Teachers and students could leave behind their traditional roles and become partners in their own learning, establishing a process whereby they actively learnt from each other and removed the notion of dependency and passivity. This was another positive aspect of the approach since it established further links between teaching and learning in religious education with contemporary teaching and learning approaches in other curriculum areas through the latter half of the twentieth century.

Some criticisms of Shared Christian Praxis

Despite its positive aspects, there have been some concerns regarding Groome's shared praxis approach. For instance, in the fourth stage, where students were expected to recall the Christian story and vision, there is a presumption that students have a knowledge of the origins and history of the Christian story. In today's classrooms, where there are students from a variety of backgrounds, including Catholic students who are quite disassociated from the Church, this may be problematic and it has some implications for the judgements and decisions for future action that are made in the fifth stage.

Another issue related to the use of the praxis approach in the classroom, was the fact that Groome recommended that, ideally, learning should take place in small groups numbering about twelve students, as this was the most effective environment to promote the levels of trust necessary for reflection, shared dialogue and action (1980). This is not feasible in the ordinary school classroom which may have twenty-five to thirty students in some classes. Under the circumstances, it is questionable whether the open and trusting atmosphere that is a vital part of the approach can be inspired in an average classroom, especially since religious education classrooms in Catholic schools often have a captive and reluctant audience. Bezzina et al. (1996) acknowledged this problem but argued that the model can be adapted to take this feature into consideration. They cited the review of *Sharing our Story* (the Parramatta religious education guidelines), conducted by Malone, Chesterton, Ryan & Macdonald (1996) where the findings suggested that praxis was identified as a major strength of *Sharing our Story* and that its approach provided teachers with a sense of security. An associated weakness, also identified by the review, was the "tendency for teachers to see it as a lock step approach" and "a lack of understanding of the Critical Reflection movement and/or difficulty in implementing it" particularly for the inexperienced teacher (Bezzina et al., 1996, p. 10).

From these findings it would seem that the guidelines possibly provided a kind of "security blanket" for some teachers who relied on the safety provided by a "lock step" approach which did not require any real risk-taking or levels of creativity and resourcefulness that perhaps they did not have. In contemporary classrooms in Catholic schools, it often expected that religious education will be taught by most teachers, which can mean that some who have a limited background and/or enthusiasm for the subject are teaching religious education. As such, effective teaching and learning using the praxis approach can be seriously affected.

An obvious problem with shared-praxis is the one that has been raised in relation to confessional models. Groome emphasized that his approach was only appropriate for Christian religious education classes, and suggested that its applicability was wider than the school classroom. In fact, this would appear to be its strength, that is, its use in catechesis classes for groups of *voluntary, committed* youths or adults. The fact that the approach is devoted to the Christian tradition and Christian scripture raises questions about its suitability for use in the average classroom. In the current Catholic secondary school, neither assumption can be made that the classroom is indeed a "faith community" or that it is a voluntary group. Instead, many classrooms today are composed of students who come from different backgrounds and who are at different stages of faith development. Indeed, the problems relating to the multi-beliefs of students, immediately create the difficulty of using such an approach to obtain its desired outcomes. As such, it would seem to be inappropriate to merely concentrate on the study of one religion to the total exclusion of others. Equally, there appears to be little evidence that the praxis approach takes note of the teachings of Vatican II in relation to world religions. Such an oversight is surely an issue in a pluralist society such as Australia so that, while the process of the approach is educationally sound, its restricted content is problematic.

> What do you see as the strengths and/or weaknesses in Groome's Shared Praxis model for classroom religious education?

An adaptation of the Shared praxis Model: (Catholic Dioceses of Ballarat, Sale, Sandhurst and Hobart)

In 2002, the country dioceses in Victoria, together with the diocese of Hobart collaborated on a project that was known as the *Inter-Diocesan Religious Education Project* which culminated with the publication of the core document in each of the dioceses in 2005. In Ballarat, the document was *Awakenings*. In the same year, school based trials of religious education units commenced along with professional development for teachers and the development of support materials.

In an introductory statement in the *Awakenings* core document, the religious dimension of Catholic education is discussed in terms of its contribution to making Catholic education distinctive:

> In its broadest sense, Catholic education is a Religious Education. Two senses of the word "religious" are possible. From the Latin word "religere", it can mean to re-bind or to strengthen a bond. From the word "relegere", it can mean to re-read or to give a new interpretation.

A Catholic educational style, therefore, is attentive to both these dimensions. It articulates and celebrates the bonds of connectedness within all reality, human, non-human and divine, and engages the human person in that network of relationships. It also seeks to develop in learners the cognitive, affective and spiritual skills needed to "read" our personal and collective experience within the narrative horizon of the Judeo-Christian world view, and so to make personal meaning of human experience (p. 18).

Using the intention foundational to the Shared Christian Praxis model, the aim of the Ballarat diocesan religious education curriculum is to "inform, form and transform learners and teachers by engaging them with the intellectual, ethical and spiritual richness of the Catholic tradition" (*Awakenings*, 2005, p. 55). As well there is recognition of lifelong learning in Religious Education; of the need to be responsive to the communities and the world in which we live, and to remember our cultural and religious heritage. The overall intention of religious education, then, is to awaken learners intellectually, ethically and spiritually.

Consider ways in which religious education may "awaken" learners intellectually, ethically and spiritually. Provide some examples of how this may be addressed in the classroom program.

Another feature of the *Awakenings* curriculum is the attention given to developing interdisciplinary links between Religious Education and other curriculum areas, since this is a "means of making available the insights, understandings and values derived from the gospel to the public discourse of society" (2005, p. 57).

Curriculum structure

The content of the Awakenings religious education curriculum is organized into eight strands which reflect the content strands in most other Catholic religious education curriculum documents in Australia. They are:

- Christian Prayer
- Sacraments
- Religion and society
- God
- Christian Life
- Jesus Christ
- Scripture
- Church

Methodology

The methodology of *Awakenings* is an adaptation of Groome's Shared Praxis Model. It is embedded within the concept that God is ever present and active in the world and may be experienced through the community's life, drawn on its history and tradition. Religious Education, then, "promotes knowing, valuing and acting of the learner who is making meaning of his or her life" within the faith and life of the community (p. 117).

The term Praxis refers to the whole learning process in this curriculum model, from thinking about situations and experiences, reflecting critically upon them, deriving meaning from them within the context of the community's Story, which will guide them to further action.

The adaptation of the focusing activity followed by the five movements of Shared Praxis as described in the *Awakenings* curriculum document are:

- Focusing Activity
- Naming
- Reflecting Critically
- Accessing the Christian Story and Vision
- Understanding and Integrating
- Responding.

This is further broken down into the following processes:

- *Focusing activity*: This activity is intended to introduce the students to the topic that is going to be studied. It will use ideas, symbols and other resources that will generate thinking, feelings and further action that will lead to the first movement.

- *Naming*: This involves naming a particular experience that is relevant to the topic, sharing it with others, exploring aspects of the experiences by asking questions such as - How/when do we… ?

- *Reflecting Critically*: At this point, students are invited to critically reflect on the experiences that have been introduced and discussed during the first movement. The questions that are used to assist in the reflection are - Why do we do this? Why do other act in the way they do? What other options could I or others have had?

- *Accessing the Christian Story and Vision*: This is where students draw on the Christian story to enlighten and further their understanding of the experience/topic and it requires some knowledge of the Christian Story and Tradition. The question to assist learning in this Movement is – What are the beliefs of the Christian community that are relevant to this topic?

- *Integrating:* At this stage of the learning, students are invited to integrate their reflections and life experience with the Christian Story in order to deepen their understanding of the experience and Christian belief and practice. The question that applies here is: So what?

- *Responding:* In this final movement, the aim is for students to respond to their learning in the topic by living an authentic Christian life. The questions to generate further thoughts and actions are – How can we… / How will we… ?

Take some time to visit the *Awakenings* website:
http://awakenings.balrt.catholic.edu.au/

Click on the curriculum box and then, at the bottom of the curriculum page, under Available documents, click on the Scope and Sequence Box.

The Scope and Sequence chart shows how the different Content Strands will be addressed across the year levels and provide a list of unit titles for each year level

Applying the Shared Praxis model to lesson planning

Unit Title: Celebrating religious diversity

Level 6
Strand: Religion and Society

Level Outcome:
By the end of Year 10, students should be able to recognize and analyse the nature, significance and role of religious places, persons and ethical codes in the faith and practice of some Christian denominations and world religions.

Doctrinal concepts:
Religious freedom is a fundamental right
A religious perspective can influence personal and communal codes of ethics and morality.

(The information given above was taken from the *Awakenings* website:
http://awakenings.balrt.catholic.edu.au/ accessed 27th August, 2007)

Some suggested activities that incorporate the Praxis model

Focusing activity

Find an image / photograph which shows an act of intolerance. Ask students to view it and then write down ten words that come to mind. They must not think too long over this. It is meant to be a spontaneous activity.

Students follow this up by sharing their words in small groups to discover similarities and differences of perceptions and explore the reasons why this may have happened.

Have some discussion about the divisiveness that can occur as a result of different religious beliefs and practices and use examples from contemporary situations.

The aim, here, has been to lead into the next movement which will focus on religious and cultural difference.

Naming

In small groups, students are invited to share their own or another's experience of tolerance and intolerance that relates to religious and cultural difference.

Individually, students are asked to reflect on a time when they may have been tolerant or intolerant of another person's difference. They are to write down their thoughts about this experience.

For HW students are asked to find some current newspaper articles, pictures etc. which show intolerance and prejudice as a result of religious difference.

Reflecting critically

Students are to present their article/images to their respective groups and explain the context.

They are to examine each example and ask questions such as: Why did this happen? Why do people behave like this? Do I ever behave like this - Why? What are other solutions or alternative ways of addressing the situation? And so on.

In the process students should examine and reflect on:
- What they already know about the topic;
- How do they feel about the situations that have been discussed;
- How are their thoughts and feelings influenced by their own beliefs;

- What are some of the prejudices that they might have and why do they have these prejudices;
- What are their attitudes and how do these affect their behaviour.

Students are to select one of the situations discussed by their group and present a freeze frame that reflects the feelings of the victim of intolerance. They will need some time to prepare this, and after viewing each group's presentation, students are to write a paragraph in their journal that reflects on what their thoughts and feelings are and what they have learned through the whole process.

Accessing the Christian Tradition

Select some relevant Scripture passages or Church teachings. For instance:
- 1 Cor 1:4-18 Salutation
- Jn 17:20-23 Jesus prays for his disciples

Or take the following passages from the Vatican II documents:

The Vatican Council declares that the human person has a right to religious freedom … the right to religious freedom is based on the very dignity of the human person as known through the revealed word of God and by reason itself (*Declaration on Religious Liberty, Dignitatis Humanae*, Flannery (Ed), 1996, pp. 552-3).

The Catholic Church rejects nothing of what is true and holy in these religions. It has a high regard for the manner of life and conduct, the precepts and doctrines which, although differing in many ways from its own teaching, nevertheless often reflect a ray of that truth which enlightens all men and women … The Church, therefore, urges its sons and daughters to enter with prudence and charity into discussion and collaboration with members of other religions. Let Christians, while witnessing to their own faith and way of life, acknowledge, preserve and encourage the spiritual and moral truths found among non-Christians, together with their social life and culture (*Declaration on the Relation of the Church to Non-Christian Religions, Nostra Aetate*, Flannery (Ed), 1996, pp. 570-1).

Students are to read and analyse these passages in light of what they may mean for Christian practice in the contemporary world.

For instance, the sentence: The Catholic Church rejects nothing of what is true and holy in these religions.

- How should this passage be interpreted?
- Does the interpretation depend on the context in which it is read? For instance, did this have a different meaning at the time of Vatican II from what it might mean today?
- What do we mean by 'true' and 'holy'?
- What does this mean for Christian practice in the pluralistic society in which we live.

Students are to write 300 words in response to the reading and discussion indicating what they have learnt and understood from the task.

Integrating

At this stage, students should be encouraged to learn more about different religious and cultural beliefs to gain a deeper understanding of how it may impact on people's attitudes and practices. Students should consider their own learning and understanding through these activities in light of their own experiences and Christian teachings

Some resources which could be useful are:
Guest speakers or visits to different religious centres.

As well, Arts resources would be particularly useful here: For instance:
From nothing to Zero: Letters from Refugees in Australia's Detention Centres, Lonely Planet Publications. 2003.

Silma's School, DVD, about a Muslim school in Sydney.

From memory to hope. Tears for the future Published by the Mercy Hospital for Women and the Northern Migrant Resource Centre.

Further, there are many excellent documentaries on the study of religions for schools. For instance:
The Worlds of Faith Series – Produced by North South Productions for Channel Four Television, UK, 1996.
Heaven on Earth, SBS, 2004.

Other useful and relevant resources may be current affair programs, the WWW, magazines and films, children's stories and so on.

Responding

In this final stage of the Praxis movement, students are encouraged to act on their learning and understanding.

- They could create posters to place around the school that promote tolerance for religious and cultural diversity;
- They could become penfriends with students from a school with a different religious orientation where they can exchange ideas and experiences of religious practices and beliefs;
- They may write a play that explores the notion of tolerance for religious difference which promotes Christian teachings on the subject.
- They may create a collage showing a movement from intolerance to tolerance through words and images.

A useful activity throughout this unit would be a reflective journal in which students record their thoughts and feelings as they develop new learning and understanding of the topic. This can be through writings and drawings. They should also be encouraged to find poems, quotations, scripture passage, drawings and so on which relate to the topic to put in their journals.

From the list of units on the *Awakenings* website, select one topic and write an overview that shows the process of the Praxis model that may be used to teach the topic.

References and Further Reading

Bezzina, M.; Gahan, P.; McLenaghan, H. & Wilson, G. (1996). Shared Christian Praxis as a basis for religious education curriculum: The Parramatta experience. Paper presented at the *Annual Conference of The Australian Association for Religious Education*. Southport.

Catholic Diocese of Ballarat (2005). *Awakenings. Core document: religious education P-12 curriculum*. Ballarat: The Catholic Diocese of Ballarat.

Fowler, J. (1981). *Stages of faith: The psychology of human development and the quest for meaning*. Blackburn: Dove.

Groome, T. H. (1980). *Christian religious education: Sharing our story*. San Francisco: Harper.

Groome, T. H. (1991). *Sharing faith: A comprehensive approach to religious education and pastoral ministry*. San Francisco: Harper.

CHAPTER 9

Planning a Religious Education Lesson

Kath Engebretson

This chapter draws on material written by Kath Engebretson and originally published in Engebretson, K., Fleming G. and Rymarz, R. (2002). Thriving as an RE teacher. Melbourne: Thompson Learning.

Initial considerations

Before you begin to plan a religious education lesson for any year level, you need to consider the following questions.

- What has the group already covered in this unit or series of lessons?

- How does this lesson link to previous lessons?

- What do I know about the students:

- Their level of knowledge of the topic

- Their interests and life experience

- Their abilities and the kinds of activities they enjoy

- Their religious experience and background?

- What implications do my responses to the previous questions have for the religious education lesson I am now planning?

- What specific content do I plan to cover in this lesson?

Year 9 at St. Carthage's Beacon Hills is studying a unit on Prayer. They have researched various definitions of prayer, and have explored a range of prayer customs in a variety of religions. For the last three lessons they have concentrated on Christian prayer, and in particular they have explored prayer as it is spoken of and taught about in the gospels. The students have very little historical or theoretical knowledge of the topic, although they are used to participating in prayer services, and they usually enjoy these, especially if they are given a role in the preparation and carrying out of the service. They are a lively but interested group, who respond best to activity based learning. There are five Muslim students in the group who have already shared their experience of family prayer in previous lessons. There are also three students from the Maronite rite within Catholicism, and the rest of the class are Catholic although few regularly attend Church. The students are quite interested in the topic but have tended to think about prayer in terms of *asking for* things.

What content might you plan to cover with this group for the next three lessons and why?

Planning a lesson

Learning outcomes

Having decided on your content, the first and crucial step is to set cognitive and affective learning outcomes. As described in an earlier chapter, cognitive learning outcomes describe the knowledge and skills that a student will have by the end of the lesson. They will cover all the content that will be included as well as the skills it is hoped that they student will gain or use. It is helpful to use a stem such as: *By the end of this lesson students will be able to: ...* in order to keep your learning outcomes as specific as possible. While cognitive learning outcomes deal with objective knowledge and skills, affective learning outcomes refer to the inner processes that it is hoped are taking part as the cognitive work proceeds. Therefore they are couched in terms of growing in the ability to reflect, growing in aware of or sensitivity towards, participating in, appreciating and learning to value, and they are expressed as hopes.

Lesson plan format

Here is a generic lesson plan format that will suit most religious education lessons. Like most recipes or plans it is useful only until you are ready to forget it. In other words, the more skilled you become in planning and teaching religious education the less need you will have of such formats. However, as a starting strategy this is a good basic format.

Introductory or opening strategy

This quite brief step will link this lesson with the lesson or lessons that have gone before, and will orient the minds of the students towards the content of this lesson. When we consider this purpose, it is not difficult to think of suitable strategies to use as introductory steps in the lesson. The following list gives some ideas to which you will be able to add.

- A quick quiz revising the content of the previous lesson
- A few well chosen questions which help the students to recall what they covered or what activities they did in the previous lesson
- Students write words or draw symbols to recall the previous lesson
- Students work in pairs to come up with questions they still have about the content covered in the previous lesson
- Brainstorm activity where the topic for the lesson is given and the students contribute what they already know about it
- A newspaper clipping, poem, story, or brief video clip is used to introduce the topic to be covered.

List other activities or strategies that may be used to introduce a lesson.

Presentation of the topic

At the beginning of this step the teacher informs the students of the topic to be covered in today's lesson, and spends time presenting the topic. This presentation may be done through "teacher talk" or direct presentation, through the showing of a film or documentary, through presenting a text for analysis, through working with a selected section of a textbook, through using a content sheet, through telling a story, having a student give a presentation, using a guest speaker or a variety of other ways. The intention here is to present the material to be covered so that it may be deepened and further explored.

Explore the topic

The aim of this procedural step is to deepen understanding of and extend the material that was presented in the previous step. The activities will now be varied to use strategies that will allow the students to take the material further. For example, material provided in text, film, or story may be analysed and discussed through a variety of questions, which invite the students to use and develop a range of skills. Students may be given a discussion and analytical task to complete in pairs or groups, based on the material presented in the previous step. Students may be asked to develop questions about the material and use these questions with other students. Students may undertake a brief research activity to deepen their knowledge of the material. The teacher may conduct a class discussion aimed at deepening understanding.

Student response

In this step the students respond to the material they have learned in the two previous steps. This will involve the students actively engaging in oral or written responsive activities which may take the form of written summaries, creative writing responses, such as poem, story or letter writing, art or symbolic activities, presenting a group report, completing a summary or revision sheet, answering questions about the material covered in oral or written form.

Conclusion

Finally there is a brief step which is designed to bring together, recapitulate or conclude the lesson. Here the students may share their work with each other, or selected students may share their work with the rest of the class. The teacher might give a summary of the lesson or through questioning students might summarise the lesson. Students may be asked to write down their key learnings from the lesson and then share this with their classmates. This step rounds off and concludes the lesson.

Using the plan in a variety of ways

This generic plan may be used in a variety of ways. It may be used as a lesson plan to structure a 50-minute lesson. In this case, the structure of the lesson may be timed loosely in this way:

- Introductory strategy (5 minutes)
- Presenting the topic (15 minutes)
- Exploring the topic (15 minutes)
- Student response (15 minutes)
- Conclusion (5 minutes)

Many schools have block timetables where there are 90 to 100 minutes of class time in a subject area. In this case the proportions of time on each step would be adjusted. The "steps" may become lessons in themselves so that they represent a learning sequence over a series of days. Here are examples of each of these.

Year 8 – Introduction to social justice

Introductory strategy

There is a class brainstorm of the notion of fairness as it applies in the lives of the students. This centres on the following questions:

- What does it mean to treat someone fairly?
- Recall a time when you were treated very fairly. Tell the class of your experience?

- Have you ever been treated unfairly? Share your experience in pairs or with the class?
- In what situations is fairness extremely important and why?

During this discussion a blackboard summary is built up.

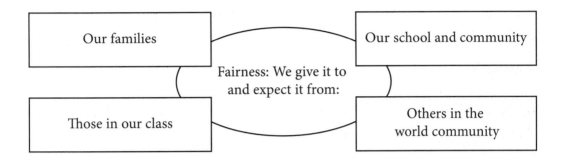

Presenting the topic

The teacher introduces the concept of fairness through the notion of human rights. This is done by giving background information about the United Nations Declaration of Human Rights and introducing the students to a summary of the main statements in the declaration. Together the class studies the declaration, with individual students contributing to the reading and class discussion centring on any unfamiliar worlds or concepts.

Exploring the topic

Students are given a worksheet, which introduces them to key principles of the Catholic encyclical: *Pacem in Terris* (John XXIII, 1963).

> John XXIII says that all human rights and duties flow from one principle, that is **the dignity of all human life**. People are full of human dignity because they have been created in the image of God and redeemed by Christ.
>
> *Each individual is truly a person. Theirs is a nature that is endowed with intelligence and free will. As such they have rights and duties, which together flow as a direct consequence from human nature. (par 7).*

Group work for this step:

1. Express in your own words the fundamental principle that Pope John declared in this passage.

2. What are rights and duties, and how do the two go together?
3. What violations of human dignity do you see in the world around us?
4. What do you think would be the characteristics of a society where human dignity was fully respected?

General class discussion centring on these questions.

Student response

The students choose one of the following questions to write about in ten lines or less.

- Which of these human rights do you really value and care about for yourself? Give reasons for your response.
- Which rights do you think are sometimes violated in Australia or around the world? Give examples of particular situations.
- Do you think Australia is a country that is concerned with protecting human rights? Give reasons for your answer.

Conclusion

Some students share their work with the class.

A "block" or "double" religious education lesson: What is Mission? Year 10 (90 minutes).

Introduction

View the film "Steven Bilong Sundown" a production of Catholic Mission, Melbourne. This brief (25 minute) film introduces the students to some basic concepts of Christian mission, such as the importance of the indigenous Church and the need to work with the community on health education and economic issues. After the film, compile a list of ideas about Christian mission that came from the film.

Present the topic

Use a worksheet containing the following text to introduce ideas about the importance of mission in the lives of all Christians.

The word 'mission' comes from the Latin word *to send*. Just as Jesus Christ was sent by his Father into the world, to share the life of God with people, so missionaries are sent **out** to bring the Christian gospel to others. Missionary activity in Christianity goes back to when Jesus sent out disciples two by two to proclaim his teaching about the Kingdom of God to their fellow Jews (Matt 10: 1-15; Mark 5: 7-13). At the end of the gospel of Matthew, Jesus is shown commissioning the Apostles to take the gospel to the ends of the earth. He promises to be with them as they carry out this work (Matt. 28:19-20).

The gospel claims that all Christians are called to **mission,** that is to sharing the Christian good news with others. At first this statement seems very unrealistic. Few people are able to, or want to, leave their lives, families and friends to go to a faraway place to be a missionary. The statement that all Christians are called to mission, however, does not require this. Each individual Christian is called to mission through Baptism, a call that is renewed at Confirmation. However, the mission of the individual Christian takes place in the time and circumstances of his or her life, and therefore involvement in mission will be different for each individual.

Some Christians will choose to work in missionary projects away from their own homes, but for most, mission will be carried out in the ordinary circumstances of daily life. In every case it is connected to the commandment of Jesus Christ to *love one another as I have loved you*. Through Baptism, Christians are called and sent on this mission of love in the name of Jesus Christ.

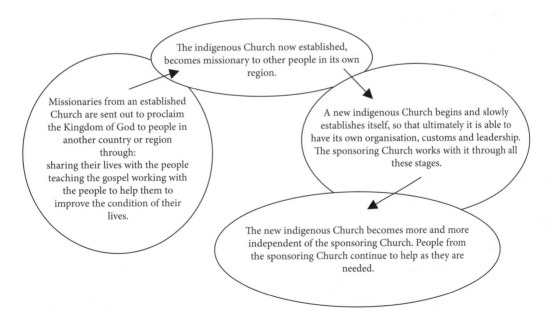

The indigenous Church now established, becomes missionary to other people in its own region.

Missionaries from an established Church are sent out to proclaim the Kingdom of God to people in another country or region through:
sharing their lives with the people
teaching the gospel working with the people to help them to improve the condition of their lives.

A new indigenous Church begins and slowly establishes itself, so that ultimately it is able to have its own organisation, customs and leadership. The sponsoring Church works with it through all these stages.

The new indigenous Church becomes more and more independent of the sponsoring Church. People from the sponsoring Church continue to help as they are needed.

Teacher and student together work through the three gospel texts, (Matt 10: 1-15; Mark 5: 7-13) and (Matt. 28:19-20). In class discussion the following question is addressed. *According to this text, what is mission about?*

Explore the topic

Students choose one of three tasks:

Task 1

Missionary activity today is carried out in many different ways. Here are some of them.

- The direct preaching of the Christian gospel to people who haven't heard it before.
- Bringing people into the Church through the sacraments of Christian initiation.
- Training indigenous priests, religious men and women and lay people, to work as preachers and teachers in the local community.
- Helping in the development of good education, health and social welfare.
- Setting up Christian schools, hospitals and other helping agencies.
- In countries where the direct preaching of Christianity is not permitted by the government, missionaries witness to Christianity by their lives and by entering into conversation with the religion of the country.
- Working with the people to change unjust situations and thus empower the people to improve their lives.

Write a pen portrait of a missionary showing the qualities they would need to have to carry out this work.

Task 2 – Internet search

- Use the following Internet sites to find out more about the various kinds of missionary work.

  www.catholicmission.org.au
  www.palms.org.au
  www.ozvol.org.au

Task 3 – Missionaries around Australia

Here are some other descriptions of real missionaries who work in aboriginal communities.

- Roeburne is a small inland town in Western Australia, and its population is almost entirely aboriginal. Two Catholic sisters of the order of Daughters of Charity, Sisters Olive and Kath, live there among the aboriginal people, many of whom are Catholic. The sisters spend time at the government run school attending school assemblies and offering their support to the teachers and students. They have an open house policy in their own home before and after school, and during the day for adults who want to come to talk. They are involved in many simple ways in the community, such as helping to provide food for community events, joining and leading prayer and visiting aborigines in prison.

- A lay missionary, Jack Ryan, visits the prison in Geraldton twice a week where 120 of the 170 inmates are aboriginal. If there is a suicide in the prison the authorities call Jack. He stays with the prisoners through the night, calms them down and allays their fears. Jack has virtually 24 hours 7 days a week access to the prison, a situation of trust that he has built up over the years because of his dedication.
- A Presentation sister, Sister Bridie, lives at Carnavon in the Geraldton diocese. As well as teaching in the school, she runs a reading programme for aboriginal youths between 8 and 18 who have been in trouble with the police.
- Sr Maureen Donnelly RSJ runs a centre for elderly aboriginal people in Port Keats.
- A Christian Brothers centre in Port Keats educates young aboriginal men for leadership in their communities.
- Sr Yvonne Gleeson, FDNSC works with aboriginal families that have been devastated by alcohol abuse, in a programme called Alcohol Awareness and Family Recovery.

Interview

Imagine that you are one of the missionaries mentioned here. Give a two minute talk on the challenges of your work, and why you think it is important.

Student response

The students work in groups to prepare a poster entitled Mission is: The activity is directed in his way.

Make a class poster for display with the heading *Mission is,* and include on it all the words you have encountered in the course of this lesson. Use symbols and other pictorial representations as well to convey a sense of what you understand by the work of missionaries.

Closing activity

A Prayer for Missionaries.

Planning a unit of work

The generic lesson plan may also be used as a structure for planning a unit of work. Use the following table to sketch out the kinds of strategies you might use in a unit of work on **Mission,** or on another topic of your choosing.

Introductory strategies	1	2	3	4
Present the topic	1	2	3	4
Explore the topic	1	2	3	4
Student response	1	2	3	4
Concluding activities	1	2	3	4

References and further reading

Elliott, T P. (Ed.). (2001a). *To know worship and love Years 7 teacher companion.* Melbourne, Australia: James Goold House.

Elliott, T P. (Ed.). (2001b). *To know worship and love Years 9 teacher companion.* Melbourne, Australia: James Goold House.

Elliott, P. (Ed.). (2002a). *To know worship and love teacher companion year 8.* Melbourne, Australia: James Goold House.

Elliott, P. (Ed.). (2002a). *To know worship and love teacher companion year 10.* Melbourne, Australia: James Goold House.

Engebretson, K. (2002). Writing church-sponsored religious education textbooks. *British Journal of Religious Education 25* (1), 33-45.

CHAPTER 10

Assessment in Religious Education

Marian de Souza

Through the1970s and 1980s, assessment policies in religious education often created tension for many teachers. The fact that, for several years, religious education had been perceived by many as a faith oriented subject with one aim being to increase a student's faith and commitment to the Tradition, meant that people were uneasy and unsure about what and how to assess in the subject. One theorist who examined assessment in Religious Education was Marie Macdonald (for instance, see Macdonald, 1988, 1990, 1995). Macdonald's (1988) conclusions in her doctoral thesis advocated that the religious education curriculum needed regular review and evaluation as well as appropriate forms of student assessment, since religious educators were accountable to the Catholic school community for the basis and development of the religious education curriculum. Further, she discussed the concept of accountability as it related to professional practice, which was to ensure that there was provision of adequate learning experiences to achieve the learning objectives. Finally, Macdonald stressed that religious education teachers were not accountable for the faith response and commitment of their students since faith was seen as a gift of God which required a free response from the individual.

> Do you agree that assessment should be an important part of the religious education curriculum? What justification would you give for your responses?

What is assessment?

Assessing students' learning is an essential aspect of teaching practice and it needs to be done with care and precision. The most important purpose of assessment is to provide feedback about the progress and performance of the student to themselves, their parents and their teachers. Sound assessment practice should identify the students' various strengths and weaknesses, so that the teacher will be able to prescribe appropriate strategies to assist them to improve their learning and performance. Further, it should be a natural extension of teaching and learning, As such it should not be imposed on classroom practice but show flow from the learning activities.

From the *Awakenings* (2005) curriculum document in the Victorian diocese of Ballarat, we learn that assessment is the process of gathering and interpreting information about student progress for a variety of purposes. These include:

- To encourage more effective learning
- To foster students' reflection on their learning
- To indicate the degree to which students are progressing
- To achieve the program goals and level outcomes
- To highlight the needs of individual students
- To assist teachers to improve their teaching methods
- To provide information that will assist in the evaluation of the Religious Education program and of individual units and activities
- To provide a basis for reporting on student progress to parents and students.

(Awakenings, 2005)

Similarly, in the curriculum document from the archdiocese of Melbourne, *Coming to know, worship and love*, 2005, assessment is recognized as essential to better teaching and learning:

> It is critically important in the cycle of teaching and learning that students can articulate what they have leant and what still needs to be learnt. In addition, teachers are required to demonstrate that they can ascertain what children have learnt and can report on that to the student and their families (p. 6).

Finally, Ryan and Malone (1996) offered the following principles for assessment in Religious Education:

- The faith response of students is not a matter for classroom assessment
- Assessment should achieve the same goals as other curriculum areas
- Assessment procedures used in other Key Learning Areas can be used to assess religious education variety of assessment procedures should be used to determine student's achievements in religious education
- Assessment of students should be determined according to established criteria, not by competitive class rankings or normal distributions of scores or grades
- Assessment and reporting policies and procedures established by schools need to be communicated to parents and other interested members of the school community (pp. 106-7).

What understandings about assessment have you gained from the excerpts presented in the above section? Identify five key points about effective assessment.

Types of assessment

Assessment is often carried out at the end of a unit of work and this allows the teacher to gauge whether the learning outcomes have been achieved. However, this practice alone is restrictive for learning and teaching since there may be little effort to measure the student's progress throughout the unit. Therefore, there is a need for assessment to take place at different periods of the learning process and there are three kinds of assessment that should be used:

- *Diagnostic assessment* ascertains a student's prior knowledge, perceptions and misconceptions, and monitors student learning progress. This can inform teaching practice and curriculum planning.
- *Formative assessment* focuses on ongoing constructive feedback from the teacher and on developing the student's capacity to self assess and reflect on their learning.
- *Summative assessment* makes judgements about what the student has learned in relation to the teaching and learning goals. It should be comprehensive and reflect the learning growth over the period assessed.

You have just met your Year 10 religious education class for the first time and the first unit you have to teach is a Scripture unit. For instance, see the Chapter 9 - The Good News of Mark pp. 193-217 from *To Know, Worship and Love Year 10,* the religious education student text book in the archdiocese of Melbourne:. Or look up the *Awakenings* curriculum in the Ballarat diocese: Level 4 – Who is Jesus?
(see the website http://awakenings.balrt.catholic.edu.au/).

1. Consider some of the information you need to know about the students' prior learning before you can begin the study of the topic, and develop a diagnostic assessment task with which you can gather this information.
2. Suggest some formative and summative assessment tasks that you can use as the study of the unit progresses. You will need to look at the content of the unit in order to do this (for instance, see above references).
3. Finally, develop one assessment task that can be used to measure what the students have learned at the end of the unit.

What should we assess in Religious Education?

Our understanding of the task of religious education and the nature of faith as a free gift of God which requires a free response on the part of the person, has significant implications for how we approach student assessment in the subject. To begin with, we need to consider the three dimensions of learning in religious education:

Cognitive – to develop the knowledge and understanding of the role of religion and of the content and practices of the faith tradition in particular (*Instruction*).
The purpose of assessment here is to determine and report on the individual student's progress in terms of knowledge, skills and understandings and to provide relevant information for the evaluation of the learning and teaching process

Affective – to provide opportunities that may allow students to respond affectively to their faith tradition and to develop students' appreciation of the faith heritage of the Catholic/Christian community (*Invitation*). The ultimate purpose of this form of assessment is not to assess the individual's personal attitudes, values and beliefs, but rather to ascertain whether certain changes are taking place in the group of learners (Macdonald, 1990). Therefore, data gathered may form the basis of curriculum evaluation and improvement. In fact, the term used by Macdonald is *evaluation* rather than *assessment*. She argues that that kind of techniques teachers may use to evaluate the effectiveness of their lesson or unit, such as observation, anonymous open-ended questionnaires, reflective writing and other techniques are the ones to be used for this aspect of the curriculum.

Spiritual – to provide opportunities for students to reflect on the gospel message and what their faith tradition might mean for them which may lead to transformed action (*Invitation*).

Although this dimension is critical in terms of its inclusion within the learning and teaching process, it is not possible to assess particularly as the learning may not be evident within the set period of a lesson or over the time that the unit of work is being studied. Ultimately, this learning should be the transformative factor.

If we examine the verbs we use for the outcomes in each of these domains, it becomes clearer as to why we would find it difficult to assess learning outcomes in the other two domains with any degree of accuracy.

Cognitive (thinking)

By the end of this unit students will be able to
define, describe, recall, recognize, illustrate, interpret, explain, apply, relate, demonstrate, distinguish, analyse, compare, contrast, formulate, communicate, articulate, plan, evaluate, judge…

Affective (feeling)

By the end of this unit students will have had the opportunity to
show awareness of, experience - , accept, appreciate, participate, display interest, become involved, respond to, feel valued, reflect, show enjoyment of, show enthusiasm for, display an attitude of…

Spiritual (inner reflecting and transformed action)

By the end of this unit student will have had the opportunity to
develop a sensitivity to, empathize, develop compassion, reflect inwardly, experience, accept responsibility, contemplate, meditate, develop self-knowledge, connect with, show a commitment to, dream, imagine, create, wonder, be peaceful, develop some resilience, change existing attitudes or behaviours…

Using the verbs for each of the dimensions of learning (or think up some others), write learning outcomes for each dimension for one of the following topics from the Melbourne diocese textbook, *To know, worship and love, Year 9*:

The story of the Passover
The Kingdom of God in the early Christian Communities
Martin Luther

Or you may choose a topic from another diocesan curriculum.

From these descriptions, it is clear that there is one dimension of learning that may be assessed accurately – cognitive learning, that is, the knowledge and skills that are the expected outcomes in the lesson or unit of work. While the affective and spiritual dimensions of learning are desired outcomes of the process, it would be difficult to achieve accurate measurements of this kind of learning. This was noted by Macdonald (1990, 1995) who made the point that while the cognitive dimension of religious education should be assessed in similar ways to other subject areas, there was a case to evaluate the potential achievement of affective outcomes or "hopes" as they are more accurately called, since religious education aimed not only at learning but also at developing attitudes, values, feelings and emotions. Macdonald acknowledged that affective evaluation was quite difficult to engage in, less valid and reliable and more controversial but that was not sufficient reason to neglect measurement in this area of learning. Indeed, there was a need to carefully and methodically evaluate students' progress in relation to the affective outcomes as a group, which then provided useful data for broader curriculum evaluation. Such evaluation needed to respect the privacy and freedom of the student, and at no time was it meant to identify individual students or to assess their personal responses involving faith, beliefs, attitudes, values and practices. Further, Macdonald suggested that self-assessment techniques were the most appropriate strategies to use for this kind of assessment.

Macdonald's proposal to evaluate the potential achievement of affective learning was received with mixed reactions, however, her work was influential in alerting religious educators to the importance and necessity of conducting appropriate and carefully planned assessment in religious education.

> Can you provide some reasons for and against the use of techniques to evaluate the potential achievement of affective learning?

One important factor to consider when evaluating affective learning is that comments should be qualified and supporting evidence should be presented. For instance, if a comment is made about the interest shown by a student, reasons for this should be given, such as:

> Mary showed interest and enthusiasm for this topic because she visited the library and found a great deal of information which she, then, shared with her class mates.

How do we assess in Religious Education?

In general, classroom assessment involves collecting information about how the knowledge and skills students have gained, and making judgments about their level of learning. Both these aspects of assessment may be achieved in a variety of ways. For instance, in an attempt to determine how much learning has occurred for any student, class tests, oral responses and presentations, essays and reports and problem solving exercises can be utilized. To judge the level of the performance of a student, the teacher is able to compare it to other students' work, or to particular criteria which is set for each task.

Some strategies/learning activities that can be used to assess in the cognitive domain are:

- word searches
- crosswords
- cartoons
- story maps
- picture sequence
- tasks requiring the use of a skill – e.g. locating Biblical reference
- constructing time lines

In groups, choose a topic from the Year 7 – 10 curriculum from any of the dioceses and develop three different learning strategies/activities that can be used for assessment of knowledge and skills.

Some strategies that can be used to evaluate potential learning in the affective domain are listed below:

Student Self Assessment techniques

- Rating scales – Interesting -- Boring
- Open-ended questions – What does Baptism mean to you?
- Closed Item questions – The story of Easter is very meaningful to me. True/False
- Attitude inventories
- Moral dilemma discussions
- Observation of student interaction/group work - For instance, it is possible to make comments on the 'level' of participation of a student in class work and group work providing the criteria is clearly stated.
- Self reflective statements – When I learnt about the parable of the Good Samaritan I began to understand…
- Open –ended written questionnaire

Here is an example of writing learning outcomes for a 2-hour lesson on Creation - Gen 1:1 - 2:4 and selecting appropriate learning activities and assessment tasks.

Note: The summative assessment task will occur at the end of the unit of work not at the end of this lesson.

Learning outcomes

Cognitive

By the end of the lesson students will:
- demonstrate their understanding that biblical stories are about something sacred;
- compare and contrast some creation stories to determine common features;
- explore the meaning that the creation story (Genesis 1:1 – 2:4) may have for the contemporary world.

Affective

By the end of the lesson there will be opportunities for students to
- be invited to regard the Bible as a source of God's Word;
- appreciate that there are many similarities amongst the creation stories of different cultures;
- reflect on how biblical stories can have relevance for today's society;
- express in a creative way a personal response to an aspect of creation;

Spiritual (transformative)

By the end of the lesson there will be opportunities for students to
- experience a sense of wonder at the beauty of God's creation;
- accept responsibility for their own role as stewards of creation;
- pursue a course of action to save the environment/beautify their school grounds etc.

Lesson Content

In order to teach to these outcomes, the content could include
- Creation stories from different cultures - Aboriginal, Celtic, Indian, Chinese, Babylonian, American Indian, African etc.
- Creation Story from Genesis (1:1 – 2:4)

Learning Activities

In small groups students will read a creation story and identify particular structural features (20 minutes).

Each group will present their story to the class and write up the features they have noted on the b/board (20 minutes).

Drawing on the above activity, students will complete a worksheet that identifies common features that occur in the different stories (10 minutes).

In a class group students will read Gen 1:1 – 2:4

Teacher-directed discussion that
- explores the sacred theme of the biblical story, and
- focuses on the relationship between the human person and God's Creation which should lead to humans having a caring attitude towards all aspects of Creation. (15 minutes);

Students, individually, write reflective responses to the following:
- What do I understand from this story?
- Does it share common features with other creation stories?
- How did God feel about each stage of Creation? How do I feel about Creation?

Some students may read out their response to one of the above questions (15 minutes).

Students to start planning a personal response to an aspect of Creation through poetry, music or art work or they may work as a small group to respond through drama or dance (25 minutes). To be completed next lesson.

Students are asked to think about a relevant group project they can undertake over the duration of the unit. This will be discussed at the next lesson (5 minutes).

Homework
- Students to think about a group project that can incorporate some form of action that involves caring for an aspect of creation. To bring their ideas to the next lesson.
- Also, to think further about the personal response activity which will be completed during the next lesson.

Assessment tasks: formative
Participation and response to discussion and worksheet (cognitive – showing knowledge of the content; and affective/spiritual evaluation and recflection – based on participation and displayed interest). Personal response activity (affective evaluation – participation and student's self reflection)

Summative
Group project - some action to care for creation which could involve, research, planning, writing up reports as well as other skills that may be needed to complete the project (cognitive assessment according to criteria set for completing the task).

Finally, there is an important factor that must be kept in mind when planning assessment tasks. At all times the focus should be on the achievement of knowledge and skills, and sometimes, comments may be made about student participation.

Below are some examples of activities that may address the three dimensions of learning in a unit of work on the Early Church. They reflect a way of teaching affectively to promote cognition. Examine them and then respond to the questions below each:

The aim for the first activity is for students to learn the content relevant to St. Paul's journeys and to present it in a rap song. Below is an example:

The story of St Paul (can be sung or recited to a rap rhythm)

Saul was a teacher of Jewish law and a tent-maker by trade
He was known for persecuting Christians, he really had it made.
He was on his way to Damascus when Jesus said to him –
'Why do you persecute me, Saul?' So he became a Christian.
He changed his name to Paul and traveled far and wide
To preach the message of Jesus Christ, to Jews and Gentiles alike.
He made three journeys o'er land and sea, and so the Gospel was spread
But Paul became known as a trouble-maker, and people wanted him dead.
He went to Rome to plead his case; Asked the Emperor to spare his life,
But was beheaded, became a martyr, around AD 65.

What criteria would you use to assess the rap song presentation? Remember that you must always focus on the content learnt and presented. The actual musical skills and other skills of presentation are not the focus here. They are only a medium whereby the students may present the content, not much different to writing an essay, report or some kind of oral presentation.

The next strategy is one whereby each group of students could focus on a different topic in the overall unit of work. So the overall unit may be Early Church, and different topics would be:

- St Paul's Journeys
- Kingdom of God
- Christian life in the first communities
- Persecution in the Early Church

The activity presented here focuses on the persecutions in the Early Church. This time, the content needs to be researched and presented in a board game. The key to the board game will be drawn from the content that has been researched.

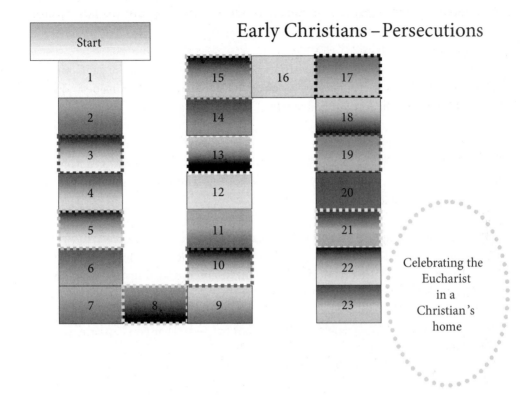

Early Christians: Persecution – Key

3. You decide to attend a Christian gathering to hear a disciple preach about Jesus' teachings. Move forward 3 steps.

5. You refuse to buy meat from a Roman butcher because you suspect that it has been used as a sacrificial offering to Zeus, a Roman god, at the big festival the previous day. Miss a turn.

8. You refused to take part in the birthday celebrations for the Roman Emperor because of some of the pagan rituals. The Emperor is offended and has ordered that you will be whipped and put in gaol. You need to throw a 6 to get out of gaol.

10. You are a jeweller who refused to decorate the statue of Diana, a Roman goddess, so your shop is closed down. Miss the next three turns.

13. You spend the evening praying with other Christians and become inspired by the Holy Spirit. Have another turn.

15. The adult male members in the family have been granted an exemption from joining the armed forces. You are so glad that your prayers have been answered that you show Christian charity by getting someone out of gaol.

17. Things have been so bad for the Christians, some of your friends are in gaol, others have been stoned to death of crucified, you wonder if God is really on your side and whether you should pray to the Roman gods instead. Go back three steps.

19. You are a builder who provided a lot of support to your Christian community to help build the new Church but this has offended the Romans. One morning, a Roman mob lie in wait for you as you are on your way to the site and they take you to the edge of town and stone you to death.

21. Nero, the Roman Emperor, has decided to blame the Christians for the burning of Rome. He has done this to divert suspicion away from himself because most people think that he is responsible. You are one of the many Christians rounded up and crucified along the sides of the road. At night, you and the others are set alight and burnt to death.

23. Hooray! You have made it safely to a Christian house so that you can pray with them and celebrate the Eucharist.

The usefulness of using such a strategy is that is involves the students' thinking, feeling and inner-reflecting abilities. It provides them with a challenge but, at the same time, is a fun-filled activity. Ultimately, time can be set aside when students are allowed to play board games from different groups and at the end, they should write responses that indicate their learning of the content of the different topics. As well they should reflect on any feelings and insights that may have emerged through the learning process. However, once again, there needs to be clear criteria that can be used for assessing the learning that has been achieved.

> Write up some criteria which you can use to assess the preceding task. Remember you need to concentrate on the knowledge and skills. However, you may like to include one criteria statement that addresses the presentation of the work and weight it accordingly.

References and Further Reading

Macdonald, M. (1988). *Assessment in religious education in Catholic secondary schools*, unpublished thesis, D. Theol., Melbourne: Melbourne College of Divinity.

Macdonald, M. (1990). Assessment of affective objectives in religious education. *Word in Life.* 38 (1), pp. 22-26.

Macdonald, M (1995). Assessing knowledge and evaluating faith: dual approaches to determining outcomes of religious education. *Word in Life.* 43 (2), pp. 9-14.

Cornerstones of Catholic Secondary Religious Education

CHAPTER 11

Planning a Unit of Work in Religious Education

Richard Rymarz

Some of the material in this chapter is drawn from Rymarz's writing in Engebretson, K., Fleming, G. and Rymarz, R. (2002). Thriving as an RE Teacher. Melbourne: Thompson Learning.

Lesson planning in religious education is considered in this book in Chapter nine. Although a standard part of teacher training and a rite of passage, developing a lesson plan is, nonetheless, a somewhat artificial part of a new teacher's skills. Teachers in schools rarely have the time to plan lessons individually. A teacher may have to plan up to thirty lessons a week, and even with the best intentions it would be hard to plan them all in detail. A more important job, therefore, is the successful planning of a *unit of work*. This is a sequence of lessons covering a number of weeks of the school year. A unit of work enables the teacher to think in terms of a broader range of topics and outcomes, and to develop teaching and learning strategies along graded and sequential lines. This more diffuse focus is educationally relevant because good teaching requires a consistent effort over a period of time, and this is difficult to do if a teacher is concentrating on a series of single lessons.

Locating the unit

Imagine that you are teaching a topic with which you have some familiarity.

- How, in general terms, would you teach this to 12 years olds as opposed to 17 years olds?
- List some of the teaching strategies that you think are appropriate for the younger students.
- What assessment tasks are more suited to older students?
- Are there any generic aspects of teaching that apply to all ages?
- What, if any, are some of the differences you need to consider in presenting a religious education topic to students of different ages?

The first task in planning a unit of work is to locate the unit within a teaching context. The most basic questions to ask here are; how old are the students, and how long is the unit to be? The age of the students is easy to determine, but in planning a unit some thought

---

should be given to how the age of the learner impacts on the way the unit is developed. Before planning a unit at a particular year level, religious education teachers should ask how they would approach the same topic if the students were older or younger. This practice helps the teacher to develop the habit of seeing students as a differentiated body, and not a generic mass.

This is illustrated when we consider a typical religious education unit dealing with some aspect of Scripture. In planning a unit on this theme at Year 7 level, consider how it may be taught at Year 10. This brief consideration of units of work across the curriculum gives the teacher a sense of the developmental character of the discipline, and can generate useful questions about the specific needs of learners at particular ages. It is also helpful to have an idea of where the curriculum and the learner are going in terms of what is expected of them in later years.

Ascertaining prior learning

Consider the following statement:
My students know nothing about the Eucharist – I have to start from scratch!

What implications does this statement have for planning a unit of work in this topic?

In planning a unit of work it is essential to ascertain prior leanings. This can be done formally by consulting the curriculum of the school to see what the students have covered in previous years. Asking other teachers or the Religious Education Coordinator (REC) is another way of gaining valuable information about prior learning. Students themselves are another source of information, but be cautious with this. Students can have a tendency to downplay what they know about a certain subject. This seems, anecdotally, to be a problem in religious education. RECS recall many occasions when new teachers have earnestly told them that their Year 7 classes know *nothing* about the content that they are supposed to be covering. Year 7 is an interesting educational landmark, signalling the transition from primary to secondary school. It would be much harder, although by no means impossible, for a teacher at this level to ascertain prior learning from the school's curriculum documents or from asking others. Nonetheless, claims of stupefying ignorance on the part of students at this level, as at others, need to be regarded with a healthy dose of scepticism. If we take the example of a unit of work on the Sacraments – a staple of Year 7 religious education in many schools – students can be expected to have some understanding of this topic. A large proportion of students in Catholic secondary schools, for example, have attended Catholic primary schools. It is almost inconceivable that students who have completed seven years of Catholic primary school education, have not attended a celebration of the Eucharist, or heard something about what the Catholic Church teaches about this sacrament. Most

Catholic primary schools, for example, devote a good part of many years to sacramental programs. The students may not immediately recall much about a topic, or thy may be reluctant to indicate their true level of understanding, but this should not be confused with a lack of familiarity.

How long should a unit of work in religious education be?

One of the great advantages in planning units of work is that it allows for the development of large *chunks* of material. How long the unit should be depends on the local condition of the school, and the demands of external educational agencies. A general principal is that it should cover from between 10 and 15 lessons or contact periods of 50 minutes or so.

The unit of work as a detailed instruction to a fellow professional

One way of describing a unit of work is as a set of instructions that, when given to another teacher, can provide them with all they need to teach the sequence of lessons provided. This is analogous to what scientists try to do when they prepare an experimental report. Another scientist who reads it should be able to successfully replicate the experiment. A good unit of work should be able, without much further explanation, to be used by another religious education teacher. It should contain enough instructions, activities, explanatory notes and additional exercises to be useful. The core activities should be highlighted and superfluous information relegated to the appendices. Just as trying to duplicate an experiment can be marred by too much detail, the efficacy of a unit of work in religious education can be hindered by a lack of focus, or presenting too much material that has not been properly analysed or edited.

Preliminary stages

In the preliminary stages of planning a unit of work in religious education the following steps are necessary.

1. Consult the school religious education curriculum. Be sure of what precedes and follows the unit. If the curriculum is insufficiently developed, at least, be clear in your own mind what precedes and follows this unit in your class.
2. Discuss your unit with the REC and other experienced religious education teachers.
3. Examine whether there are Guidelines or other curriculum documents that are relevant to the topic you are teaching. Read them carefully and let them inform what you are planning?
4. Do some background reading or other research on the topic you wish to cover. This is an important step, especially if you are venturing into unfamiliar territory. If you do not know a lot about a particular area it is essential to research it, and even if you think you know enough, it is still necessary to make sure your knowledge is up to date and comprehensive.

5. Consider the question; why am I teaching this unit? In the process of planning, the answer to this question should become clearer.

Developing the plan, part 1: The first draft

Step one: Quickly sketch out how you think the lessons in the unit will be sequenced. It is important from the very outset of planning a unit of work in religious education to envisage it as a sequence of lessons, and not a collection of individual lesson plans. Try to include at least one cognitive outcome and one teaching activity for each lesson. This will help you quickly identify those areas that are crucial and those which need further development. Write out this outline in table form. A table, which uses the example of a unit on St Paul aimed at junior secondary, is given below.

Lesson 1	Lesson 2	Lesson 3	Final Lesson
One key outcome – eg students identify who St Paul was One key activity – read a short account of the life of St Paul	Outcome – further explore the life of Paul Activity – students find examples of Paul's ministry in the Acts of the Apostles)	Outcome – identify key themes in Paul's writing Activity. Hand out to students one example of Paul's teaching from the Acts of the Apostles – choose something that is not too advanced	Outcome – summarise what we know about Paul Conduct an interview and write this up with a companion of Paul

Attempt to compile an outline table for the unit of your choosing. Remember to identify the year level of the students and give some thought to their prior leanings, then follow the steps below.

Step two: Identify a number of lessons in the unit that you consider to be pivotal and develop these, again without going into complete detail. This stage enables you to get something on paper that gives you a reference point for more detailed lesson plans. This is helpful in developing the unit as a plan of action, and not just a conceptual framework.

Step three: Give some thought at this stage to teaching and learning activities, assessment tasks and the further outcomes you hope to achieve in the unit. Make preliminary lists of all of these. These are the things that *leap out at you* by being obviously relevant to the unit.

Step four: Go back to the lesson plans that you developed in step 1. Now fill these out with some of the activities, assessments and outcomes that you listed in the previous step. You are now at a stage where most lesson plans have outcomes, activities and assessments ideas included.

Developing the plan part 2: The final version

You are now ready to complete a final version of the unit using the four steps listed above as a preliminary template. Begin at step four, but now give greater attention to detail. This means, initially, identifying more carefully what exactly you are going to do in the lessons in the unit. Your attention here should be to generate teaching and learning strategies that *work*, that is, meet the demands of students and also the specified learning outcomes. Good teaching is largely typified by teachers using effective teaching and learning strategies. This sounds like a truism, but it needs to be said nonetheless. Inexperienced religious education teachers often find it difficult, at least initially, to generate good teaching and learning strategies. One way of selecting good teaching activities is to consider assessments tasks. Which ones will be used and when will they be given in the sequence of lessons you have planned? For example, if you would like to use a cumulative work diary as part of your assessment, think about what the students will have to include in their diaries. If the students are expected to complete, amongst other things, a glossary of key words and phrases, you will need to allocate part of your unit to activities that enable students to meet this assessment task.

> Suggest some teaching and learning strategies that will enable students to complete a glossary of key terms by the end of a unit.
>
> Imagine that you are teaching a Year 7 unit on St Paul. Students are asked to conduct an interview with a companion of Paul. How would your classroom teaching enable students to meet this assessment task?

The link between assessment and teaching activities is one way of getting ideas about how to develop lessons in a unit. At this stage of unit preparation, audit all the activities and assessment tasks. It is helpful to list these again, as this gives a clear indication of the teaching and learning strategies and assessment tasks that you are offering. When these are listed, a bias towards one type of activity or assessment is more obvious. At the end of step five you should have lesson plans that have detailed strategies and assessments included.

Developing cognitive and affective learning outcomes

Now return to some of the outcomes you listed in step one. The outcomes that you initially listed now need further development, and usually they need to be made much

---

more specific. As the lesson plans begin to take shape, outcomes such as *students will understand ...* transform into far more specific ones that include verbs such as *list, describe, compare, analyse* and *locate*. At this stage the number of outcomes increases and this is a helpful consequence of greater specificity. At this stage the unit should be taking definite shape. Include approximate times for each strategy you have included. This may alter your lessons, as timing an activity also makes you think more carefully about it, and whether to add or eliminate some detail. It is better to include too much information and not finish everything that you have planned, rather than be struggling to fill in time. It is important, however, to be clear about what the key strategies are. These may not follow in sequence but are, in your judgement, pivotal to the success of that particular lesson. Rather than skip over these, leave out other more peripheral teaching and learning strategies. This is especially important if the key activities are toward the end of the lesson. In your completed unit of work, you may wish to highlight the key activities in a distinctive colour so that they stand out. A series of activities from a unit on Church history aimed at junior secondary, with approximate times is given below.

Activity 1: Students read an account of early Irish settlement in Australia. Students are asked to respond to the question *How were the Irish regarded?*	Reading 5 minutes, response 5 minutes Total 10 minutes
Activity 2: Give students a worksheet that explains the conditions in Ireland in the nineteenth century. Questions are included as part of the worksheet.	Reading, answer questions and review. 15 minutes
Activity 3. In small groups, students discuss the severity of the penal laws and what impact this had on the Irish leaving or being deported to Australia	10 minutes
Activity 4. *Make the punishment fit the crime.* Ask students to propose prison sentences for offences that resulted in deportation in earlier times. Ask them to rank these in order of the seriousness of the crimes and justify their answers. Work individually and then as part of a whole class discussion	10 minutes

Timing

Note that any plan for a lesson in a unit of work estimates the length of time that activities will take. This is a help for the planning process, and is not intended to stifle an unexpected vein of interest. For example, in the table above, activity four could take significantly less time, or far more, depending on how students react to it. This is difficult to predict accurately. If an activity works well and students embrace it enthusiastically, you should stick with this, provided that the pivotal parts of the lesson are identified and not neglected. This may mean returning to a pivotal activity in another part of the unit.

Resources

Now prepare the resources that you will need for the unit. How this is done depends on the type of teaching and learning strategies that you have chosen. An important general principle is to try and make all resources that you include in your unit as concise as possible. If, for example, you plan to give the students some background information from a book, prepare only the relevant part of the source document. Do not hand out to students wads of paper that are only remotely connected to your teaching plan. A similar point can be made about using other resources such as audio-visual aids. A video can be a very appropriate teaching aid. It is unlikely, however, that students need to see a long section of a video. It is far better to nominate the exact section of the video that you will be watching.

Developing unit outcomes

The unit of work should now be almost complete. It should include outcomes for each lesson as well as a variety of teaching and learning activities. Now try to compose some outcomes which span the whole unit. This is another way of making sure that the unit is a developmental sequence. In general, if a unit is well integrated, it is relatively easy to see the main focus of the unit, and then to specify this into a number of unit outcomes. This is the time to consider the affective outcomes for the unit, that is the more personal outcomes that are embedded in the unit of work. One or two of these across the unit should be sufficient. Chapter six of this book gives a detailed treatment of cognitive and affective outcomes. Now list all of the cognitive and affective outcomes that will cover your unit of work. The final step is to present it professionally and share it with other teachers.

Evaluation of the unit of work

All reflective teachers are constantly engaged in a process of thinking about their work, judging how effective their teaching is and taking steps to improve it. This reflection may be as simple as the thinking of the teacher as he or she walks to the staffroom after a lesson. His or her internal talk may go something like this. *How did that lesson go? Why didn't that activity I planned seem to work as well with this class as when I used it last week with another class? Why didn't I get through all the work I'd planned? How could I have presented that teaching point better?* On the other hand, it may be formal, intentional and structured, such as when a religious education faculty or year level team gathers to consider a unit of work or curriculum, assess its strengths and weaknesses and make plans for its improvement. This is **educational evaluation**, and while it takes place naturally in an informal way, it must also, at certain times, be formally and intentionally carried out.

All of the following have a place in the evaluation of religious education units of work:

Teacher reflection. This is the natural, responsive evaluation of his or her work by the thoughtful teacher. It refers to internal questions such as: *Why did that class work well and yesterdays didn't? Why couldn't Nine Red do that activity I gave them? How could I vary my approach to this topic? What is the inattention of the students telling me? That was a great class: what did I do right?* If used well, such reflection will lead to improved preparation, delivery and assessment of religious education curricula.

Informal discussion among teachers. Although informal, this is a very valuable part of overall evaluation in education. Religious education teachers often informally discuss their work in the staff work area or lunchroom, talking over difficulties, sharing ideas for resources, and discussing ways in which a particular unit can be approached. This is valuable at any time, but when it takes palace among religious education teachers working at the same year level in a school, it can lead to real curriculum development.

Analysing student work. Analysis of the class work and assessment tasks completed by students through the unit will give the religious education teacher much information about the efficacy to the teaching learning processes. If the student work, including assessment tasks, indicates that the cognitive learning outcomes of the curriculum have been achieved, the teacher can be confident that the unit or curriculum has been effective. On the other hand, if the work of the students seems to indicate that many have missed key points, or if the work is not completed, or generally is of a poor standard, the teacher knows that he or she must consider where the teaching learning unit is weak, and seek ways to improve it. If, however, all the students seem to compete the work set in a short time, and to a very high standard, this might suggest that the unit of work or curriculum is not challenging enough, and needs to be developed further.

Seeking feedback from students. As part of unit evaluation, it is very important to seek feedback from the students either informally or systematically. A brief survey of student opinions at the end of a unit can be very useful. For example, a teacher might give a simple survey such as the following to the students at the end of a unit.

- Were you pleased with your work in this unit? Why or why not?
- Did you find the unit interesting? Why or why not?
- What lessons or activities did you like best and why?

- Which didn't you like and why?
- How could I improve this unit for next year?

Formal evaluation by teams of teachers. Ideally, at the completion of each unit, the team of teachers who has taught it will gather to formally evaluate the unit, and devise plans for its development and improvement. Questions that teachers may consider in an end of unit evaluation include the following.

- What cognitive learning outcomes did we set? Were they all achieved? Did we set too many or too few?
- Did the teaching / learning strategies we set match the cognitive outcomes?
- Was there a clear sequence in the unit? Does the sequencing need to be improved?
- Was there enough variety in the teaching / learning strategies?
- Did we have enough resources and were the resources we used effective? Which are the most effective resources and which are the least effective? Do we need any further resources?
- How did we assess the students work? Were the assessment tasks effective and how well did the students do them? Did we have too many or too few assessment tasks? What did the students work on assessment tasks tell us?
- Do we want to keep this unit in the curriculum? Why or why not?
- What steps do we need to take to develop and improve this unit for next year's curriculum?

Why can it be claimed that evaluation is a necessary and integral part of teaching and learning in religious education?

Devise a set of strategies that you might use to evaluate a religious education unit.

References and Further Reading

Nolen, B. (2002). Developing an RE unit: Challenging and stimulating students. *Journal of Religious Education* 50(1): 45-49

CHAPTER 12:

Teaching Scripture in the Catholic Secondary School

Kath Engebretson

Basic principles in approaching Scripture

Catholic teachers' tools for understanding Scripture

Just as Scripture is foundational in a Catholic view of Revelation, it is central to the religious education curriculum in a Catholic secondary school. Therefore Catholic religious education teachers need to have an adequate knowledge of the content of Scripture, should be able to apply appropriate methods to analysing it and should be prepared to develop these knowledge and skills constantly. Pope Pius XII's 1943 encyclical *Divino Afflante Spiritu* (DAS) challenged Catholic biblical scholars to use the "historical method," to analyse Scripture. Catholic scholars were called to re-investigate questions of authorship, dating of biblical books and sources used by authors — all with the goal of coming as close as possible to the original intention of the writers. This is the meaning of this except from *Divino Afflante Spiritu*.

> Being thoroughly prepared by the knowledge of the ancient languages and by the aids afforded by the art of criticism, let the Catholic exegete undertake the task, of all those imposed on him the greatest, that namely of **discovering and expounding the genuine meaning of the Sacred Books**. In the performance of this task let the interpreters bear in mind that their foremost and greatest endeavour should be to discern and define clearly that sense of the biblical words which is called literal. Aided by the context and by comparison with similar passages, let them therefore by means of their knowledge of languages search out with all diligence the literal meaning of the words; ...so that the mind of the author may be made abundantly clear.(#23)

In 1993, the document of the Pontifical Biblical Commission, *The Interpretation of the Bible in the Church*, re-asserted the fundamental principle of *Divino Afflante Spiritu* when it called for analysis of scriptural texts in order to come as close as possible to the intention of the writers. The method for doing this is referred to as the *historical-critical method*.

In the extract from DAS given above, how is the word "literal" used?

What is the historical-critical method?

The historical-critical method is a term used for a collection of ways of approaching Scripture. It is based on recognition of the fact that each of the books of the Bible developed in a particular historical, social, cultural and religious environment, that this environment can be studied and understood, and that it has had a direct influence on the final content of the books. The intention of the historical-critical method is to uncover the meaning of the text as the author intended it. The historical -critical method contains the following elements.

a) Textual criticism

Textual criticism is the process of attempting to retrieve as much of the original text of the biblical book as possible. In ancient times writing was a very specialised skill, and the biblical books would have been committed to writing by scribes writing on behalf of the author. This writing often contained errors in spelling, inaccurate expressions of certain words or ideas, or inaccurate corrections. In copying the text, errors would be made, or certain parts accidentally left out. There may be insertions in the text made by the scribe and a range of other changes to the original. Scholars who use textual criticism, go back to the earliest possible manuscripts of the same text in order to come as close as possible to the most accurate reading.

b) Source criticism

The beginning of source criticism is attributed to the 17th century biblical scholar, Richard Simon. He noticed that there were repetitions, discrepancies in content, and different writing styles in the Pentateuch (the first five books of the Bible) and realised that this meant that Moses could not have been the single author of these books as was commonly believed. Source criticism attempts to identify the various "sources" that have been put together to form a particular book or series of books. In the 19th century there developed the "documentary hypothesis," which claimed that four sources have been intertwined with each other to form the Pentateuch. These were the Yahwist narrative, (J), the Elohist narrative, (E), the Deuteronomic narrative (D) and the Priestly narrative (P) which was used by the final editor to provide an overarching structure of the five books.

In similar fashion, different "sources" can be identified in the four gospels. The gospels of Matthew, Mark and Luke are referred to as the *synoptic gospels,* meaning that they are summaries of the life and teaching of Jesus, with a similar outline. Almost ninety percent of Mark's gospel can be found in Matthew and about half of it in Luke. There is also material in Matthew and Luke that is virtually identical, but it is not from the gospel of Mark. From where did the authors get their material? Did they copy from each other? Source criticism applied to the synoptic gospels can be used to argue that Mark's gospel was the first to be written, and that the authors who wrote the gospels of Matthew and Luke knew and used Mark's gospel. At times they took passages from Mark's gospel exactly, and at other times they re-shaped the material to give it a particular meaning for their own communities. However, there is material in Matthew and Luke that is identical, yet is not in Mark. It is argued by some scholars that the writers of Matthew and Luke had access to another document, which they also used, in putting together their gospels. This document appears to have been a collection of the sayings and teachings of Jesus, now lost. This is often referred to as the *Q Source*, Q standing for the German word Quelle meaning *source*. However, other scholars believe that there was no such document. Of course, in addition to the material from Mark and Q, Matthew and Luke also have a great deal of material that is unique to their gospels which they have taken from other independent sources.

John's gospel is quite different from the three synoptic gospels. The author of this gospel may have been aware of the gospels of Matthew, Mark and Luke, but did not use them in the composition of his own gospel. Instead, the gospel of John is based on a particular oral and written tradition unique to the author or the community from which it came. The following diagram summarises the possible links between the four gospels:

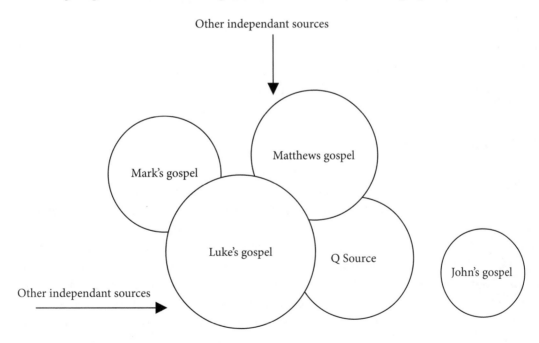

While source criticism is useful in identifying the underlying documents that go to make up the final text, it does not pay attention to the message of the text, and so the next step in the historical-critical method is form criticism.

In the first two chapters of the Book of Genesis two accounts of creation are given. Read each one through and identify the evidence that they are not by the same author.

c) Form criticism

Form Criticism is a method of literary analysis that seeks to identify the genre of a biblical book and the various genres that are included within it. Herman Gunkel (1852-1932) first introduced and developed form criticism, drawing attention away from the analysis of whole books, the concern of source criticism, to the smaller units (or pericopes) within them. As an example of what can be learned applying form criticism, Gunkel discovered that the book of Psalms contained songs for liturgical use. They were not meant to be used for private prayer, but were the prayers of the community of Israel to be used in Temple worship. Gunkel then distinguished sub-genres within the genre of psalms and these were: psalms of praise, psalms of lament, thanksgiving psalms, entrance songs and royal psalms. Similarly, within the overall genre of gospel, there are historical narratives, miracle stories, parables, announcement stories, call stories, allegories, infancy narratives and other literary forms. However while it was and remains helpful to distinguish genres within genres, interesting questions are raised by the ways in which the pericopes have been put together. Clearly this was not a random process, and analysing this process is the subject of redaction criticism.

Try to name the genres of each of these New Testament passages
Romans 16: 25-27; Acts 9: 36-43; Luke 14: 7-11; Luke 1: 26-38; Mark7: 31-37

d) Redaction criticism

Redaction criticism is the study of the how biblical books were edited. It shows how the sacred writers have put together sources and genres in their composition of the book, or series of books, and why they have done it this way. Redaction criticism therefore is concerned with the overall viewpoint or theological message of a book or books. Therefore the person using redaction criticism is particularly interested in the community from which the texts emerged or to whom they were addressed. The cultural, political, social and religious environment of this community will have greatly influenced the editing. For example, redaction criticism applied to the synoptic gospels would seek to understand the context of the community for whom a particular gospel was written, and then to analyse, in light of this, why certain passages have been included and others not, and why the passages are put together in this way. Ultimately it is concerned with the author's theological intentions.

What do you understand by the phrase "the author's theological intentions"?

The historical-critical method put together

As the document *The Interpretation of the Bible in the Church (IBC)* argues, the four steps of textual criticism, source criticism, form criticism and redaction criticism make up the historical -critical method. Together they give us the most reliable method of approaching Scriptural analysis.

> When this last method was brought into play, the whole series of different stages characteristic of the historical-critical method became complete: From textual criticism one progresses to literary criticism, with its work of dissection in the quest for sources; then one moves to a critical study of forms and, finally, to an analysis of the editorial process, which aims to be particularly attentive to the text as it has been put together. All this has made it possible to understand far more accurately the intention of the authors and editors of the Bible as well as the message which they addressed to their first readers. The achievement of these results has lent the historical-critical method an importance of the highest order. (IBC section1)

Give your own reaction to the historical-critical meted as a tool or series of tools for understanding biblical literature.

Applying the historical-critical method

The historical–critical method can be applied to a biblical text using a series of questions.

1. What can you learn about the source of the text?
2. What is the genre of the text and for what purpose is it this genre used?
3. Where does the text come in the book and what reason may there be for this?
4. What were the historical, religious, social and political conditions for the community at the time the text was written?
5. What then do you think was its original purpose?
6. What are the theological ideas in the text? (Ideas about God, people, the universe and the relationships between these; ideas about the Kingdom of God or about Jesus?)
7. What may it have to say to a contemporary Christian?

Try these questions with Luke 18:9-14.

A note about fundamentalism

The fundamentalist interpretation of Scripture arose as a result of the Reformation, and the Protestant concern to argue for the literal meaning of Scripture. It insists that everything in the Bible is literally true, treats the text of the bible as if has been dictated word by word from God, and rejects symbolic or figurative meanings. It argues that the Bible is the only source of truth, and rejects the authority of anything that has come after, including the Tradition of the Church. It rejects any kind of critical research into the bible, and does not concede that the development of the biblical text was influenced by historical, religious and political circumstances which explain its structure, language and intention. It often describes as historical, material which was never intended to be seen in an historical way. In relation to the gospels, it confuses the final written products with the actual words and deeds of the historical Jesus, and so overlooks the theology of the first Christian communities from whom the gospels came, and which is the real treasure of the gospels.

The document *The Interpretation of the Bible in the Church* has this to say about biblical fundamentalism, words which make it clear that this approach to Scripture has no place in a Catholic school.

> In its attachment to the principle "Scripture alone," fundamentalism separates the interpretation of the Bible from the tradition, which, guided by the Spirit, has authentically developed in union with Scripture in the heart of the community of faith. It fails to realize that the New Testament took form within the Christian church and that it is the Holy Scripture of this church, the existence of which preceded the composition of the texts. Because of this, fundamentalism is often anti-Church; it considers of little importance the creeds, the doctrines and liturgical practices which have become part of Church tradition, as well as the teaching function of the Church itself. It presents itself as a form of private interpretation which does not acknowledge that the Church is founded on the Bible and draws its life and inspiration from Scripture.

> The fundamentalist approach is dangerous, for it is attractive to people who look to the Bible for ready answers to the problems of life. It can deceive these people, offering them interpretations that are pious but illusory, instead of telling them that the Bible does not necessarily contain an immediate answer to each and every problem. Without saying as much in so many words, fundamentalism actually invites people to a kind of intellectual suicide.

It injects into life a false certitude, for it unwittingly confuses the divine substance of the biblical message with what are in fact its human limitations. (IBC, par.)

Why would the Pontifical Biblical Commission argue that the fundamentalist approach to the understanding of Scripture is "dangerous"?

What does it mean that the Bible is inspired?

The Catholic Church believes that the Bible is the inspired Word of God. This does not mean that God literally wrote the Bible, for it is clear that the Bible is the work of human beings. However the Church believes that the Bible is *the words of God in the words of these human beings*. In other words, under the guidance of the Holy Spirit, and using their own intelligence, knowledge, experience and insights, the biblical writers wrote what God wanted. The Second Vatican Council summed this belief up in this way:

> In composing the sacred books, God chose people, and while employed by Him they made use of their powers and abilities, so that with Him acting in them and through them, they, as true authors, consigned to writing everything and only those things which He wanted (Dei Verbum, par. 11).

This belief in the inspiration of the Bible means that it can be read by believers with confidence that it is truly the communication of God to people.

Does this mean that we will not find any error in the Bible? Does *inspiration* mean that it is absolutely historically accurate or does it mean something more than this? To what aspects of biblical writing does *inspiration* apply?

Exploring the Bible

The Canon of the Old Testament

The Bible is a collection of books that is organised into Old Testament (often also referred to as Hebrew Scriptures) and New Testament (often also referred to as Christian Scripture). The Old Testament tells the story of Israel and the Jewish people up to the era in which Jesus Christ was born, and the New Testament tells of the birth, life, death, resurrection of Jesus Christ, and the beginning of Christianity. The Catholic Church recognises 46 books of the Old Testament, and these are grouped into different categories such as the *Pentateuch*, the *Historical* books, the *Prophets,* the *Wisdom* books. The word *Canon* is used by the Church to describe the full and final list of writings which the Church believes are inspired by God, and which belong to the Catholic Bible. The Canon of books that comprise the **Old Testament** was decided during the fourth century, and reaffirmed after the Protestant Reformation by the Council of Trent.

The Canon of the New Testament

As explained earlier in this chapter, different groups of early Christians probably had their own oral (spoken) traditions, stories and collections of Jesus' deeds and teachings. When written accounts of Jesus' sayings did begin to circulate, writers within various Christian communities supplemented these with other traditions, thus developing their own gospels. Eventually these expanded writings spread through other communities, until some were recognised as accurate and having authority. In 185 AD Bishop Irenaeus of Lyons pronounced the four gospels that we have today as authoritative, and they began to be referred to by their present titles. The four gospels of the New Testament are the gospels of Matthew, Mark, Luke and John. The four gospels were used along with various letters, stories and other documents, according to what the particular Christian community found helpful and reliable in their understanding of Jesus Christ. The Church finally reached agreement on which writings were truly authentic, and represented the tradition of the Apostles.

The New Testament contains 27 books which are:

- The four gospels.
- The Acts of the Apostles
- Fourteen letters of St. Paul
- One Epistle of St James
- Two Epistles of St. Peter
- Three Epistles of St John
- One Epistle of Jude
- The Book of Revelation

When was the Bible written? – Old Testament Time-line.

The various books of the Bible were written at different times by different authors. In most of the biblical books we need to think about:

a) the time the book is written **about.**
b) the time **at which the book was put into its final form.**

These are usually two completely different times as the following time-line shows.

BC	What happened?	Characters	Putting the books together
2000 - 1500	Patriarchs	Abraham, Isaac, Jacob, Joseph.	
1250	Exodus: the central event	Israel is formed as a people, liberated from slavery and led back to Canaan by Moses. Occupation of the Promised land	
1000	Kingdom of David and Solomon	Peace and stability	Writing the stories of the past begins
933	Division of the Kingdom into North and South	North is attacked and destroyed in 721. Prophets Amos and Hosea in the north; Isaiah, Micah and Jeremiah in the south.	
587	Exile in Babylon	Prophets Jeremiah, Isaiah and Ezekiel	The books of the Torah, Genesis, Exodus, Leviticus, Numbers and Deuteronomy were finally put together. The Books of Proverbs and the Psalms were gathered together. The books of Joshua, Judges, Ruth, 1&2 Samuel, 1&2 Kings were gathered.
537	Return from Exile	Rebuilding of the Temple	The first and second book of Chronicles and the book of Ezra put together at this period.
333	Greek domination		The Books of Sirach, Ecclesiastes and Wisdom composed at this period, perhaps also Job. Book of Daniel. Book of Judith
63BC-66AD	Roman occupation	Jesus Christ born in c 4BC.	

When we realise that some books of the Old Testament took their final form up to 800 to 1000 years after the events that they describe, we need to ask these questions.

- Can we expect this to be an absolutely accurate historical account?
- What may have been the intention of the author or authors in writing or editing the material at that time?
- Could the account be influenced by the situation of the people of Israel at the time at which it was written?

The following passage from the Book of Exodus is a significant one for Jews and Christians.

> Now Moses was keeping the flock of his father in law Jethro, the priest of Midian; he led his flock beyond the wilderness and came to Horeb, the mountain of God. There the angel of the Lord appeared to him in a flame of fire out of a bush; he looked and the bush was blazing but it was not consumed. Then Moses said: "I must turn aside and look at this great sight, and see why the bush is not burned up." When the Lord saw that he had turned aside to see, God called to him out of the bush: "Moses! Moses!" And he said, "Here I am." The he said, "Come no closer! Remove the sandals from your feet, for the place on which you are standing is holy ground." He said further: "I am the God of your father, the God of Abraham, the God of Isaac and the God of Jacob." And Moses hid his face, for he was afraid to look at God.

> Then the Lord said, "I have observed the misery of my people who are in Egypt; I have heard their cry on account of their taskmasters. Indeed I know their sufferings and I have come down to deliver them from the Egyptians and to bring them up out of that land, to a good and broad land, a land flowing with milk and honey, to the land of the Canaanites, the Hittites, the Amorites, the Perizzites, the Hivites and the Jebusites. The cry of the Israelites has come to me; I have also seen how the Egyptians oppress them. So come, I will send you to Pharaoh to bring my people, the Israelites out of Egypt." But Moses said to God, "Who am I, that I should go to Pharaoh and bring the Israelites out of Egypt?" He said, "I will be with you. And this will be the sign to for you that I have sent you; when you have brought the people out of Egypt, you shall worship God on this mountain"

> But Moses said to God, "If I come to the Israelites and say to them 'The God of your ancestors has sent me to you,' and they ask me, 'What is his name?' what shall I say to them?" God said to Moses, "I AM WHO I AM" He said further: "Thus you shall say to the Israelites: 'I AM has sent me to you.' " God also said to Moses, "Thus you shall say to the Israelites, 'The Lord the

God of your ancestors, the God of Abraham, the God of Isaac and the God of Jacob, has sent me to you.' This is my name forever, and this is my title for all generations. Go and assemble the elders of Israel and say to them, 'The Lord the God of your ancestors, the God of Abraham, of Isaac and of Jacob appeared to me saying: "I have given heed to you and to what has been done to you in Egypt. I declare that I will bring you up out of the misery of Egypt to the land of the Canaanites, the Hittites, the Amorites, the Perizzites, the Hivites and the Jebusites, a land flowing with milk and honey." *(Exodus 3: 1-17. trans New Revised Standard Version).*

- Write down your first impression of the text.
- At what time in Israel's history is it written about?
- At what time was it actually written down?
- What was happening in the life of Israel at the time that it was written down?
- When this text was finally written and put together with the Book of Exodus, the people of Israel were scattered from their land, some in exile in Babylon because of the Babylonian invasion of their land, in which their Temple was destroyed. In what ways may this have influenced the way the story was told?
- What do you find in the text that tells you something of the feelings of the Israelite people in their exile in Babylon?
- What are the theological ideas in the text? (i.e. ideas about God).

When was the Bible written? – New Testament Time-line

The following time-line gives approximate dates for the writings of the New Testament.

Date	Event
3-5 BC	Birth of Jesus
27-30 AD	Death and resurrection of Jesus
33-65AD	Journeys and ministry of St. Paul; writing of his letters. Period of oral tradition and some writing about Jesus between his death and the time the first gospels were written. Headquarters of the Church moved from Jerusalem to Rome.
49AD	Council of Jerusalem where it was decided that discipleship of Jesus would be open to Gentiles as well as Jews.
50-67	Writing of Mark's gospel with other early gospel material.
64-67	1 Peter written in Rome. Sts Peter and Paul martyred at about this time in Rome.
65-80	Gospel of Luke and Acts of the Apostles written.
75-90	Gospel of Matthew written or completed.
81-96	Book of Revelation written.
90-110	Gospel of John written or completed. Epistle of Jude written.
125-350	Period of Christianity during which the Bible was assembled

The four gospels were written at different times and in different communities. They certainly tell the story of the life, death and resurrection of Jesus Christ that had been handed down in the Christian communities, but each gospel tells this story in a different way. For example, the way the story is told in each gospel has been partly influenced by the kinds of problems and issues the community was dealing with at the time of writing.

Stages in the writing of the gospels

We can identify three stages in the writing of the gospels.

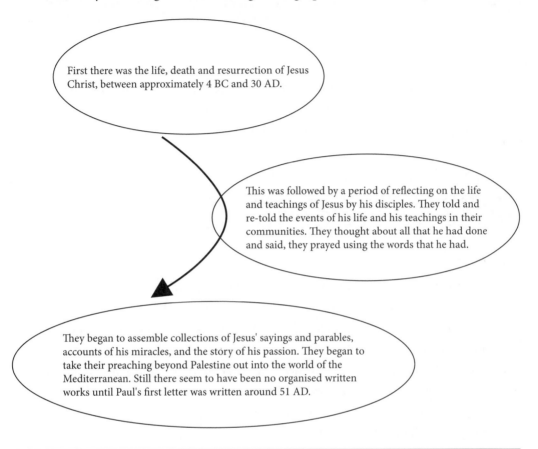

First there was the life, death and resurrection of Jesus Christ, between approximately 4 BC and 30 AD.

This was followed by a period of reflecting on the life and teachings of Jesus by his disciples. They told and re-told the events of his life and his teachings in their communities. They thought about all that he had done and said, they prayed using the words that he had.

They began to assemble collections of Jesus' sayings and parables, accounts of his miracles, and the story of his passion. They began to take their preaching beyond Palestine out into the world of the Mediterranean. Still there seem to have been no organised written works until Paul's first letter was written around 51 AD.

What implications does this three stage process have for the final written products?

The Gospels are documents of faith

Almost all books tell us what they are about in the opening sentence or paragraph. We only have to read the opening lines of each of the gospels to know that the writers were not trying to give a disinterested account of the life of Jesus Christ. The gospels were written by authors who believed that Jesus was the Messiah and the Son of God. Their gospels set out to demonstrate and explain this. This is obvious from the very first sentences. Complete some or all of the following analytical exercises.

Mark's gospel opens with the line: *The beginning of the good news of Jesus Christ, the Son of God (Mark 1:1).*

- There are three key phrases or words in this opening sentence: *good news, Christ* and *Son of God*. Remember that *Christ* is the Greek form of the word *Messiah*.
- What points about Jesus is Mark making at the beginning of his gospel? What will you expect to find as you read the rest of the gospel?

Matthew's begins in this way: *An account of the genealogy of Jesus the Messiah, the son of David, the son of Abraham (Matt1:1).*

- Read the rest of the opening passage of Matthew's gospel, verses 1-17.
- In one word, what do these first seventeen verses deal with?
- In the first verse, which two famous Jewish leaders are mentioned? What was each of them famous for?
- Who might the author of this gospel be writing for, that would cause him to point out that David and Abraham were the ancestors of Jesus?
- Judging from his opening sentence, what is the writer of the gospel of Matthew going to emphasise in his gospel?

Luke addressed his gospel to a Greek convert to Christianity, Theophilus

Luke's gospel is an instruction to this convert, so that the new Christian would understand more deeply the things in which he had been instructed. Luke was also concerned to provide a truthful and accurate account of the events of Jesus' life, death and resurrection.

Since many have undertaken to set down an orderly account of the events that have been fulfilled among us, just as they were handed on to us by those who, from the beginning, were eye witnesses and servants of the word, I too decided, after investigating everything carefully from the first, to write an orderly account for you, most excellent Theophilus, so that you may know the truth concerning the things about which you have been instructed (Luke 1:1).

Theophilus may or may not have been a real person. His name in Greek means *one who loves God*. However, he represented the community for whom Luke's gospel was written, many of whom were Gentiles recently converted to Christ.

- What reason did Luke give for writing the gospel?
- Did Luke imply that his account of the life of Jesus may be rather different from those written before?

The author of John's gospel teaches that Jesus is the eternal Word, who was with God from the beginning, equal to God in all ways.

In the beginning was the Word, and the Word was with God, and so the Word was God (John 1:1).

- When John speaks of the *beginning*, to what beginning is he referring? Did the world already exist at this *beginning*?
- Read verses 1-6 of the first chapter of John's gospel. What does John claim that Jesus was involved in at the beginning?
- If this is so, what does this mean about Jesus?
- For what purposes do we human beings use words? How do our words reveal our own characters and personalities?
- What might John mean when he says that Jesus is the Word of God?

	Mark	Matthew	Luke	John
Write out the opening sentence in each gospel				
What is the message of the the gospel, judging by its opening passage?				
What are the first words spoken by Jesus in each gospel?				
What do these words of Jesus tell us about what the gospel is going to be about?				

The context of the synoptic gospels: The gospel of Mark

According to tradition, the author of the gospel of Mark was John Mark, a disciple of St. Peter. The community for which he was writing, based in Rome, had probably known the Apostle Peter very well, and had been influenced by him until his martyrdom in approximately 64AD. It is most likely that the gospel was written in Rome, and that it was written for Christians of non-Jewish origins (Gentiles). He explains all the Jewish customs that he mentions and explains Aramaic words (the language spoken by Jesus). There are Latin words scattered throughout his gospel. The community in Rome was under threat of persecution by Roman emperors, especially Nero who had already killed Sts Peter and Paul by 67AD. The community would have been afraid and distressed, not only by the persecutions but also by the war between Rome and Israel, the place where Christianity had its roots. Many would have wondered if this were the end of time, the time for the

Second Coming of Christ. Some "pretenders" may even have claimed to be Christ come again.

Applying the historical-critical method on a story from Mark's gospel

We will use the historical-critical method now to analyse the story of Jesus calming the storm, which is told in Mark 4: 35-41.

> On that day, when evening had come, he said to his them; "Let us go across to the other side." And leaving the crowd behind, they took him with them in the boat, just as he was. Other boats were with him. A great windstorm arose and beat into the boat, so that the boat was already being swamped. But he was in the stern, asleep on the cushion: and they woke him up and said to him, "Teacher, do you not care that we are perishing ?" And he woke up and rebuked the wind and said to the sea "Peace! Be still!" Then the wind ceased and there was dead calm. He said to his them: "Why are you afraid? Have you still no faith?" And they were filled with great awe and said to one another "Who then is this that even the wind and the sea obey him?" (trans NRSV)

Here are the key questions to apply to the text:

1. What can you learn about the source of the text?
2. What is the genre of the text and for what purpose is it this genre used?
3. Where does the text come in the book and what reason may there be for this?
4. What are the historical, religious, social and political conditions for the community at the time the text was written?
5. What then do you think was it original purpose?
6. What are the theological ideas in the text? (Ideas about God, people, the universe and the relationships between these; ideas about the Kingdom of God or about Jesus?)
7. What may it have to say to a contemporary Christian?

Read the story of Jesus calming the storm in Mark 4:35-41, then expand on these responses.

Source: only in Mark's gospel

Genre. This is a nature miracle. It is used to show the power and divinity of Jesus as Son of God.

Where it comes in the text: The story comes quite early in the gospel, to prepare the reader for the coming account of the passion and death of Jesus, through which their faith will be tested. It comes at the end of a chapter which contains parables about the coming Kingdom of God, the second coming of Christ for which the Christians were hoping?

Context. Mark's community was suffering under persecution by the Roman Emperor, Nero, and in fear of the consequences of the Israel-Roman war. They hoped for the coming of the Kingdom of God but their future seemed dangerous and uncertain, their leaders killed and their destiny unclear.

Meaning for the original community. The story calls the Christians of Mark's community to put their faith in Jesus. He is truly the Son of God and he knows and cares about their situation. He will bring them peace in their troubles. Because he is with them they will come safely to the Kingdom of God.

Contemporary meaning. Today's Christian can also find in this story a call to faith in Christ through all the difficulties and doubts of their lives.

Use this method now to interpret one or more of the following texts.
Mark 7:24-30
Mark 10:35-42
Mark 10:28-31.

The context of the synoptic gospels: The gospel of Matthew

Tradition ascribes this gospel to the Apostle Matthew. It is written for "second generation Christians" perhaps by a Jewish convert to Christianity who was familiar with the Jewish law and traditions, the writings of the prophets and with the hopes of the Jewish people for a Messiah. The gospel was possibly written after the destruction of the Temple in Jerusalem in 70 AD. It is uncertain where it was written, but most scholars think that the place of its composition was the city of Antioch in Syria, to which many Jewish-Christians had fled after the destruction of Jerusalem. The author of the gospel frequently refers to Jewish Law, Jewish Scripture and traditions, which suggests that he is writing primarily for Jewish converts to Christianity. Jesus is shown as the Messiah for whom Israel waited, and at other times as a new Moses who brings a new Law for the Christian communities.

Matthew's gospel was written in a period of settling down for the Christian community. The Jewish Christians had separated from their fellow Jews, and they no longer attended synagogue as they had in the earlier years of Christianity. The threat of immediate persecution had passed, but there may have been conflict in the community between Jewish Christians and Gentile Christians. In this settling down period, the early Church was beginning to put together what it believed about its life and mission. The first Trinitarian formula in the New Testament is given to us in Matthew's gospel, probably a formula used in baptism in this early Christian community.

Go therefore and make disciples of all nations, baptising them in the name of the Father and of the Son and of the Holy Spirit (Matthew 28:19).

Use the following structural outline to complete the activity below.

Matthew's gospel can be divided into these sections.

1. The Prologue: the birth of the Messiah: Chapters 1-2
2. The New Law: Chapters 3-7
3. Christian discipleship: Chapters 8-10
4. The reign of God: Chapters 11-13
5. The Church: The beginning of the Kingdom: Chapters 14-18
6. Judgment: Chapters 19-23
7. Epilogue: the death and resurrection of Jesus: Chapters 26-28

Work in groups of 4 or 5, and select one of the sections from the outline given above. Write out in order what is in the chapters and give a short spoken report on the section.

Read two or three of the following passages and for each one write in a few words what point the author is making in the passage.

- Matthew 21:5-11: Jesus as the Messiah and King.
- Matthew 27:54: Jesus as the Son of God.
- Matthew 10:1-5; Matthew 28:18-20. Jesus passes his authority on to his Apostles.
- Matthew 13:1-9. Some hear the word of God and others do not.
- Matthew 17:1-8. Jesus fulfils the Law and the Prophets.
- Matthew 16:17-19. The leadership of Peter.

Use the historical-critical method that we used earlier in this chapter to analyse the story of the transfiguration, Matthew 17:18

1. What can you learn about the source of the text?
2. What is the genre of the text and for what purpose is it this genre used?
3. Where does the text come in the book and what reason may there be for this?
4. What are the historical, religious, social and political conditions for the community at the time the text was written?
5. What then do you think was it original purpose?
6. What are the theological ideas in the text? (Ideas about God, people, the universe and the relationships between these; ideas about the Kingdom of God or about Jesus?)
7. What may it have to say to a contemporary Christian?

The context of the synoptic gospels: The gospel of Luke

The author of the Gospel of Luke is thought to have been a Syrian, named Luke, from the city of Antioch, who was a physician and friend and fellow traveller of St. Paul. His gospel may have been written after the destruction of the Jewish Temple, between 80 and 90 AD. It is almost impossible to know where it was written, but scholars have suggested one of the cities in Greece, perhaps Corinth. Luke is clearly writing for Gentile Christians. The person to whom his gospel is addressed has a Greek name, Theophilus, and he declares throughout the gospel that the salvation of Christ is offered to non-Jews. The author is clearly deeply influenced by the Old Testament, even though he seldom quotes it directly. Luke is writing in a period of great expansion for the infant Church. The early Christians have accepted that the Second Coming of Christ may not occur for a long time, and they have learned to concentrate on issues of day to day Christian life, work, Christian love and prayer. The most important theme of Luke's gospel is that Jesus is Saviour for all, Gentiles, outcasts and sinners alike.

Analyse the following passages in terms of the questions of the historical-critical method given above.

1.	Luke 4.14-6.49
2.	Luke 7:1-9:50
3.	Luke 9:51-12:59.
4.	Luke 13:1-16:31
5.	Luke 17:1-19:27.

Luke's parables

A parable is a short instructional story, which makes a clear point about Christian life or belief. Luke has some wonderful parables in his gospel, many of which are not in any other gospel.

Choose up to three of the parables listed below and interpret them using the chart provided.

Parable of the yeast (Luke 13:20-21).

The Wedding Banquet (Luke 14:16-24)

The Lost Sheep and the Lost Coin (Luke 15: 3-10)

Faithful Servants (Luke 12:35-48)

The Pharisee and the Tax Collector (Luke 18: 9-14)

The Rich Fool (Luke 12:13-21)

Places at the Table (Luke 14:7-14)

Analysing a parable

- What is the setting of the parable? Who are the characters? To whom does Jesus address it? What has led up to it? Does Jesus tell it to defend his teachings or actions? Did Luke put it here because he is developing a certain idea or theme?
- What is the parable about just as a story? Re-tell the story in your own words.
- Find the main point of the parable. It is usually at the end, and may be posed as a question or statement. Is Jesus teaching in this parable about God, salvation, himself, Christian prayer, forgiveness?
- Try to state the theme in one sentence using "Just as…so." For example, "Just as the shepherd went looking for the sheep he had lost, so God welcomes and forgives sinners."
- What links are there between this parable and the life situation of the community for which Luke wrote his gospel?

Analyse the parable of the Good Samaritan (Luke 10: 25-37) using the historical-critical method.

Write down your key learning as a religious education teacher from this chapter.

References and Further Reading

Abbott, W. (1966). *The Documents of Vatican II. De Verbum. The Dogmatic Constitution on Divine Revelation.* London: Geoffrey Chapman.

Pope Pius XII. (1943). Encyclical. *Divino Afflante Spiritu.* http://www.vatican.va/holy_father/pius_xii/encyclicals/documents/hf_p-xii_enc_30091943_divino-afflante-spiritu_en.html

Pontifical Biblical Commission (1993). *The Interpretation of the Bible in the Church.* http://www.catholicculture.org/docs/doc_view.cfm?recnum=561

Catechism of the Catholic Church (1994) Pars 78-139.

CHAPTER 13

Teaching Hard Topics in Religious Education

Richard Rymarz

The neglected topics in the religious education curriculum

Brainstorm the following questions:
- What do you think is a hard topic in RE?
- What makes it hard?
- What, if any, was your experience of studying complex topics such as the Trinity or the Incarnation in secondary school?
- Do topics such as these have a place in the contemporary religious education curriculum?

One key to a strong religious education program in the school setting is balance. A good way of determining what is in the religious education curriculum is to simply lay it out and to note what topics are covered and how much time is devoted to them across a number of year levels. When this exercise is completed one tendency that is often revealed is that the curriculum is too heavily weighted to topics that lack cognitive depth and a clear religious education focus. These are topics for which religious education teachers often have an intuitive feel, and do not require specialist theological information. A curriculum that devotes too much time to experiential themes such as relationships or the importance of family at junior secondary level, or constant units on social justice at middle to senior level to the detriment of other important topics, does not provide sufficient intellectual challenge for students. The result of this is that it makes religious education uninteresting, as it becomes a discipline that dos not bear academic comparison with other subjects in the school curriculum. This is not an argument for a religious education curriculum in secondary schools which would challenge a university undergraduate, but one for balancing the curriculum with sufficiently demanding academic themes.

There can be a tendency in religious education to avoid difficult themes and this may have been occurring for some time. Here is how two contemporary religious education teachers recalled the religious education that they were exposed to as secondary school students. (Rymarz, 2001).

There was a lot of focus on discussing issues. We didn't have a textbook; we didn't look at the Bible. Religious Education was based on your own personal development. What you want to do when you leave school. How are your relationships? Are you acting like a Christian person? It was values based. (EC 2)

I don't really remember a lot about the religious education classes. Like I can remember liking probably mid-secondary school the RE classes, but they weren't really RE. It was more development as to the type of person you are. We didn't really discuss religious issues, it was more life issues and was based on that. (AS 3)

> How would you teach a topic, such as "Who is Jesus" at various levels in the secondary school. How would you make it progressively more challenging for older year levels? What aspects of the topic might you develop as a sequence?

The need for students to tackle topics in religious education that place strong demands on them and their understanding of the Catholic tradition is debated, but at least two ideas can be advanced that support this emphasis. First, the dominant educational paradigm used in religious education in Australia and elsewhere for at least the past two decades has been an "educational" approach. An important aspect of this approach is that religious education should be able to use the language and tools of general educational discourse, and apply these to religious education. An important part of this discourse is the spiral curriculum, or the idea that as students progress through the school they are presented with more and more complex presentations of key topics. A corollary of this is that difficult ideas are also tackled in as educationally sophisticated a way as possible. If religious education is educational, it must be able to demonstrate a commitment to developing students' understanding in a sequential manner, and also not to avoid areas which require a high level of teaching expertise. It is hard to imagine another discipline not doing a conceptually important area because it was just too hard.

A more philosophical argument arises from the need to provide students in religious education with an understanding that is coherent. For a position to be coherent two conditions are essential, consistency and explanation (Everitt and Fisher, 1995). Coherent beliefs are consistent, and have some explanatory power. An example of a core theme in religious education in Catholic schools is teaching about Jesus. If difficult notions such as the Catholic belief that Jesus is both human and divine are not covered, then much of what Catholics believe about Mary, and about the passion and the resurrection of Christ do not follow. A well grounded understanding of what Catholics believe about Jesus will explain many factors of Catholic life, and provide an entry into other areas of the faith tradition. The religious education curriculum needs to be balanced with topics which have a strong cognitive, base and which are pivotal to understanding the faith tradition being investigated. Study of these topics, which many teachers often describe as hard, is likely to meet students' needs, to extend them and help then negotiate their own identity in relation to the home tradition. They do not exclude an experiential emphasis when required. The fact that students find some topics in religious education difficult is not a reason for excluding them from the curriculum. Students find many disciplines difficult, but this is an indication that the study has serious academic and intellectual claims. An important part of the role of religious education should be to broaden and deepen the understanding of students in topics that are a critical part of the Christian tradition. The key question is how to teach hard topics better.

Below is a section from a widely used Catholic religious education textbook (To Know Worship and Love, Book 8). Critique this passage. With what age level should the text be used?

Jesus in Matthew's gospel

Jesus is presented as the Saviour who has come to fulfil the Law not to abolish it. Matthew's gospel was written for an audience who would have been familiar with the Old Testament and this is frequently quoted in this gospel. Matthew makes the point that Jesus is the Messiah that Israel had hoped for. Jesus is referred to as the Messiah, the Christ, the Son of David and King of Israel. He is presented as a great teacher who brings the New Law just as Moses had been the one who brought the Jewish Law to the people.

Jesus as the Glorified Lord

In Matthew's gospel Jesus is presented as the promised Saviour. This portrait stresses the power of Jesus. One example of this theme is the mythological story of the three wise men (Magi). Read this in Matthew 2: 1-11

- What do the Magi do when they see Jesus?
- What do they give Jesus?
- Why does Herod want to stop them?

Look through Matthew's Gospel. List as many references to the Old Testament as you can.

Jesus in Mark's gospel

Mark's gospel presents Jesus through the eyes of Peter. Jesus is described with his disciples. He eats, prays and travels with them. They are present when he preaches; he spends time in their homes and families. Because Mark's gospel reflects the views of someone who was very close to Jesus, this account stresses the humanity of Jesus. He experiences pain and rejection and is presented as the suffering Messiah. Disciples of Jesus must also share Jesus' suffering and death before sharing the glory of his Resurrection.

Jesus as One who suffers
Mark's gospel presents Jesus as the suffering Messiah. Throughout this gospel Mark reminds his readers that to be followers of Jesus is to experience pain and suffering, just as Jesus did. Read Mark 8: 34-38

- What does Jesus ask of His followers?
- What does it mean to gain the whole world and forfeit your life?
- Name some "crosses" that people have to bear in their lives.

The most important part of Mark's gospel deals with Jesus' passion and death. Read Mark 15: 16-24.

- Draw a flowchart, which illustrates his suffering before he was crucified.
- Draw a symbol that you think represents how Jesus is portrayed in Mark's gospel.

Hard topics require theological knowledge and an understanding of a range of cross-disciplinary concepts and complex ideas. They are difficult to explain to others and require excellent pedagogical skills on the part of the religious education teacher. In addition, they often do not have a ready expression in human experience. Most people, for example, have some ideas on relationships, (a topic often done to death in religious education) but a more complex topic such as the challenge posed to a literal approach to the Book of Genesis by Darwin's theory of evolution, cannot be prepared as the teacher walks down the corridor to his or her religious education class. Hard topics require research, sequential planning and a sustained approach over a number of lessons. Finally and perhaps most importantly, hard topics are often of critical importance in defining what makes Christian thought and practice distinctive. They establish distinctions between what Christians believe, and what others believe. For this reason hard topics make demands on the content knowledge of religious education teachers, especially in areas that relate to the religious tradition that they are working within.

An approach to teaching hard topics

The first step in developing pedagogy for hard topics in religious education is a commitment to tackling these issues in the curriculum. Without this, it is unlikely that any satisfactory program can be developed, due to the inherent difficulties that many of these topics present to religious education teachers. The schemas outlined below gives some ideas for approaching hard religious education topics.

Step	Description
Recognition	Make a clear commitment to teach hard topics in the curriculum. This does not mean that every lesson should involve such themes, but teachers should have a firm realisation that these should be intentionally planned.
Orientation	Examine the existing curriculum to see how the particular topic has been covered in the past, and recognize that it may be covered again in the future. Hard topics often require a number of treatments in a four or six year program. Ask yourself what aspect of the topic will be covered now and what will be done later. Be aware of the age and prior learnings of students.
Research	Identify a number of key resources in the area. These can be divided into two types: first, teaching resources used by others to teach this topic, and second, sources that help teachers understand the topic themselves. A good deal can be achieved here by some guided selective reading. Whilst higher degree qualifications are always desirable for religious education teachers, the aim is to improve teaching and learning about hard topics and not to become experts in one particular theoretical area.
Focus	Working with others if you can, try to encapsulate as briefly as possible the heart of the issue. What is it that makes this topic hard and why do students have trouble understanding it? What is their thinking about the topic and especially what common misconceptions exist?
Response	Repeat the focus step, but now try to correctly encapsulate Catholic teaching on the topic.
Educational goals	Develop cognitive learning outcomes, that is write down what you expect of students who have completed this unit of work. Some teachers may prefer to do this step after completing the teaching strategies step which follows.

Teaching strategies	This is the critical step. You are now at a stage where you ready to start developing a series of teaching and learning activities that will engage students. Rely here on your knowledge as a skilled teacher. Give some thought to the number of lessons you are going to devote to the topic. It is important to note the role of direct instruction. With hard topics, no amount of student group work or research is going to communicate the heart of the topic as well as skilfully presented teacher input, using any resources that will help with this. While this should not be very long, it is often the missing strategy in religious education lessons. Plan assessment strategies that will enhance the learning of the students.
Review and consolidation	Try to make a judgement regarding the success of your lesson sequence and record what was successful. Begin to develop a pool of resources that have been helpful so that when this topic is taught again you have a starting point.

A worked example: Teaching about Jesus in junior secondary classes

Step	Description
Recognition	Obviously teaching about Jesus is an important aspect of religious education in Christian schools. It should include something of the complexity of the topic, and how the Church has understood Jesus over the centuries. This example covers the teaching of the Council of Nicea, (325 AD), later re-affirmed in the Council of Chalcedon (481 AD) that Jesus is both God and Man. We will study the natures of Jesus in Years 9 and 10 with a focus on the development on the doctrine about Jesus in the senior years. We plan to spend five lessons on this topic.
Orientation	Currently Jesus is presented at two stages in the curriculum. In Year 7 there is an emphasis on Jesus the storyteller. In Year 11 Jesus is presented as part of the school's internal religious education programme. The teaching strategies that have been identified as currently in use all rely on presenting Jesus as a human figure and role model. Students are presently asked to consider statements such as "What would Jesus do in this situation?" but are never really told what the Catholic Church believes and teaches about him.

Research	A useful resource book for teachers is Young, F. (1983). *From Nicea to Chalcedon: a Guide to the Literature and its Background.* London: SCM Press.
Focus	The central issue is that of Jesus as God and Man. It is easy if you stress either the humanity or the divinity of Jesus, but to combine both is a challenge. Many secondary students see Jesus as a kind of superman, with great powers but different from the creator God. Some are inclined to see Jesus as just "pretending" to be human.
Response	Jesus and God are the same essence. Jesus was not created but has always existed. He is the pre-existent Word of God incarnate.
Educational goals	*By the end of this unit students will have:* • Participated in a role play that depicts the character and views of Arius and Athanasius; • Viewed and made notes from a video on the Council of Nicea; • Produced a timeline that depicts the key events leading up to and following the Council of Nicea; • Correctly identified Catholic teaching on the relationship between Jesus and God the Father; • Contrasted the Catholic view with that of Arius; • Explored some of their questions about the origins of Jesus; • Discussed some of the difficulties and objections associated with the teaching of the Council of Nicea; • Listed and defined some of the key terms used in Christological discussions.

Teaching strategies	• Give some historical background; introduce the key characters of Arius and Athanasius. Have students interview each character and try to draw out their different understandings of who Jesus is; • Show a video which gives some background to the Council of Nicea; • Brainstorm the question, "Who do you think Jesus is?" • Use artwork to communicate how artists have interpreted Catholic teaching about Jesus. Many icons represent Mary and Jesus. The depiction of Jesus here is quite different from what students may be used to. The man/child Jesus sitting enthroned on the lap of Mary is a powerful image of Jesus as God; • Provide students with a simple statement of Catholic understanding of Christ's origins; • Design a worksheet that helps students define some key Christological terms; • Use selected scripture passages that are relevant to the topic: e.g. Philippians 2: 5-11. • Invite students to record in their diaries or journals how they react to the idea of Jesus as God; Discuss the how it is different to say that one thing is **similar** to another, from saying that something is **identical** to another. • Imagine that you are speaking to the greatest expert on Jesus in the world. What questions would you ask? • Research one aspect of the historical period under review, themes such as the Council of Nicea, the Emperor Constantine or another position such as Docetism.
Review and consolidation	When this topic was covered in class, the strategy of the argument between Athanasius and Arius was very successful. Students could really relate to the personalities. They found some of it difficult, especially how the divine Jesus could coexist with the human Jesus. We will come back to this topic in Year 9. The main assessment tool was the cumulative work diary submitted at the end of the unit. The students submitted two worksheets, a narrative dialogue between Arius and Athanasius, a report on the video of the Council of Nicea, an analysis of two scripture passages, a timeline for the period before and after the Council of Nicea and a statement of the Catholic teaching about who Jesus is.

Try developing a unit of work along the lines suggested above on a challenging topic in religious education. Some areas that you may wish to consider include:

- The interface between science and religion
- The Trinity
- Creation theology
- Catholic ethical perspectives on human life issues
- Catholic teaching about the Communion of Saints.

References and Further Reading

Buchanan, M.T. (2005). Pedagogical drift: The evolution of new approaches and Paradigms in religious education. *Religious Education 100* (1), 20-37.

Rossiter, G (1997). A cognitive basis for affective learning in classroom religious education. *British Journal of Religious Education.* 4(1). 4-11

Rymarz, R (2001). When I was at School. *British Journal of Religious Educa*tion 24(1) 20-32

Walshe, K (2005). *What do young people today really think about Jesus?* British Journal of Religious Education 27(1) 65-78.

CHAPTER 14

The Professional Responsibilities of Religious Education Teachers in Catholic Secondary Schools

Richard Rymarz

(In this chapter Rymarz has drawn on material he wrote for a similar chapter in Engebretson, K., Fleming, G. and Rymarz, R. (2002). *Thriving as an RE Teacher. A handbook for secondary religious educators.* Australia: Social Science Press.)

Some of the greatest anxieties that religious education teachers face are concern how to deal with issues that are *controversial*. These include matters that relate to the personal and professional lives of teachers, as well as a number of specific topics that can be covered in religious education.

The most important advice for religious education teachers dealing with controversial issues, is to make sure that they discuss their concerns with others in the school. The first person to approach is usually the Religious Education Co-ordinator or someone in a similar position. Part of the role of this person is to support religious education teachers when controversial issues arise. Religious education teachers often make situations far more difficult for themselves if they do not communicate their concerns early enough. Some issues that arise in the contemporary religious education class can be difficult for an inexperienced teacher to deal with alone. These are not problems, however, that occur in isolation. They have been faced before and can be dealt with effectively provided concerned parties are informed about what is going on.

Professional responsibilities and the private lives of religious education teachers

Consider the following scenario:

"I teach RE at the local Catholic school. I also live with my partner and we are not married. I realise that this conflicts with Church teaching and am afraid that my students will ask me about this."

- *What are some of the issues that are brought into focus by this case?*

When it comes to forming and fostering moral attitudes in the young, teachers influence their pupils more by what they are and do, than by what they merely say. Because of the important teacher-student relationship, teaching cannot be a value-free profession. Undoubtedly the known behaviour of a teacher, both in and out of school, may affect the moral outlook of his or her pupils. Pupils cannot be favourably influenced, when they know that the behaviour of their teacher in private life conflicts with the moral formation taught or inculcated by the school. The danger is greater if the children are more impressionable than older tertiary students or adults. It would be contrary to the professional ethics of a schoolteacher to allow such a conflict fraught with moral danger for the school's pupils, to arise. (Ford, 1986:14)

- *What implications does this extract have for the case above?*
- *What is your response to this quote?*

The scenario provided above raises a number of issues for the religious education teacher. The first is the conflict for the teacher in living a lifestyle that does not accord with Catholic teaching. The private life of the teacher is one for the individual involved, and the school has no right to inquire about these matters provided they remain out of the public domain. More particularly, the students have no right to ask about these matters. A teacher who allows himself or herself to be quizzed by students about how they live their lives, is not respecting the boundaries of proper teacher-student relationships. The situation here is similar to a teacher asking students about their personal lives. A teacher who enters into this dialogue is being intrusive as well as foolish.

However, the teacher must respect the integrity of the school and its relationship with the Church. Catholic schools belong to the mission and function of the Church. People who work in Catholic schools are expected not to contradict what the Church teaches, since this belongs to the identity and ethos of the school. This is especially important for religious education teachers in the classroom. Mutual respect and professionalism is required. If the religious education teacher does not agree with a particular aspect of Church teaching, they are entitled to this opinion, but it should not become a forum for disagreement in the classroom or other forums in the school. The classroom is not the place for religious education teachers, or any other teachers for that matter, to air their disagreements with the Church.

Being honest

> "But I feel really strongly about this and feel my job is to be honest with the students. How can I be true to myself and not speak out?"
>
> • *How would you answer this question?*

If a religious education teacher decided to speak about an issue in a way that was not in conformity with Church teachings, he or she is behaving unprofessionally by contradicting the message that the school itself is trying to promote. If a teacher feels obliged to argue for such a position, it would seem that the teacher would be more suited to teaching in an unaffiliated institution. The issue here is not so much whether the teacher can be honest about expressing his or her opinion, but whether they can be honest about agreeing to support the ethos of the school which is a condition of employment in Catholic schools. No teacher is obliged to give his or her opinion about any issue at all, nor is a teacher obliged to give details of his or her personal life to students. In most cases, in fact, it would be very unwise to do so.

Answering questions

An important aspect of the role of the religious education teacher is that of witness. This can be especially relevant when teaching about the integrity of the Christian life. Religious education teachers are often asked questions like, *do you pray, or do you go to Mass on Sunday?* Teachers may well, and have the right to, refuse to become involved in this kind of conversation, as it impinges on their private lives. It is also perfectly appropriate for teachers to answer such questions affirmatively. If this is done, however, it is important to be aware that a precedent has been established. The teacher has let the students know that he or she is prepared to reveal to them aspects of their own faith life. Later on it may become more difficult to reverse this policy. Be aware also of the acceptable bounds of questioning and disclosure. Questions, for example, about the sexual activity of teachers are inappropriate, irrespective of the answer, and school leaders should be informed when these questions are asked.

I just can't agree with this

"I really support the ethos of the school and love teaching RE. There are some things however, in Church teaching and ethics that I have a problem with. What can I do?"

• *How would you answer this question?*

As well as personal issues, some topics in religious education can cause conflict for religious education teachers. These are often related to sexual, moral and ethical issues because these areas often have the most obvious *overlap* with everyday life. Religious education teachers are more likely to be challenged on the Church's teaching on relationships, than on a more purely theological topic such as the nature of the Trinity. In dealing with both topics however, the same principles apply.

The first principle is **not to defend the indefensible**. There are many instances in the history of Christianity where Christian behaviour has been much less than ideal. The role of the religious education teacher is not to provide unswerving apologetic support for everything that Christians, including Church leaders, have done over the centuries. A sanitised telling of the story of the Church will stifle the interest of students who value an educational approach to religious education. Students today are well aware that Christians and consequently the Church are not perfect, for the Church lives out its mission in the world of people and events. Some decisions that are made are not correct and many individuals in the Church fall well short of what is expected of them. With an appropriate awareness of the dangers of judging other eras by the standards and values of our own, religious education teachers should discuss the history of the Church in a way that does justice to a Church that is striving for perfection but always falling short. A strong example of this attitude to Christian heritage was provided by Pope John Paul II. In a visit to Greece in 2001 Pope John Paul II expressed his regret and sorrow for the destruction of Constantinople during the fourth crusade. Here is a report of part of his speech.

> Some memories are especially painful, and some events of the distant past have left deep wounds in the minds and hearts of people to this day...I am thinking of the disastrous sack of the imperial city of Constantinople, which was for so long the bastion of Christianity in the East. It is tragic that the assailants, who had set out to secure free access for Christians to the Holy Land, turned against their own brothers in the faith. The fact that they were Latin Christians fills Catholics with deep regret. (Zenit News Agency infoenglish@zenit.orgt 4/5/01)

A second principle is to be aware of the complexity of issues.

I once observed a religious education teacher teach a lesson on embryonic stem cell research. Actually, teach is not the right verb to describe what happened. The lesson consisted of the teacher making some superficial comments, then directing students to a series of articles of varying quality, and then asking them to report on their findings. Needless to say the students emerged from this situation none the wiser. The general conclusion of the lesson was that embryonic stem cell research was a positive boon for humanity because it was going to provide a cure for Alzheimer's disease.

- How would you prepare to teach a unit on bioethics (or another complex issue)?
- What issues would you need to consider?
- Under what circumstances would you consider it to be unadvisable to teach a particular complex issue?
- What is your role in relation to teaching about the Catholic position on these issues?
- What does a professional approach to the teaching of religious education require of you?

Religious education teachers need to approach complex issues with caution. They can get into some difficulty by launching into areas which require, at the very least, careful preparation and background reading. Teaching bioethical issues well, for example, is very dependent on having a clear understanding of terminology and argumentation. This frequently means relying on more than newspaper accounts and other secondary sources. In areas such as these, it is not enough to ask students to research matters and come up with their own conclusions. If the religious education teacher wants to move into complex areas, and there is nothing to say they should not do this, they must be prepared to help guide students through some of the difficult concepts involved. This is especially true when teachers take upon themselves the responsibility of speaking about what the Church believes and teaches. This is a very necessary role for the religious education teacher. For example, when a teacher says *the Catholic Church teaches…* he or she is making an objective statement. These are to be encouraged because they give students a firm position on which their own understanding can grow. Nonetheless, it is the responsibility of the religious education teacher to be accurate when he or she makes these objective statements. Statements about what the Church believes and teaches need to be checked for accuracy perhaps with the Religious Education Co-ordinator or other suitable qualified people. Religious education teachers must do their homework thoroughly.

A third principle is that **the teacher is the one who makes responsible decisions about what will be discussed in the religious education lesson.** What should the religious education teacher do in response to issues that arise, usually unexpectedly, some of which can have a significant impact on the Church's mission? These often come up in the electronic media and hence have a very wide circulation. One example of such material is the welter of comment about sexual abuse by priests and religious. Bearing in mind the comments in previous sections of this chapter about the incarnational nature of the Church, how should a religious education teacher deal with this? If such issues arise in the course of a lesson, some further comment is appropriate. Certainly an expression of sorrow and an acknowledgment of the deep hurt that has been caused can be made. Depending on the age of the students, some deeper analysis may also be given. There is, however, no easy answer to many current and topical issues. It is unlikely that discussing them at great length will assist in resolution or significant progress. There is also the danger that the purposeful teaching of the religious education curriculum will be disrupted if too much attention is given to issues as they arise. The religious education teacher should be responsive to student enquiry about issues of the day, however, this should not become the main focus of the classroom. It is not advisable to allow the classroom to become dominated by discussion of issues that have arisen in the most recent blockbuster movie or segment on current affairs shows. Ideally many of these topics could be discussed within the existing curriculum where they can be placed in an appropriate educational context.

A fourth principle is to acknowledge when there is disagreement.

"My parents think that the Church is wrong and should change its position on...My uncle who works for the Church says the same thing. When is the Church going to move forward?"

- Fill in the dots in the statement above. What issues could be referred to in this context?

In many ways, the most difficult thematic issues that can arise in religious education are matters on which there is some disagreement amongst Catholics. These are often issues that give rise to passionate argument and can be very divisive. Within the Catholic tradition topics such as contraception, the ordination of woman, teaching on homosexuality and issues of ecclesial governance are examples where many Catholics favour a change in Church teaching. How should a religious education teacher in a Catholic secondary school handle topics such as these which are likely to arise in a number of places in the curriculum? This difficulty is particularly acute when it confronts a teacher who may also disagree with the Church teaching but wants to be supportive of the school ethos.

If the religious education teacher ventures into these areas then professionally, he or she must faithfully and attractively present the teaching of the Church. This assumes, of course, that the teacher understands the Church teachings and can articulate this understanding well. It is also appropriate to acknowledge difference of opinion on these matters amongst Catholics. If the religious education teacher does not do this, then it is almost assured that his or her students will point out these disagreements. It is important, when students raise questions in these areas, not to *squash* the questioner. Students need to feel that their comments will be dealt with respectfully and in an atmosphere that values the search for truth. The religious education teacher should, however, be mindful of the context of the question and the need, on occasion, to defer dealing with a specific issue until it can be dealt with as part of the school's religious education curriculum. None of this prevents the teacher from having his or her opinion about the issue, but normally this should not be shared with students in class.

When discussing contentious issues, it is worth bearing in mind that the secondary school is not a proper theological forum where *cutting edge* discussion can take place. This is simply an acknowledgment of the age of the students. Religious education teachers can assume a level of maturity and interest that does not reflect the attitudes of students in front of them. For example, lessons on the latest theory in scripture scholarship, the content of which would challenge most undergraduates, should not be directed at unsuspecting adolescents. There is a vast range of topics that can be taught in religious education that are both interesting and stimulating, and that fall within a general theological consensus. Similarly, it is not the role of the secondary religious education class to forge new directions in Catholic moral theology. An intelligent grasp of key Catholic moral principles and the ability to apply them in a variety of situations is an extremely worthwhile achievement for secondary students.

Controversial issues: A final word

It is important that good and able teachers not be discouraged from teaching religious education because they are anxious about what have been called in this chapter, *controversial issues*. Many teachers, especially inexperienced ones, often have an exaggerated fear about the frequency with which these issues arise. In a school with a well thought out and implemented religious education curriculum, the focus of classroom tends to be on meeting educational goals. With this focus, controversial themes, when they arise, can be dealt with in a proper context. Nonetheless, by understanding some of the issues that may arise and being able to respond well, the religious education teacher can work with confidence in these areas. By way of summary when dealing with controversial issues RE teachers should:

- Be prepared to discuss issues when they arise with the relevant people in the school, such as the REC or members of the school's leadership team.
- Be familiar with and prepared to support the ethos of the school.
- Understand the professional responsibilities of religious education teachers.

- Not let students overstep boundaries by asking about personal matters.
- Recognise the complexity of some issues and the need to research these thoroughly.
- Be conversant with Church teaching and be prepared to ask for help when this is needed.
- Understand the specific instances when their personal opinion is and is not an appropriate response.

References and Further Reading

Engebretson, K (2005). Editor. *Catholic Ethical Thinking for Senior Secondary Students*. Melbourne: James Goold Publication.

Ford, N. (1986) Professional responsibility and the private lives of teachers in Catholic schools. Homebush: St Paul's Publications.

Rymarz, R (1999). Knowledge and the RE teacher: *Journal of Religious Education*. 47 (4) 48-54.

CHAPTER 15

What Catholics Believe

Kath Engebretson

Introduction

To say that one believes something, means that one gives assent to a proposition that cannot be empirically or scientifically proved. To teach religious education in a Catholic school, it is essential to have at least a basic knowledge of what Catholics believe. This chapter gives a limited introduction to Catholic beliefs on which teachers can build. Throughout the chapter the term "Catholic" is used, but it is important to remember that many of the beliefs discussed here are held by all Christians.

What do you already know about what Catholics believe? Remember that beliefs are cognitive propositions, not rituals, moral stances or values.

Revelation

The first and most basic belief that Catholics hold is that there is a loving, personal "other" whom they call "God". Moreover, this God seeks to be in communication with people. The self disclosure of God to people is referred to as **Revelation.** Revelation has two dimensions. First, it is God's unwarranted, loving, invitation to people to enter into friendship with God. Second, it is the communication of a body of truths about God and human beings that is referred to as "the deposit of faith". Catholics believe that the self- disclosure or "revelation" of God comes to human beings in the following ways:

The **first way** in which God has communicated with people is through the story of salvation history as recounted in the two testaments of the bible. This story begins with Abraham, the forefather in faith of the Jewish people, then tells of the covenant God made with Israel, and of the ups and down of Israel's history. Finally it tells of the life, death and resurrection of Jesus Christ and the beginning of the Church as it moved beyond Judaism. Catholics read the stories, historical narratives, parables, prayers, prophecies and other forms of literature in the Bible in order to come to know what God communicates through Scripture to the Church as a whole, and to them as individual Catholics.

God's self-disclosure (Revelation) is centred of Jesus Christ. Catholics believe that the story of salvation as told in the Bible culminated in the life, death and resurrection of Jesus Christ and the beginning of his Church. Moreover, they believe that Jesus Christ, whom they believe is the Son of God, is God's ultimate and full revelation, the one who reveals in his own person exactly what God is like. "In the past God spoke to our forefathers through the prophets at many times and in various ways, but in these last days he has spoken to us by his Son, whom he appointed heir of all things, and through whom he made the universe" (Hebrews 1: 1-2). Jesus Christ is therefore the **second** and the ultimate, way in which God's self-communication comes to people.

A **third way** in which God reveals himself to people is through the Tradition of the Church. Over two thousand years, the community of the Catholic Church has reflected on and taught about the events recounted in the two testaments in the Bible, and as a community has come to understand them as having life-giving meaning. The reflection of the Church on Scripture, and its teaching about this reflection over the centuries, is referred to as Tradition. A large body of doctrinal and social teaching belongs to Tradition. The teachings of the Tradition of the Church are found in the writings of the early Church fathers and the saints, and also in the writings and teaching of the Popes and Councils of the Church through the centuries. Catholics study the documents of the Tradition of the Church because they believe that through this tradition God continues to communicate with the world. Therefore, for Catholics, Scripture and Tradition are closely connected. Scripture refers to the whole story of salvation history as told in the books of the Bible and Tradition refers to the Church's reflection on, and teaching about the truths of Scripture over the 2000 years of her history.

While Catholics recognize that in Scripture, Tradition and ultimately the life death and resurrection of Jesus Christ there is the fullness of foundational Revelation, they do not believe that Revelation is just in the past. God continues to speak to people especially through "created realities". (Dei Verbum, #3). This term refers to the universe and its history, its ecology, the rich range of plant and animal species that inhabit it, and to human life in its individual and community aspects. Catholics believe that it is through their lives in the world that God continually communicates with them and calls them to friendship with him. This is the **fourth** avenue of God's self-disclosure or Revelation.

What do you understand by the terms Revelation, the deposit of faith, Tradition of the Church, foundational Revelation, created realities?

Why can it be argued that the belief in a God who communicates with humankind is fundamental to Catholic belief?

Salvation (Redemption)

Belief in Salvation is very closely tied to Revelation. It refers to God's work of reconciling humankind with himself, and restoring to humankind the privileges of complete unity with him, with each other and with the created world that are naturally theirs and which were broken by sin (Gen, Ch 3). This reconciliation and restoration is achieved through God's gift of himself incarnate (made flesh) in Jesus Christ. As a human being, Jesus of Nazareth lived in complete obedience to God's plan as he discerned it, and this faithful self surrender, even to death, was validated in his resurrection. In Jesus Christ and his resurrection, humanity can hope for deliverance **from** the consequence of sin which is eternal death, and deliverance **for** God's salvific gift, which is eternal life. As Christ's Body on earth, the Church continues God's work of salvation, reconciling people with God, with each other and with their world through Jesus Christ.

Catholics believe that the salvation of Christ is offered to all. For a scriptural analysis of the Judeo-Christian belief in salvation read St. Paul's letter to the Romans , 5: 12-21.

Faith

Faith is the graced but free human acceptance of God's communication in Christ as mediated through the Church. (Cook, 1995, p. 510) To say that it is "graced" means that faith itself is a gift from God, and it cannot be earned. While it is a God-given gift, it is also a free acceptance of what God has revealed, and this acceptance is intellectual, emotional and deliberate. It involves saying "yes" in the deepest part of oneself to God's faithful love, and responding to that love with trust and hope. For the Catholic, faith is a response to God's revelation as mediated through the Church. It is not an individualistic "Jesus and me" experience, but one that impels the Catholic into relationships with others, and to share in Jesus' mission to build up the Kingdom of God. The intellectual, emotional and practical response to God's revelation which is faith is lived out in the community of the Church.

What does it mean to say that faith has intellectual, emotional and practical aspects?

The Trinity

The Trinity is a specifically Christian way of understanding God. Catholics believe that God is one in three persons, Father, Son and Holy Spirit. This Trinitarian belief in God is revealed through the New Testament, and was given specific shape by the Councils of the Church up to the fifth century. In the Trinity, Catholics acknowledge God the Father, the first person of the Trinity, creator of the universe, the God who invited Israel into covenant, and whom Jesus of Nazareth worshipped. In the New Testament God is constantly referred as the Father of Jesus Christ. Catholics acknowledge God the Son, the second person of the Trinity, the pre-existent Word of God made flesh in Jesus of Nazareth, who lived and died in surrender to God and was raised by God from the dead. Finally they acknowledge God the Holy Spirit, the third person of the Trinity, the advocate, teacher and counsellor sent by the Father to guide and teach the Christian community. These are not three Gods but one God revealing three different persons. Each person of the Trinity **is** the fullness of God's nature, and the Trinity is one in substance, although diverse in persons. Catholics address God as Trinity in many of their prayers, for example in this traditional prayer: *Glory be to the Father, and to the Son, and to the Holy Spirit. As it was in the beginning , is now, and ever shall be, world without end. Amen.*

Catholics believe in a Trinitarian God, that is God who is in community within God's nature. What implications does this have for the living out of the Catholic life?

The Incarnation

The Incarnation is the belief that while human in every way, Jesus Christ is God in flesh. In his person the human and the divine are fused. One nature does not dominate the other, but the two natures are one in the person of Christ. It follows from this that in the mystery of the Incarnation, all that is human is permeated by the divine, and the divine becomes human. The words that the Catholic Church has used to define the Incarnation since the Council of Chalcedon in 451, are that Jesus Christ is "true God and true man". In the very earliest years of the Church St. Paul expressed the Christian belief in the Incarnation in the poetic words of this ancient Christian hymn.

Let the same mind be in you that was in Christ Jesus,
Who though he was in the form of God,
Did not regard equality with God
As something to be exploited,
But emptied himself,
Taking the form of a slave,
Being born in human likeness.
And being found in human form,
he humbled himself
and became obedient to the point of death
—even death on a Cross.

Therefore God also highly exalted him
And gave him the name that is above every name,
So that at the name of Jesus
Every knee should bend,
In heaven and on earth and under the earth,
And every tongue should confess
That Jesus Christ is Lord,
To the glory of God the Father. (Phil 2: 5-11)

The mystery of the Incarnation has implications for the way in which Catholics view their humanity and their lives in the world. Can you spell out some of these implications?

Mary

In believing that Jesus Christ is true God and true man, Catholics believe that Mary his mother is the *Theotokos,* that is God-bearer or Mother of God. The title affirms that Mary did not just give birth to Jesus' humanity, but that in giving birth to the child Jesus she gave birth to the Son of God, and is therefore the Mother of God. This fundamental Catholic belief about Mary was declared at the Council of Ephesus in 431. Other Catholic beliefs about Mary are the virgin birth which asserts that Mary was a virgin before, during and after the birth of Christ, the Immaculate Conception which declares that Mary was conceived and born free from of the "original" sin that is the heritage of all humankind, and the Assumption, which asserts that Mary was taken to heaven in body and soul after her death.

While Catholics hold Mary in great esteem and love, they do not worship her as a goddess. Rather she is seen to have an intercessory role, and many Catholics ask her to intercede for them or to bring their prayers before God. What traditional prayers or devotions do you know through which Catholics honour Mary?

One baptism

"There is one body and one Spirit, just as you were called to the one hope of your calling, one Lord, one faith, one baptism, one God and Father of all who is above all, and through all and in all" (Ephesians, 4: 4-6). Baptism is the sacrament through which one becomes a member of the Christian community. There is one Christian baptism, and a person who has been baptized in any Christian Church, does not repeat the sacrament if he or she wishes to join the Catholic Church. Christian baptism is in the name of the Trinity.

From the earliest centuries, baptism was only for adults, but later infant baptism became much more common, with the first recorded mention of this being around 200 AD. The Second Vatican Council (1962-1965) encouraged the restoration of adult baptism (the catechumenate) in the Rite of Christian Initiation for Adults (RCIA).

The high point of the baptismal ritual is the symbolic washing of the candidate in baptismal water, in the name of the Trinity, and the sealing of the baptism with the oil of thanksgiving. The act is believed to both cleanse the person from sin, and bring the person to life in Christ and to union with Christ's resurrection. In adult baptism the newly baptized join the community to take part fully in the Eucharist for the first time. In infant baptism this "sealing" of the baptism takes place later, in the sacrament of Confirmation.

The ritual enacts and expresses the meaning of the sacrament. Baptism is identification with Christ in his death in order to experience his resurrection. The baptized person "puts on" Christ, and this involves the acceptance of his suffering as well as of his resurrection, with all of the consequences that come with this acceptance, in the midst of and in identification with the Christian community.

> What advantages or difficulties do you see with infant baptism and why do you think it began in the Church?

The Kingdom of God

In the *Our Father*, perhaps the best known of all Christian prayers, Christians pray that the Kingdom of God will come. The Kingdom of God was central to the teaching of Jesus, and is central to Christian belief today. The term (also referred to as the Reign of God) expresses metaphorically the conviction God is the ruler of the universe and human history, in its past, present and future. This rule is generous, loving, creative, redemptive and eternal. The Kingdom of God is beyond time, unable to be measured in history as political kingdoms can be, and it is eternal. In early Christian times, the writer of the letter to the Hebrews stated this belief: "While all other kingdoms will someday be destroyed, God's kingdom cannot be shaken, and will never be destroyed (Heb 12;29).

The people of Israel saw the reign of God in their history. God gave people the universe in all its beauty, and offered them the promise of redemption when they sinned. God called Abraham to be the father of Israel and of the nations, and journeyed with Moses and the people from Egypt back to the promised land. God remained with his people through the many disasters of their history, and comforted them in their sufferings. The early Christians saw the reign of God in the life, teaching, death and resurrection of Jesus. A powerful image of Jesus' Kingship is found in the gospel of John, where his courage and dignity during his trial and persecution mark him as more kingly than those whose power had been conferred on them by state and religion (Jn 18). His kingdom, not one of power and politics, is a kingdom that is "not of this world" (Jn 18:36), present now but realized fully in the world to come.

The New Testament shows how John the Baptist prepared for the Kingdom with the words "Repent, for the Kingdom of God is near" (Mt 3:2).At his baptism by John, Jesus appears to have had a profound experience of his relationship with God as a son with his father, a relationship that was the basis of his mission. This is represented in the gospels metaphorically in the opening of the heavens, the appearance of the Holy Spirit and the proclamation from heaven that Jesus is God's beloved son. (Mt 3: 13-17). From the time of his baptism which was the initiation of his public ministry, the focus of Jesus' teaching was the Kingdom of God, which he saw as both present in time and yet still to come. Metaphors that he used to show this present but "still to come" Kingdom were the tiny mustard seed that grew ultimately into a huge tree (Mt 13:31); the handful of yeast that leavens the whole loaf (Mt 13:33); a treasure hidden in field which brings joy to the one who finds it (Mt 13:44) and the pearl of great value for which someone sells all that he owns (Mt 13: 45).

The kingdom belonged, Jesus taught, to those who were not wedded to their possessions, (Mt 5:3), those who were small in the eyes of the world (Mt 5:10) and those who were humble like children (Mt 18: 1). People of the Kingdom did not expect or assume God's gifts, they trusted in God (Mt 6:32) and strove first for the kingdom of God and for holiness in its service (Mt 6:33). They were not motivated by desire for power (Mt 18:4). Jesus taught that the Kingdom of God was for all, not just for the Jews, and that those considered to be outsiders would also take their place at the table of the Kingdom of God (Matt 8: 5-13, Mt 22:1-14). Entry to the Kingdom of God was not determined by birth and status, but by a life of loving service to others (Mt 25: 31-46). He taught his twelve close disciples to work as he did, healing the sick and proclaiming that the Kingdom of God had come (Mt 10:7).

The task of the Christian and of the Church is to advance the Kingdom of God, just as Jesus and his disciples did.

> The Kingdom of God is one of justice, love and peace. What are the implications of this belief for the work of Christians in the world?

Resurrection of the body

Belief in the resurrection of the body is grounded in the resurrection of Christ, in which Christians believe all will be made alive. As St. Paul has put it: "Christ has been raised from the dead, the first fruits of those who have died. For since death came through a human being, the resurrection of the dead has also come through a human being. For as all die in Adam so all will be made alive in Christ." (1 Cor: 15:20-23). Christians believe in and hope for a future after death when they, like Christ, will live for eternity in union with God.

Read and discuss all of 1 Cor; Ch 15, which contains St. Paul's theology of the resurrection of the body.

The Church: one, holy, Catholic and apostolic

Catholic faith is not individualistic, but is lived out constantly in the in the community of the Church. This community includes all those in the local and Australian Church as well as those who belong to the universal Church. It includes all who have gone before in previous generations, the saints and martyrs, and those who have died in the Catholic community. It has past, present and future dimensions.

Almost all Christians profess their faith in "one, holy, catholic and apostolic Church", the words of the Nicene Creed that were ratified in the Council of Constantinople in 381. "One, holy, catholic and apostolic" are said to be the "marks" or "notes" of the Church. The Church is **one** because of her source, the unity within the Trinity, because the reconciling salvation offered by Christ is offered to all, and because the Holy Spirit is received in baptism by all Christians. However the Church is one in diversity. Within the unity of the Church a multiplicity of people and cultures belong. There are different gifts and ministries, and particular churches that retain their own traditions. The Church is also one in division, with many Christian Churches having separated from the Roman Catholic Church throughout history.

The dogmatic Constitution on the Church, *Lumen Gentium*, teaches that there is only one Church of Christ, united in faith, in worship and in apostolic succession, and that this Church of Christ is not co-extensive with, but **subsists** in, the Catholic Church. In other words, the Church of Christ, the historical Church of the New Testament, which Christ entrusted to Peter and the apostles, continues to exist and is still to be found in the Catholic Church, but a real though imperfect communion binds together *all* the Christian Churches and ecclesial communities, which in various ways participate in the reality of the one Church of Christ (UR#3, LG#15). The Church of Jesus Christ, though divided, is one, all Christians are urged to work together to overcome the misunderstandings that divide Christian communities. This work of ecumenism is unfolding today, along with a growing desire of Christians to understand their fellow human beings who belong to religions other than Christianity.

The Church is **holy**, because it was founded by Jesus Christ, the incarnate Son of God, and is sanctified and guided by the Holy Spirit. However, the Church is also a human institution. Individuals within it, even people in whom trust and authority is vested, often cause hurt and scandal by their actions. Nevertheless, the fact that individual Catholics are sinners does not diminish the holiness of Christ's Church as a human institution which is a sign in the world of God incarnate. This fact however does challenge individual Christians and all Christian communities to struggle daily to be overcome sin and evil in their daily lives, and as it is found in the world.

The Church is **catholic.** This term essentially refers to the mandate given at the end of the gospel of Matthew, (Matt 28: 16-20) that the followers of Christ were to take the gospel to the ends of the earth, baptizing in the name of the Trinity and working for the coming of the Kingdom of God. This missionary outreach continues today, with the Catholic Church being involved extensively in development work around the world.

The Church is **apostolic**. The Catholic Church began with Jesus and with his earliest disciples. The impulsive and faith-filled (Matt 16:16) Peter was commissioned by Jesus to be the shepherd and leader of the group of disciples. The "keys of the kingdom of heaven" (Matt 16:19) symbolized the responsibility and authority which Jesus conferred on Peter. He was the "rock" on which the Church was to be built (Matt 14:30, Matt 16:18, Matt 16: 22, Matt 17:4; Matt 19: 27; Matt 26: 29, Matt 26:33). Today Catholics claim that under the Pope, the bishop of Rome, who is the direct successor of Peter, they can trace an unbroken line of authority back to Peter and thus back to Christ. This apostolic succession, the Church claims, is unique to the Catholic Church . However the apostolic succession challenges the Church to continually return to its roots, to the faith and simplicity of the first Christian communities.

> What key issues do you think the Catholic Church must face in the twenty-first century?

Conclusion

The Nicene Creed is the statement of faith which all baptized Catholics recite at the Sunday Eucharist.

We believe in one God, the Father, the Almighty, maker of heaven and earth, of all that is seen and unseen.

We believe in one Lord, Jesus Christ, the only Son of God, eternally begotten of the Father, God from God, Light from Light, true God from true God, begotten, not made, one in being with the Father. Through Him all things were made.

For us and our salvation He came down from heaven: by the power of the Holy Spirit, He was born of the Virgin Mary , and became man. For our sake He was crucified under Pontius Pilate; He suffered, died, and was buried. On the third day He rose again in fulfilment of the scriptures: He ascended into heaven and is seated at the right hand of the Father. He will come again in glory to judge the living and the dead, and his kingdom will have no end.

We believe in the Holy Spirit, the Lord, the giver of life, who proceeds from the Father and the Son. With the Father and the Son, He is worshiped and glorified. He has spoken through the Prophets.

We believe in one, holy, catholic, and apostolic Church. We acknowledge one baptism for the forgiveness of sins. We look for the resurrection of the dead, and the life of the world to come. Amen.

References and Further Reading

Catholic Church Documents

Gaudium et Spes. (1965). The Pastoral Constitution on the Church in the Modern World. Second Vatican Council.

Lumen Gentium. (1965) The Dogmatic Constitution on the Church. Second Vatican Council.

Pope John Paul II. (1992). *Catechism of the Catholic Church.*

Other references

Cook, M. (1995). Faith. In Richard P. McBrien (gen ed). *The Harper Collins Encyclopedia of Catholicism.* San Francisco: Harper Collins.

Sullivan, F.(1988). *The Church We Believe In. One, Holy, Catholic and Apostolic.* NY: Paulist Press.

CHAPTER 16

The First Eleven Centuries of Christianity

Kath Engebretson

The first Christian community in Jerusalem

By the time of the birth of Jesus of Nazareth in about 4BC, the Jewish people had been ruled by many different powers. During Jesus' lifetime they were ruled by the government of Rome, at a time when the Roman Empire was at its height. It was under the Roman government, around 33AD, that Jesus of Nazareth was executed by crucifixion, for the crime of sedition. Very soon after his death, his disciples, both men and women, came to a profound belief that he had been raised from the dead by God. This belief appears to have been based on certain experiences of Jesus as risen, that occurred for the disciples both individually and as a group, and that are told in the gospels. The belief to which these experiences gave rise, that Jesus had indeed conquered death, was the defining belief of the tiny community that ultimately became the religion we know today as Christianity.

Read at least one story of the resurrection appearances: Luke 24: 13-35; Luke 24: 36-49; John 20:11-18; John 20: 19-23; John 20: 24-29; John 21:1-14.

What are the common ideas or themes in the stories?

The first followers of Jesus, who congregated in Jerusalem after his death and resurrection, would not have thought of themselves as "Christians". Like Jesus, they were observant Jews, who would have seen their discipleship of Jesus as compatible with their Jewish identity. The story of Pentecost (Acts 2: 1-13) which is often referred to as "the birthday of the Church", significantly took place on an important Jewish feast day. Jesus had been crucified just outside Jerusalem at Passover time. Normally, the pilgrims who had come to Jerusalem for the Passover would stay there for the feast of Shavu'ot, also known as Pentecost, which was celebrated on the fiftieth day after Passover, and which gave thanks for the harvest, and the gift of the Torah by God on Mount Sinai (Ex 19:16). According to the Gospel writers, Jesus had promised to send the Holy Spirit to his disciples, so that they would come to understand all that he had taught. On the day of Shavuot the disciples were gathered in Jerusalem with Mary the mother of Jesus. The powerful symbols of fire, thunder and lightening had accompanied the giving of the Torah to the assembled Israelites at Mount Sinai (Ex 19:16). Luke, the evangelist credited with the writing of the Acts of the Apostles, employed the same symbols of wind and fire to illustrate the power and presence of the Holy Spirit coming to the infant Church and its members. In his use of these symbols, the evangelist linked the coming of the Holy Spirit with the most momentous event of Israel's religious history, and presented the gift of the Holy Spirit as a new "law" which would guide the infant Christian community.

Read Acts 2:1-4.

Why is this story told and re-told so often in the Church today?

The mission to the Gentiles

As noted above, at first, Christianity was a movement within Judaism, and the disciples would certainly have seen themselves as good Jews, going to the Temple and to the synagogue, keeping the food and other laws outlined in the Torah, and continuing to pray as Jews. The spread of the movement which was to become Christianity, occurred gradually, as the disciples carried the teachings of Jesus to the many Jewish communities along the Mediterranean coast. At first they taught only fellow Jews, until a particular group of disciples led by a deacon, Stephen, broke with this practice and began to preach to the Gentiles. Stephen's criticism of the Jewish leaders led to his death by stoning, and he was the first of many Christian disciples to die as a martyr (Acts Chs 6 & 7). Stephen's followers began to preach the gospel wherever they travelled, no longer seeing the message of Jesus as belonging only to the Jews.

After the destruction of the Temple in Jerusalem in 70AD, a new centre of Judaism was established in Jamnia. Jewish leaders began to be stricter about the differences in thought and practice that had been a part of Judaism before the destruction of the Temple. Now there was officially only one Judaism, and soon the early Christians found that they presented a problem to their fellow Jews. In 49 AD the decision of the Council of Jerusalem, led by the Apostles Peter and Paul, allowed gentiles to join the Christian community without needing to observe all of the rituals and laws of Judaism (Acts 15:7-11). Through these and a series of other events, the Church gradually moved away from its Jewish origins. When the Temple in Jerusalem was destroyed in the Jewish Roman war of 70 AD, the Christian community in Jerusalem scattered, and Jewish Christians fled throughout the Empire. As a result of the missionary activity of the Apostle Paul, whose journeys and teaching around the Empire had led to the establishment of many infant Christian communities, Christianity now spread quickly beyond Jerusalem. By the end of the first century there were many Christian communities all around the coastline of the Mediterranean sea. In each place the Christian community adapted itself to Greco-Roman customs and culture. It adopted the organisational patterns of the Roman Empire, and, like the empire, had its own centre at Rome, the place where it was believed Peter (Christ's closest disciples and the first bishop of Rome) and Paul had been executed and buried.

What may have been the future of Christianity if the decision to allow gentiles to become Christian had not been made?

Some practices of Christianity in the first three centuries

The Apostles (the original twelve disciples of Jesus) appointed leaders in each community, these being the president or bishop and the elders or presbyters, later known as priests. They taught, led prayer and worship and saw to the day to day management of the communities. Within each community the presbyters formed a council around the bishop, who was regarded as the successor of the Apostles. By the end of the first century, a single bishop had replaced this council in each Church community. Thus began the role of bishop as we know it in the Church. The role of deacons was to look after the daily administration of the community, so that the Apostles would be free for teaching. Deacons had the task of assisting at the "breaking of the bread", and distributing the Body and Blood of Christ to the assembled Christians. They assisted at baptisms, took care of the sick and managed the community funds. Women often took leading roles in the management of particular communities, and it also appears that there were men and women who were prophets and teachers. Believing themselves to be called by the Holy Spirit, these men and women moved freely from community to community, teaching and preaching, while the bishops, presbyters and deacons lived in their own communities.

Early forms of the sacraments existed in these first Christian communities. From this very earliest time Christians would confess their sins before taking part in worship. "The breaking of the bread", based on the actions of Jesus at his last supper, was the most important sacrament and it was only for those who had been baptised. Baptisms were celebrated after a long period of instruction, study, reflection and prayer, and were usually by full immersion in a pool of water. Indeed, the roots of the seven sacraments of the Church can be found in the history of these early Christian communities.

What similarities or differences do you see between these early leadership roles and those in the Church today?

Persecutions of Christians in the first three centuries

During the first century, Christians began to attract the disapproval of the Jewish leaders and also of the Roman rulers. This seems to have been arisen from the tendency of Christians to keep themselves apart from many public activities because of their beliefs. For example they would have nothing to do with occupations that put them into contact with Roman gods; they would not visit hospitals where there were prayers offered to Roman gods; because of their pacifist beliefs, they would not attend gladiatorial contests or serve in the army; their practice of "eating" the body of Christ and "drinking" his blood led some to refer to them as "cannibals". In addition, the first generation of Christians believed that Christ would come again in their lifetimes, and some, waiting for this second coming, did not work. Even Paul corrected such Christians with the advice: *Do not let anyone have any food if he refused to do any work.* (2 Thessalonians 3:10) Finally it was almost impossible for the polytheistic Romans to understand a strictly monotheistic religion, and to accept the apparent secrecy of the rituals of the Christians.

In 64AD, the Roman Emperor Nero used this climate of dislike to begin persecuting Christians. A great fire had broken out in Rome, and many Romans suspected Nero himself of causing it. To deflect blame from himself, Nero accused the Christians of arson. From that time Christianity was regarded as an illegal religion, and numerous Christians suffered for their belief in Christ. Although the religion was never officially outlawed, Christians were under suspicion, and could be raided by the Roman police at any time, or convicted for refusing to worship a statue of the Roman emperor. Gradually, the worst of the persecutions died down, but they continued sporadically for the first three centuries.

What does this have in common with other religious persecutions about which you may know?

East and West

Finally, under the Emperor Constantine, Christianity became a legal religion (313AD), and Christians were able to worship publicly. When he became Emperor, Constantine moved the capital of the Empire from Rome to Constantinople, (now Istanbul), and so from this time there were two centres of Christianity, the west with its centre in Rome and the east with its centre in Constantinople. By the time the western Roman empire fell in 476 AD, the centre of the Empire had transferred to the east, often called the "Byzantine" Empire, which retained its independence until 1453 AD. In 324 Constantine became sole Emperor of the Roman Empire, ruling both east and west. In the following year, he called a Council of the Church at Nicea, now the city of Iznik in modern Turkey. This Council clarified the doctrine of the Trinity, settled ongoing questions about the person of Jesus Christ and his divine and human natures, and drew up the Nicene Creed which is still today recited by Christians every Sunday. These doctrines were further ratified in the Council of Constantinople held in 381 AD. At the time of Constantine's death, Rome and Constantinople were the major centres of Christianity, and the other key centres were Antioch, Jerusalem and Alexandria.

Gradually Christians took over some the old pagan temples and public buildings and built beautiful ornate Churches, such as the Basilica of St Peter in Rome and Sancta Sophia in Constantinople. As representatives of both God and the Emperor, bishops were powerful and privileged. The Church received bequests from wealthy families and landowners, and itself became a wealthy landowner. Christianity was stronger in the east, with the Patriarchs of the great eastern cities enjoying power and prestige, but the bishop of Rome was recognised as the successor of St. Peter. Disagreements over power and authority, as well as over some aspects of doctrine, were at the basis of the divisions that ultimately led to the great schism between the eastern and western Churches.

What issues may there have been between east and west that had the potential to lead to division?

Divisions within Christianity

There was jealousy between the east with its capital in Constantinople, and the west with its capital in Rome. In addition, the Councils of Ephesus (449AD) and Chalcedon, (451AD) had emphasised that Jesus was both fully human and fully divine, but this "orthodox" doctrine was unacceptable to certain Christian groups in Syria and Egypt. Unable to accept the full humanity of Christ, they became separated from the rest of the Church. Today these are the Syrian and Coptic Orthodox Churches. The breakaway of these groups was only one sign of the increasing differences between the eastern and western Churches. These differences were exacerbated by language, (Latin in the west and Greek in the east) and by variations in styles of worship. In the west, the celebration of the Eucharist and sacraments was more simple than in the east. Eastern Christians emphasised the mystery of the Eucharist, concealing the altar behind curtains, and later behind a fixed screen, the *iconostasis*. In the west the congregation was able to see what was happening at the altar. There were also differences in the use of sacramentals, (objects such as vessels, vestments, kinds of bread and music that were used in the liturgy) and about whether it was right to use images of Jesus, Mary and the saints. Many beautiful images were destroyed by over-zealous Christians (iconoclasts) who believed that the use of icons constituted the worship of false gods. Later the use of icons was restored in the east, but the scars remained. Furthermore, the eastern Churches continued to ordain some married deacons to the priesthood, but the western Church increasingly insisted on the celibacy of all the clergy.

Perhaps the greatest disagreement was over the authority of the Pope (bishop of Rome) to speak and make decisions on behalf of the whole Church, east and west. The Roman Church expected that it would have this authority because Jesus had appointed Peter as head of the Church, and Peter had made Rome the Centre of Christianity. In Constantinople it was argued that since that city was the capital of the empire, the authority of the Church should reside there. This disagreement had come to the fore in the controversy over the wording of the Nicene Creed. The original Nicene Creed (composed at the Council of Nicea in 325) stated that the Holy Spirit "proceeded from" the Father. During the seventh century, a group in Spain unofficially added the phrase "and the Son", to this. As a result the Nicene Creed now said that the Holy Spirit "proceeded from the Father and the Son." The Emperor Charlemagne who identified with the western Church, insisted that this should now be the wording of the Creed, and by the eleventh century this was the wording used throughout the western Church, with the approval of the Pope. The Church in the east objected strongly that there should be no change to the wording, and that any alteration to the Creed was forbidden. The eastern Churches did not believe that the Pope had the right to make such important decisions on behalf of the east.

As a result of the many differences between the eastern and western Churches particularly over this issue of papal authority, there was a parting or schism in 1054 AD, with both condemning each other through a mutual excommunication. The eastern form of Christianity, generally known as the Orthodox east, became progressively separated from the western form of Christianity, led by the Pope. However, some eastern Churches never lost unity with Rome, and later other separated communities re-established unity with the Pope. Today the eastern Churches that are in full communion with Roman Catholic Church are: the Armenian Catholic Church, the Chaldean and Assyrian Catholic Churches, the Coptic Catholic Church, the Melkite Greek Catholic Church, the Ukrainian Greek Catholic Church, the Russian Catholic Church, the Maronite Catholic Church and the Syrian Catholic Church. Other eastern Christian Churches that remain separate from Roman Catholicism are the Greek Orthodox Church, the Russian Orthodox Church, the Ukrainian Orthodox Church, the Holy Apostolic Catholic Assyrian Church of the East, the Coptic Orthodox Church, the Armenian Apostolic Church, the Antiochian Orthodox Church, and the Syrian Orthodox Church.

Working for reconciliation

The Second Vatican Council (1962-1965) called all Christians to work for the unity of the Church. In 1965 Pope Paul VI met with the Eastern Patriarch Athenagoras, and together they issued a statement of regret for the misunderstandings of the past, and revoked the sentences of excommunication they had issued against each other. In 1995, Patriarch, Bartholomew I, Archbishop of Constantinople and the Ecumenical Patriarch, paid an historic, friendly and respectful visit to Pope John Paul II in Rome. In 1996 the Patriarch paid his first visit to Australia where he was warmly welcomed by members of his own

Churches, as well as by the leaders of other Churches and the Australian government. In 1995, Pope John Paul II wrote an important encyclical devoted to Christian Unity (*Ut Unum Sint*). He declared: "The Church must breathe with her two lungs!... The vision of the full communion to be sought is that of unity in legitimate diversity." (Ut Unum Sint, 54)

During his visit to Turkey in 2006, Pope Benedict XVI and Patriarch Bartholomew I signed an historic common declaration which contained the following words:

> We give thanks to the Author of all that is good, who allows us once again, in prayer and in dialogue, to express the joy we feel as brothers and to renew our commitment to move towards full communion...The Holy Spirit will help us to prepare the great day of the re-establishment of full unity, whenever and however God wills it...As far as relations between the Church of Rome and the Church of Constantinople are concerned, we cannot fail to recall the solemn ecclesial act effacing the memory of the ancient anathemas which for centuries have had a negative effect on relations between our Churches. We have not yet drawn from this act all the positive consequences which can flow from it in our progress towards full unity...We exhort our faithful to take an active part in this process, through prayer and through significant gestures.

What implications does the historical material in this chapter have for your work as a religious educator?

References and Further Reading

Alfen, P. (1991).The *St. Peter Tradition in the First Three Centuries of Christianity* Dept. of Classics, University of Utah.

Garner, G. (2003). *The Expansion of Christianity in the Roman World of the First Three Centuries.* Bible College of Queensland.

Harnack, A. (1972) .*The Expansion of Christianity in the First Three Centuries, Vol. 1* Edited and Translated by James Moffatt. New York.

McBride, R. (1980). *Catholicism.* Minneapolis: Dove Communications.

Mullen, R. (2007). The Expansion of Christianity: A Gazetteer of Its First Three Centuries. *Bulletin for Biblical Research.* The institute of Biblical Research.

Cornerstones of Catholic Secondary Religious Education

CHAPTER 17

Reformation and Catholic reform: the Middle Ages to the Twenty-first Century

Kath Engebretson

Introduction

The later Middle Ages was a time of crisis in the world and for the Catholic Church. The bubonic plague which had emerged in the Gobi Desert in the 1320s, spread across Europe and Asia, killing millions of people, and sometimes exterminating whole populations. Through the 1340s the plague spread towards the west, reaching Constantinople in 1347, then Egypt where daily deaths were in the thousands. By the end of 1347 it had made inroads into Cyprus, Sicily and Italy. In the following year it reached Paris, England and Germany, with 1348 being the worst year of the plague.

Among Christians, at that time usually illiterate and often superstitious, it was easy to see the plague as the result of God's anger, and people began to seek ways in which this perceived anger of God may be appeased. Fearful of death, and at the mercy of an better educated, often wealthy and sometimes unscrupulous clergy, the people were vulnerable to exploitation With death a daily reality, many Christians were eager to make sure that they would have a place in heaven, and this was one of the factors that led to the abuse of indulgences in the Church. This abuse in turn was one of the factors that led to Martin Luther's protest and the Reformation which followed.

> Remember that in the west, Catholicism was more or less synonymous with religion, and priests and bishops now had great power. What contradictions were there between this situation and that of the early centuries of the Church?

Purgatory and Indulgences

In Catholic understanding, an indulgence is an action or prayer that can take away all or part of Purgatory for oneself or for another. Although indulgences are still part of the life of the Church, they are sought and given much less frequently now, but in the Middle Ages they were often used to exploit the fears of vulnerable, unworldly Christians.

A correct understanding of indulgences rests on the Church's teaching about Purgatory. The *Catechism of the Catholic Church* defines Purgatory in their way:

> All who die in God's grace and friendship, but still imperfectly purified, are indeed assured of their eternal salvation; but after death they undergo purification, so as to achieve the holiness necessary to enter the joy of heaven… The Church gives the name Purgatory to this final purification of the elect, which is entirely different from the punishment of the dammed (#1030-1031)

In Church teaching, Purgatory is the way in which God helps people to atone for sin which has already been forgiven. It is the state in which those who have still to atone for sin remain for time after death, before entering heaven. The prayers and good works of Christians on earth can help to reduce Purgatory for others. Therefore there is a long tradition in the Church of praying for the dead.

It is easy to see that in certain circumstances indulgences may be open to abuse, and in the history of the Church there have been many instance of this. For example, at the height of the Church's issuing of indulgences in the middle ages, some people believed that they could atone for their sins by paying someone else to do the penance for them. Some priests and bishops gave excessive indulgences to their family and friends, and some religious brothers and sisters falsely claimed that they were authorized by the Pope to forgive sins. They took money from the poor, promising than this would guarantee them a place in heaven, and release from Purgatory. In addition indulgences were sometimes "sold", so that if a person gave money to a particular cause they would be granted partial or full release from Purgatory. Indulgences did become a source of evil and corruption, sometimes with payment being regarded as the price of salvation. In the years leading up to the Reformation abuses of indulgences were rife.

In what circumstances do you think superstitious ideas and practices are apt to creep into a religion? Of what other instances in the history of Catholicism are you aware?

Martin Luther and the Reformation

Martin Luther was an Augustinian priest, who lectured on Scripture at the University of Wittenberg. When Pope Leo X and the Archbishop of Mainz promoted the sale of indulgences to pay for the construction of St Peter's basilica in Rome, through the preaching of a Dominican monk, John Tetzel, Luther took the step he had been considering for some time. On 31 October 1517, he circulated **Ninety-five Theses**, which consisted of 95 statements about aspects of Church life and teaching, and particularly about indulgences. They were discussion points, probably intended for his students. However, it appears that his students nailed them to the Castle Church door for all passers-by to see and this action prompted reactions that could never have been anticipated. Here is a summary of events as they developed.

1517

Luther circulated his 95 Theses, which were posted on the door of the Wittenberg Castle Church. The document contained an attack on papal abuses and the sale of indulgences by church officials.

1518

When Luther refused to take back his attack, Pope Leo X issued a statement outlining the Church's doctrine on indulgences, and condemning Luther's ideas.

1519

Luther wrote to Pope Leo X, stating that it was not his intention to question the authority of the Pope or the Church. The impact of the Luther-Rome dispute began to grow.

1520

By this time Luther had the support of many of the German nobility. Pope Leo X gave him 60 days to recant or face excommunication. As his books were being burned in cities throughout Germany, Luther published an open letter to Pope Leo X, apologizing to the Pope personally, but continuing to denounce what he saw as false doctrine and corruption in the Church.

1521

Luther was excommunicated, and summoned to the city of Worms to appear before a hearing at which he still refused to take back his attack on the Church. On his way back to Wittenberg, he was captured by supporters disguised as bandits and taken to safety in Wartburg.

1522

The next two years saw Luther preaching throughout central Germany.

1524

Luther was banished by the Church and the Emperor, but by this time he had great popular support. By now, certain groups without Luther's agreement were using his ideas as a reason for revolution. Luther left his religious order and married, continuing his writing and denouncing the groups that were using his ideas as an excuse for criminal acts.

1530

Many German princes and cities signed a document called the Augsburg *Confession* as an expression of the new Protestant faith.

1546

Luther died aged 62.

1555

Each German prince was given the right to choose the religion of his own territory. As a result, the Reformation swept through Northern and Eastern Europe.
Cf. To Know Worship and Love, Book 9

Luther's differences with the Church were not only about indulgences. His most important idea was that salvation could be gained by faith alone. Salvation he argued was a *gift of God*, and it cannot be *earned* by anything a person may do. Good works did not earn salvation, but were a natural outpouring of the gift of faith. However, the Catholic Church has always taught that faith *and* good works are necessary for salvation. (James 2: 17). In fact the positions of Luther and his followers and that of the Catholic Church on this belief were actually very close, and this makes even more astonishing the events that unfolded in the ensuing years.

In October 1999 the Catholic Church and the Lutheran World Federation issued a Common Declaration on this issue of faith and good works as means to salvation. The Declaration carefully set out the positions of each group, showing the different nuances given to faith and works by each, and provided a consensus that was accepted as true to both Churches. Therefore the condemnations of the past were put aside and there was a commitment made to a new openness to each other.

> The understanding of the doctrine of justification set forth in this Declaration shows that a consensus in basic truths of the doctrine of justification exists between Lutherans and Catholics. In light of this consensus the remaining differences of language, theological elaboration, and emphasis in the understanding of justification described in paras. 18 to 39 are acceptable. Therefore the Lutheran and the Catholic explications of justification are in their difference open to one another and do not destroy the consensus regarding the basic truths (#49)

If consensus could be reached in this matter of belief in 1999, what factors prevented this consensus in 1517?

The Reformation spread across Europe

The Protestant Reformation, as it came to be called, was carried on by people who modified Luther's teaching in ways that he would never have envisioned. Congregations bearing the name *Lutheran* appeared in northern Germany and Scandinavia. Zwingli, a disciple of Luther's and a Catholic priest, brought Protestantism to Zurich from where it spread through Switzerland. In Geneva, Calvin drew on Luther and Zwingli to promote a stern and demanding Christianity, emphasizing predestination, a position which appears to naturally flow from Luther's position on the necessity of the gift of faith alone for salvation. John Knox brought Calvin's Reformed Church to Scotland, where it became the Presbyterian Church, and in England, King Henry VIII also split from Rome, in 1534 making himself head of the Church in England in order to resist the Pope's refusal to grant him a divorce form his first wife, Catherine of Aragon. Henry VIII was highly critical of Martin Luther but his son, Edward VI, introduced Protestant doctrines and Protestant forms of worship into England. By the 1530s, all of Scandinavia, the British Isles, and much of Germany, Austria and France had broken with Rome. While devastating for the Roman Catholic Church, the Reformation led to the Catholic Council of Trent (1545-1563), and to a general reform of many conditions in the Church.

Catholic Reform: The Council of Trent

Pope Paul III who led the Church between 1534 and 1549 is considered to be the first Pope of the Catholic reform, and the Council of Trent (1545-1563) which he convened, is recognized today as an important watershed of reform in the Church. This Council responded comprehensively to the issues of the Reformation. It reformed the clergy, forbidding corrupt practices among priests, bishops and cardinals, and insisting that all clerics must reside in their posts, thus correcting priests, bishops or abbots who paid others to look after their diocese or parishes, while they took the profits. It stipulated that no-one was to be appointed bishop until he had been ordained for six months, and it forbade the practice of bishops taxing and receiving money from parishes that they visited. Furthermore, it condemned the abuse of indulgences a means to raise money.

Doctrinally the Council of Trent taught that salvation does indeed come from God as a pure gift, but emphasized that it also needs human co-operation. In other words, faith and good works are necessary for salvation. It affirmed traditional teaching that both Scripture and the Tradition of the Church are sources of Revelation. It reformed the sacraments, established their number and laid down specific criteria for their celebration. Finally, it regulated the education and training of priests.

New religious orders and other groups were founded to help in Catholic renewal. Some of these were the Capuchins, the Ursulines, and the Jesuits. Later in the century, St. John of the Cross and St. Teresa of Ávila reformed the Carmelite communities. St. Francis of Sales had a great influence on the faith of the ordinary people, and later St. Vincent de Paul pioneered a model for the training of priests and ministry to the poor. **What do you know about any of the orders or saint s who were so important to the Church's reform at this time in history?**

Twentieth Century Reform: The Second Vatican Council

The tridentine era, that is the period of time after the Council of Trent, came to an end with the Second Vatican Council (1962-1965). Called by Pope John XXIII, the Council has profoundly shaped present day Catholicism. Its context was the aftermath of the Second World War; the renewed emphasis on human rights as a result of the atrocities of war; the millions of displaced persons seeking safety after the war; the formation of the Untied Nations; the arms race, and the growing gap between the rich and the poor

What other social factors affected life in the 1960s?

Pope John XXIII declared in his opening address that the Council's goal was to promote peace and unity among humanity, and to find new ways in which the Church can present itself to the world. He used the Italian word, *aggiornamento*, to express the renewal and updating that he believed the Church needed in order to adapt to the changing world. The goal of the Council, he said, was to "open the windows of the Church" to allow the breath of the Holy Spirit to pervade it. He prayed:

O Holy Spirit, sent by the Father in the name of Jesus, who is present in the Church and infallibly guides it, pour forth, we pray, the fullness of your gifts upon the Ecumenical Council.

Grant that from this council abundant fruit may ripen; that the light and strength of the gospel may be extended more and more in human society; that the Catholic religion and its active missionary works may flourish with ever greater vigour, with the happy result that knowledge of the Church's teaching may spread, and Christian morality increase.

O sweet guest of the soul, strengthen our minds in the truth and dispose our hearts to pay reverential heed, that we may accept with sincere submission those things that shall be decided in the Council and fulfil them with ready will.

Renew thy wonders in this day, as by a new Pentecost. Grant to the Church that being one in mind and steadfast in prayer with Mary the Mother of Jesus, and following the lead of blessed Peter, it may advance the reign of our divine saviour, the reign of truth and justice, the reign of love and peace. Amen.

The Council produced sixteen documents, which covered the Church, liturgy, Revelation, the relationship between the Church and the modern world, communications, Eastern Catholic Churches, other religions, freedom of religions, the roles of bishops and priests, the training of priests, lay people in the Church, missionary activity, Christian education and the relationship of the Church with other Christian Churches. In particular it emphasized the engagement of the Catholic Church with the world saying that "The joys and the hopes, the griefs and the anxieties of the people of this age, especially those who are poor or in any way afflicted, these too are the joys and the hopes, the griefs and the anxieties of the followers of Christ. Indeed nothing genuinely human fails to raise an echo in their hearts" (Gaudium et Spes, 1).

What do you think was the most important topic discussed at the Council and why?

The Council developed a vision of the Church as embracing all Christians, a Church which could not simply be limited to the boundaries of the Catholic Church. The Church of Jesus Christ, though divided, is one, and the Council urged all Christians to work together to overcome the divisions and misunderstandings that divide Christian communities. This work of ecumenism is unfolding today, along with a growing desire of Christians to understand their fellow human beings who belong to religions other than Christianity.

The Reformation is over

Reflecting on the differences in the Catholic Church as a result of the Second Vatican Council whose effects, some argue, are really just beginning to be felt in the Church, Edmund Campion, the Catholic historian declared that the Reformation is now over.

> The Reformation is over and we draw sustenance where we can find it. Nothing has speeded this process so much, I think, as the protestantizing of Catholicism. When Rome shows herself willing to listen and learn form Geneva and Canterbury, then we are in a new age. The evidence for this is overwhelming; the Bible at the centre of Catholic theology, liturgy and spirituality; Catholic liturgy in a language 'understanded of the people'(as the Thirty nine Articles have it); a morality of striving for justice and mercy rather than a morality of guilt; the freeing of lay intelligence and the slow erosion of clerical control systems; a laity who set their own spiritual agenda; and ecclesial pluralism which shows that the Church is now humble enough to learn from multicultural society. Each of these was a spiritual gain of the Reformation; each has been taken on board by the Catholics. Oh yes, the Reformation is over. (Campion, 2003, 193-194).

References and Further Reading

Church Documents

The Catechism of the Catholic Church. (1994). Homebush, Sydney: St. Paul's Publications.

Gaudium et Spes. (1965). The Pastoral Constitution on the Church in the Modern World. Second Vatican Council.

Other References

Cameron, E. (1991).*The European Reformation.* New York: Oxford University Press.

Campion, E. (2003). *Lines of My Life.* Camberwell, Melbourne. Penguin Books.

Lindberg, C. (1996). *The European Reformations.* Oxford: Blackwell.

MacCulloch, D. (2004) *The Reformation: A History.* New York: Viking Press.

CHAPTER 18

The Sacraments: Signs of Faith, Hope and Love

Kath Engebretson

Some of the material on Baptism and Eucharist in this chapter has been drawn from writing done by Kath Engebretson for the Archdiocese of Melbourne World Youth Day training manual for guides.

Some basic terms

Fundamental to Catholic life are the celebrations called sacraments. Before proceeding with a discussion of each of the sacraments it is necessary to introduce some terms.

A **Sacrament** is a ritual which mediates the saving presence and activity of God through human words and actions.

Liturgy: is defined as the public worship of the Catholic Church, and it refers to formal gatherings of the Catholic community when it takes part in public rites or rituals.

Grace: refers to all that God gives, the gift of Christ, the gift of the Holy Spirit, and the gift of God's life, which allows people to share in the life of God. Christians believe that God's grace in their lives is constant. "Sanctifying" grace is the grace that brings about salvation, the forgiveness of sin, adoption as children of God, incorporation into Christ, friendship with God, participation in the divine life and the indwelling of the Trinity. "Sanctifying" grace, comes to the believer and the community through the sacraments "Actual" grace refers to assistance given for a particular need or action. It may be given in the strength to follow a particular right action, the strength to remain faithful to conscience; the strength to do the right thing in a relationship. It may be a sense of the presence of God, or a sense of confidence in God's help. Through "actual" grace the person is assisted by God in the challenges of living daily life.

Salvation: refers to God's work of reconciling humankind with himself, and restoring to humankind the privileges of complete unity with him, with each other and with the created world that are naturally theirs and which were broken by sin (Gen, Ch 3). This reconciliation and restoration is achieved through God's gift of himself incarnate (made flesh) in Jesus Christ. (See chapter 15). In Jesus Christ and his resurrection, humanity can hope for deliverance **from** the consequence of sin which is eternal death, and deliverance **for** God's salvific gift, which is eternal life. As Christ's Body on earth, the Church continues God's work of salvation, reconciling people with God, with each other and with their world through Jesus Christ.

The Kingdom of God. This was the central idea in the teaching of Jesus Christ. The Kingdom of God (also referred to as the Reign of God) expresses in metaphor the belief that God rules over creation and human history, in their past, present and future. This rule is life-giving and redemptive. It is eternal, as God himself is eternal. It has been prepared from the beginning of time, but is beyond time. It is not a Kingdom that can be measured in years, months and days, as political and military kingdoms can be, for it is everlasting. In early Christian times, the writer of the letter to the Hebrews stated this belief: "While all other kingdoms will someday be destroyed, God's kingdom cannot be shaken, and will never be destroyed (Heb 12;29). Christians work in their daily lives for the coming of the Kingdom of God and hope for its ultimate victory in life after death, and in the world to come.

In short, then, the sacraments together make up the **liturgy** of the Catholic Church and through them Catholics believe that they receive the **grace** which comes from the life, death and resurrection of Jesus Christ, and through which they will experience the life of God and work for the **Kingdom of God** in this life and in the life to come.

History of the sacraments

Until the seven sacraments we have today were finally confirmed by the Council of Trent (1545-1563) there was really no definition of what a sacrament was, or no consensus about their number. There were literally hundreds of sacred rites, from the reading of scripture, blessing oneself with holy water, making the sign of the cross, praying before a statue, receiving the ashes on Ash Wednesday, genuflecting before the Eucharist, and many others. The eastern and western Churches, with their centres respectively at Constantinople and Rome had already separated in 1054 AD (see Chapter 16). As shown in the previous chapter, the next series of separations came with the Reformation which was a movement that began in Germany through the teaching of Martin Luther (1483-1546). It was fuelled by dissatisfaction with the corruption, wealth and abuse of power that had crept into the hierarchy of the western Church. It came to be called the Protestant movement, and quickly spread across Europe, leading to the birth of numerous Christian Protestant Churches. Faced with the challenges of the Reformation, the Catholic (western) Church called the Catholic Council of Trent (1545-1563), which set out to reform many institutions and practices that had been corrupted. The seven sacraments we have today were settled upon, and given the title of **sacraments**, while other lesser rituals such as saying the rosary, blessing oneself with holy water, genuflecting, making the sign of the Cross came to be called **sacramentals.** So just as human life is marked by a number of stages from birth to death, the Catholic life is marked by sacraments that deepen the individual's belonging within the Catholic community. In this pattern of sacraments there are the sacraments of initiation, Baptism, Confirmation and Eucharist, the sacraments of healing, Reconciliation and Anointing of the Sick, and the sacraments of commitment, Marriage and Holy Orders.

The sacraments of initiation

Baptism

The history of Baptism

In the New Testament baptism is described in terms of "putting on" Christ, of becoming one with Christ in his death so as to share in his resurrection. The *Didache* was a late first-century manual for Christians and for those preparing for Baptism. It instructed Christians in this way.

> And concerning baptism, baptize this way: Having first said all these things, baptize into the name of the Father, and of the Son, and of the Holy Spirit, in living water. But if you have no living water, baptize into other water; and if you cannot do so in cold water, do so in warm. But if you have neither, pour out water three times upon the head into the name of Father and Son and Holy Spirit. But before the baptism let the baptizer fast, and the baptized, and whoever else can; but you shall order the baptized to fast one or two days before.

The text given above shows that from the earliest decades of Christianity believers were baptized in the name of the Trinity, preferably immersed in flowing water, but if this was impossible the pouring of water on the head of the candidate in the name of the three persons of the Trinity was acceptable. In the second and third centuries, the ritual took the following form. In the midst of the community the catechumens (those who had been approved to prepare for baptism) prayed and fasted for the forgiveness of their sins for a period of up to three years. During this period their faith was tested and the authenticity of their conversion to Christ was judged. Immediately before the baptism, they were called upon to formally renounce evil and accept Christ. At the first light of day the water was blessed. In a ritual very similar to that practised today, the bishop then blessed the oil of thanksgiving and the oil of exorcism, and then the candidates were called upon to renounce sin and express their faith in God the Father, Son and Holy Spirit. When they had renounced evil, they were anointed with the oil of exorcism, and then they descended one by one into the baptismal pool with the deacon, children going first. Here they were "washed", a process that was also referred to as "illumination", as the names of God the Father, Son and Holy Spirit were invoked. The washing was through a three-fold immersion in water, and with each immersion the candidate made a profession of faith in Father, Son and Holy Spirit. After the immersion, the candidates were anointed with the oil of thanksgiving, and then they joined the gathered community. Here the bishop laid his hands on the head of the newly baptized person to symbolize the gift of the Holy Spirit. They were again anointed with oil (Chrism) and sealed with the sign of the Cross on their foreheads. They were given milk and honey and a chalice of water before sharing the Eucharist with the gathered community (see Justin Martyr: (100-165AD).First Apology; Hippolytus: Apostolic Tradition (215AD)).

The ritual of baptism enacted and expressed its meaning. Baptism was seen as an identification with Christ in his death in order to experience his resurrection. The baptized person "put on" Christ and this involved the acceptance of his suffering as well as of his resurrection. The immersion in water was like going into the tomb with Christ before becoming one with him in his resurrection.

> Do you not know that all of us who have been baptized into Christ Jesus were baptized into his death? Therefore we have been buried with him through baptism into death, so that just as Christ was raised from the dead by the glory of the Father, so we too might walk in newness of life. For if we have been united with him in a death like his, we will certainly be united with him in a resurrection like his....But if we have died with Christ, we believe that we will also live with him. We know that Christ, having been raised from the dead, will never die again. Death no longer has dominion over him. (Rom 6: 1-8)

Implicit in the sacrament of baptism, now as much as then, is hope. Christian hope is focused on the promise of good things in the present life and in the life to come.

> For you did not receive a spirit of slavery to fall back into fear, but you received a spirit of adoption. When we cry Abba! Father! it is that very Spirit, bearing witness with our spirit, that we are children of God, and if children then heirs, heirs of God and joint heirs with Christ. If in fact we suffer with him so that we might be glorified with him. (Rom 8:15)

Although the catechumenate declined from the time that Christianity expanded across the Roman empire, it was revived by the Second Vatican Council (1962-1965) through the Rite of Christian Initiation of Adults (RCIA). In this rite, which is commonly practised in parishes around Australia and the world, the catechumens who seek baptism go through the periods of enquiry, catechumenate, testing, baptism at the celebration of the Easter vigil, and entry into the community as did the catechumens of the early Church. In the Catholic Church today this rite exists alongside the rite of baptism for infants, which is now often celebrated within a Sunday Mass.

Infant Baptism

Christian writings of the second and early third century indicate that Christians baptized children and infants, and by the end of the third century infant baptism was a universal practice. The Catechism of the Catholic Church encourages Catholic parents to have their children baptized as infants. "The Church and the parents would deny a child the priceless gift of becoming a child of God were they not to confer baptism shortly after birth" (Catechism of the Catholic Church, 1252).

The meaning of Baptism

Baptism is not an individualistic "Jesus and me" experience, but one that impels the Catholic into relationships with others, and to share in Jesus' mission to build up the Kingdom of God. The living out of the salvation brought by Christ, which is taken on in baptism, is done in the community of the Church. The very first Christians took the community aspect of their lives literally. They lived together, shared all that they had and prayed together daily. Today in our Catholic communities the same principles of shared belief, prayer and charity are at the heart of communal life. Catholics believe that their Church, the worldwide community of Catholics, is the Body of Christ on earth. While individuals within it show weakness, sin and even deliberate evil, it is the effective sign and instrument (Lumen Gentium #1) of God's presence on earth through Christ.

Confirmation

History and meaning of Confirmation

Confirmation is literally the sealing of Baptism. In adult Baptism, Confirmation is part of the ritual of Baptism. It is the final anointing on the head with the oil of Chrism, before the newly baptized person joins the community to share in the Eucharist. In the case of those baptized as infants, it is a separate sacrament. As the Church grew and spread across Europe, it was impossible for bishops to perform all infant baptisms, and so the ritual of infant baptism became the task of the priest. However, people still wanted the final anointing to be performed by the bishop, so the full initiation of baptized children was delayed until the bishop was available. In the Catholic Church today Confirmation is still administered by the bishop, usually when the child is around twelve years old. The ceremony begins with general laying on of hands by the bishop over the heads of the gathered candidates, while he prays that the Holy Spirit will come down upon them. Then he anoints each individual with the oil of chrism saying: "I sign you with the sign of the cross, and confirm you with the chrism of salvation, in the name of the Father and of the Son, and of the Holy Spirit." Finally, he gives each a slight blow on the cheek saying: "peace be with you". The final prayer asks that the Holy Spirit may live in the hearts of those who have been confirmed and the ritual ends with the bishop's blessing.

Chrism is olive oil mixed with perfume. It is blessed by the bishop every year at the Mass of Chrism, which is usually celebrated on Holy Thursday. It is used in Baptism, Confirmation, priestly ordination, the ordination of bishops and in the blessing of Churches and altars. The oil symbolizes the gift of strength for the journey of the Christian life, and its perfume is a symbol of the coming of the Holy Spirit. Along with the oil of the sick (used in the sacrament of Anointing of the Sick), and the oil of catechumens (used in adult baptism), Chrism is reserved in a special place in the Church sanctuary.

Reconciliation

History of the Sacrament

Also referred to as the Sacrament of Penance or Confession, this is the sacrament that gives Catholics the opportunity to confess sorrow for their sins and to be absolved from them. At first the sacrament of Penance (Reconciliation as it came to be named by the Second Vatican Council; 1962-1965) was a public ritual which could only be received once in a lifetime, and the ritual lasted for a long time, often for three years, or even up to fifteen years for extremely serous sins. In the first three centuries it had particular application for those Christians (the *lapsi)* who had denied their Christianity in the face of Roman persecution, and who now wanted to be reconciled with the Church. In time, local Churches developed their own form of the ritual, although the final step in the ritual was always the laying on of hands on the head of the penitent by the bishop or priest. The ritual was accompanied by such severe penances (such as committing to celibacy of the rest of their lives) that from 700 onwards it was rarely used, unless the person was close to death. However in England and Ireland a private form of confession and absolution developed, which was more like spiritual direction. This was practised by monks and nuns who confessed their sins to their abbot or abbess, seeking forgiveness and encouragement. When Celtic monks and nuns went to Europe at the end of the sixth century as missionaries, they took this private form of Reconciliation with them, and gradually the public form disappeared. In 1215, the fourth Lateran Council adopted the private rite as a sacrament. The Council of Trent, after the Reformation, encouraged frequent use of the sacrament, as does the Church today.

Structure of the Sacrament

The sacrament can be celebrated in four rites which are shown in the following table.

Rite 1 Individual confession	Rite 2 Communal prayer with individual confession	Rite 3 Communal Penance	Rite 4
In this rite the person (penitent) meets individually with the priest, tells him of their sins, expresses sorrow for them and then receives absolution from the priest who acts in the name of Christ. The priest usually givens the penitent some encouragement and advice.	In this rite the community gathers, is welcomed by the priest, listens to Scripture, has a time of communal examination of conscience, and then each person goes individually to the priest to recite their sins and receive absolution for them.	In this rite the entire sacrament proceeds as a communal rite with no individual confession. After an opening prayer, reading from Scripture and communal examination of conscience, the gathered penitents are asked to give a sign that they seek forgiveness of their sins. Then the priest gives absolution to all acting in the name of Christ.	A very brief, emergency rite, to be used at the time of death.
Penance. The person is set a "penance" which may be a prayer or more often advice to reflect more closely on some aspect of life or to undertake a particular action.	Penance is given as in the first rite.	Penance is given as a community with everyone present being encouraged to reflect on some aspect of their lives or to take some form of action.	

The Church encourages the use of the first and second rites, but Church law states that the third rite can only be used when there is "grave necessity" or when there are insufficient priests for everyone to have access within a given time. In Australia, since the time of the Second Vatican Council (1962-1965) up to 1998, this third rite of Reconciliation was very popular with hundreds of people coming to it before Christmas and Easter. However in 1998 the Pope asked the Australian bishops to reserve the third rite for cases of grave necessity as stated in Church law.

There is no doubt that use of the sacrament of Reconciliation has declined in Australia since the Second Vatican Council. Previously most Catholic s believed that they had an obligation to use this Sacrament approximately once a month, but the individual form of the sacraments is now not often used by most Catholics.

The meaning of the Sacrament of Reconciliation

Reconciliation is a powerful and consistent theme in the New Testament. The Christian understanding of salvation is that it is the reconciliation of humankind with God. Jesus both lived and preached reconciliation, in his constant forgiveness, his relationships with society's outcasts and in his many parables. The healing miracles of Jesus recounted in the New Testament are symbols and reminders of the spiritual healing that comes from being reconciled with God. The meaning of the sacrament for Catholics comes in the realization that sin in an offence against oneself, but it is also deeply social. It damages relationships in the community and breaks down one's relationship with God. The sacrament of Reconciliation, where the priest mediates the forgiveness of God and absolves sin, brings inward peace, and reconciliation with the community and with God. The act of "penance" is a recognition of this forgiveness and an act of thanksgiving for it.

Eucharist

The meaning of the Eucharist for Catholics

Referred to by the Second Vatican Council as the "source and summit" (see The Eucharist: Source and Summit of the Life and Mission of the Church. Synod of Bishops, XI Ordinary General Assembly. Par 1.) of Catholic life, the Eucharist is the sacrament that celebrates and makes present again the dying and rising of Jesus Christ (the Paschal Mystery). It is a celebration of praise and thanks to God for his saving work among his people, and in the Eucharist Catholics believe that they are formed into the Body of Christ on earth. The Eucharist is grounded in the historical reality of the last supper that Jesus shared with his disciples. The earliest reference to it is from St. Paul, who, as a later convert to discipleship, was not actually present at the last supper. His words represent a very early experience and memory of the Christian community.

> For this is what I received from the Lord, and in turn passed on to you: that on the same night that he was betrayed, the Lord Jesus, took some bread, and thanked God for it and broke it, and he said, 'This is my body which is for you; do this as a memorial of me'. In the same way he took the cup after supper, and said, 'This cup is the new covenant in my blood. Whenever you

drink, do this as a memorial of me'. Until the Lord comes, therefore, every time you eat this bread and drink this cup, you are proclaiming his death…
(1 Corinthians 11:23-26)

For Catholics the meaning of the Eucharist centres on remembering the life, death and resurrection of Christ, joining with his redemptive sacrifice and acknowledging his real presence in the consecrated bread and wine. This mystery of the joining of the divine and the human in Christ (the Incarnation) is made present again through the words of consecration, on the Eucharistic table. The profound and wonderful mystery of the Eucharist is that just as Jesus became human, in the Eucharist humans are caught up in the divine. All that we bring to the Eucharist, our own humanity, the loves, joys and pains and challenges of our lives, are presented with the bread and wine on the altar of the Eucharist and there are transformed.

History of the Eucharist

The early Christians gathered on the first day of the week (Sunday) to read the Scriptures, to re-tell the story of Jesus' death and resurrection, and to remember him in the blessing of the bread and wine. Christians believed and taught that the bread and wine became the Body and Blood of Christ. Early in the second century, St. Ignatius, bishop of Antioch, described the Eucharist as *the flesh of our Saviour, Jesus Christ*. These early communities met in house-churches, gathering in a room in a family's home. The unity and love experienced in *the breaking of the bread* reflected the support and care that these early Christians gave to each other. In the first twenty or so years after Jesus' death, the breaking of the bread probably took place within a meal, just as it had at the Last Supper. However, from the middle of the first century the blessing of the bread and wine was separated from the meal. The bread and wine were consecrated in a prayer, which came to be called the *Eucharistic Prayer*. After the celebration, some Christians would take portions of the Eucharist home, to receive during the week or to bring to those who could not be present, especially persecuted Christians in prison. The meal was held later and it came to be called the "agape" or "love feast".

After Christianity become a legal religion with the Edict of Constantine (313AD), Christian communities became much bigger. They built huge beautiful Churches based on the form of the basilica, the Roman law courts, for the celebration of the Eucharist, and the ritual that was celebrated in them was not unlike its order today. It consisted of:

- Gathering and preparing
- Reading and explaining the Scriptures
- Community prayers of intercession
- Preparation of the gifts of bread and wine

- The Eucharistic Prayer with the central moment of the consecration of the bread and wine
- The distribution of the Body and Blood of Christ.

The practice of taking the Eucharist to those who were unable to attend through illness or other factors was continued, and this is still practised in Catholic parishes today.

Gradually, as Christians became very numerous, the participants in the Eucharist became almost spectators, with the action being reserved to the priest who read the scripture readings and celebrated the Mass in Latin, with his back to the people. The aspect of Eucharist as a mystery was emphasized, and many Catholics stopped receiving Eucharist frequently. In fear of their own sinfulness, and in awe at the mystery of the Eucharist among other reasons, they would limit their reception of Eucharist to special occasions. Children did not receive the sacrament until they were twelve or fourteen years old, and many adults would receive it only once a year. The practice arose among many Catholics of not taking the Eucharist unless they had been to the sacrament of Penance very recently. Private devotions such as the rosary or other private prayers were pursued during Mass, and the adoration of the Eucharist outside the time of Mass became widespread. In 1215 AD, the Fourth Lateran Council decreed that it was compulsory for Catholics to receive Communion at least once a year, at Easter. As corruption of various forms (such as paying money for Mass to be celebrated for the intentions of one person) became commonplace, the Church was faced with the challenge of Martin Luther and the events that followed, which have come to be called the Protestant Reformation. The Council of Trent (1545-1563) was the response by the Church to the abuses that had in part led to the Reformation, and this Council reformed the celebration of the Eucharist.

The "Real Presence"

It was during this mediaeval period that the doctrine at the heart of Catholic belief about the Eucharist was fully formulated. This is the belief in Christ's real presence in the Eucharist. Transubstantiation, the word used to designate the transformation of the bread and wine with the words of consecration, was spelled out. Essentially this means than when the words of consecration are uttered, Christ becomes really present, body and blood, under the appearances of bread and wine. Catholics believe that while the **appearances** of the consecrated bread and wine do not change, their **inner nature** does change. This inner nature of the bread and wine becomes the Body and Blood of Christ. Today the Mass is very different from the gatherings for *the breaking of the bread* in earlier centuries, and the Latin Mass of the mediaeval and Tridentine periods, but the fundamental belief that Jesus Christ is truly present under the appearance of bread and wine has not changed.

The Eucharist and the Second Vatican Council

Further reform of the liturgy of the Eucharist came for the Second Vatican Council (1962-1966). While the Council continued to emphasize the real presence of Christ, it also noted other ways in which Christ was present in the Eucharistic celebration, that is, in the person of the priest who celebrates the Eucharist, in the Word of God, and in the gathered community. Alongside the theology of the Eucharist being the same sacrifice as that of Christ, the theology of Eucharist as the holy meal of the community, an emphasis that had been lost since the first centuries, was re-affirmed. As a result of these renewed emphases, Catholic dioceses gradually introduced various changes into their liturgies.

- The altar was brought closer and turned around so that the priest now faced the people.

- The Mass was now to be celebrated in the vernacular, the language of the people. (This did not mean than the Latin Mass disappeared, but Mass in the vernacular is now the norm).

- Communion could now be given "under two species" or as consecrated bread **and** wine.

- More emphasis was placed on the centrality of Scripture and a responsorial psalm was introduced after the first Scripture reading.

- Priests were encouraged to use the homily (sermon) to help the gathered Catholics to understand the Scripture readings.

- The General Intercessions (Prayers of the Faithful) that had been a part of the earliest Eucharistic celebrations were re-introduced.

- A Sign of Peace, a practice common in the first centuries, was re-introduced to be used just before Communion.

- Priests were given choice in the Eucharistic Prayers that they used, with four different prayers being available for use on ordinary Sundays (See the example of the fourth Eucharist prayer given at the end of this chapter)

- The people responded to the words of Consecration with an acclamation such as *Christ has died, Christ is risen, Christ will come again.*

- In most countries, it became normal for people to receive communion into their hands rather than on their tongues.

- Lay people were encouraged to take active parts in the liturgy, through reading, commentating, serving and helping to distribute Communion where needed.

The Eucharist today

The celebration of the Eucharist in the Church today has four parts. These are:

The Introductory Rites consisting of : The Entrance Song or Antiphon, the Sign of the Cross, the Greeting, the Introduction, the Penitential Rite (A time for recalling human sinfulness and expressing sorrow for it), the Gloria (A prayer of praise usually used only on Sunday), the Opening Prayer.

The Liturgy of the Word consisting of: The first reading (from the Old Testament), the Responsorial Psalm, the Second Reading (from the New Testament), the Gospel Acclamation, the Gospel Reading, the Homily, the Profession of Faith (The Nicene Creed), the Prayer of the Faithful.

The Liturgy of the Eucharist
Part 1: The Preparation of the Gifts consisting of the Preparation of the Altar, the Procession of the gifts of bread and wine, the Preparation of the gifts, the Priest's washing of hands, the Prayer over the gifts.

Part 2: The Eucharistic Prayer consisting of the Preface, the Holy Holy Holy, the invocation of the Holy Spirit, the Consecration (using the words of Jesus at the Last Supper), the Offering, the Prayers for the living and the dead, the Doxology.

Part 3: The Communion Rite consisting of the Lord's Prayer, the Sign of Peace, the Breaking of the Bread, the Commingling, the Lamb of God, the Invitation to Communion, the Priest's Communion, the distribution of Communion, the Communion Song, the washing of the vessels, the prayer after Communion.

The Concluding Rites consisting of the Final Blessing, the Dismissal

Anointing of the Sick

History of the Sacrament

The four gospels portray Jesus as a healer, who brought physical and spiritual healing to those who approached him. *And wherever he went, to village, or town, or farm, they laid down the sick in the open spaces, begging him to let them touch even the fringe of his cloak. And all those who touched him were cured. (Mark 6:56).* The gospels also show that Jesus shared this healing power with to his disciples *(Mark 6: 13)*. In the healing stories of the gospels Jesus is often shown healing by touch, usually laying his hands on the sick person. Continuing the healing work of Jesus and the Apostles, the laying on of hands and anointing with oil were administered to the sick in the early Church, in a ritual that was very like the way Catholics celebrate the sacrament today. The Epistle of James records this practice.

> If any one of you is in trouble, he should pray; if anyone is feeling happy, he should sing a psalm. If one of you is ill, he should send for the elders of the church, and they must anoint him with oil in the name of the Lord and pray over him. The prayer of faith will save the sick man and the Lord will raise him up again. And if he has committed any sins, he will be forgiven. (James 5: 13-16).

During the first eight centuries of the Church, the priests or "elders" would anoint the sick with oil that had been blessed by the bishop, lay their hands on them, and pray to the Holy Spirit to heal them. Lay people also used blessed oil to anoint sick relatives and friends, and someone who was sick may be anointed several times. During the Middle Ages the anointing of the sick was accepted as one of the sacraments of the Church, and it was affirmed as such by the Council of Trent. It was often perceived by people as the "last anointing" ("extreme unction") or the "sacrament of the departing" because the sacrament was used mostly by the dying and was usually conducted on a person's deathbed. The Council of Trent emphasized that the purpose of the sacrament was to give strength, comfort and the support of the community to a dying person, to offer physical and spiritual healing and to forgive sin. The Second Vatican Council, however, taught that it was better to refer to the Sacrament as the "Anointing of the Sick" because it was not just a sacrament for the dying. The *Catechism of the Catholic Church* points out that a person may well receive this sacrament more than once.

> If a sick person who received this anointing recovers his health, he can, in the case of another grave illness, receive this sacrament again. If, during the same illness, a person's condition becomes more serious, the sacrament may be repeated. It is fitting to receive the Anointing of the Sick just prior to a serious operation. The same holds for the elderly whose frailty becomes more pronounced (CCC 1515).

The meaning of the Sacrament

Just as the suffering and death of Jesus led to his resurrection, Christians who have been united with Christ in their baptism can hope for new life after death. This hope is central to Catholic life and spirituality. The Sacrament of Anointing allows those who are sick or dying to express faith in the resurrection of Christ and thus hope for their own resurrection. When the Christian community celebrates the Sacrament of Anointing, it affirms that God is present in suffering, even though it is often hard to see or understand this. If the person is dying, the sacrament expresses the hope that he or she will experience spiritual healing and resurrection in Christ to new life with God.

The structure of the Sacrament

Anointing of the Sick is available to all who are ill or elderly. It may be celebrated during Mass, at the sick person's home or at their hospital bed, for example before a major operation, or by the bedside of a dying person. When a person is very close to death, special prayers are included which entrust the dying person to Christ. In this form of the sacrament, the person receives his or her last Communion. Holy Communion given to a dying person is called "Viaticum" meaning "food for the journey". When celebrated outside of Mass the sacrament has this structure:

Introduction: The priest greets the sick person and the others present, sprinkling them with holy water. He gives a short introduction to the Sacrament and then there is a Penitential Rite similar to those used at Mass.

Liturgy of the Word: There is an appropriate reading from Scripture.

The Anointing: The priest begins with intercessory prayers asking for God's blessing, and for strength for the sick person. Then he lays his hands on the sick person's head. He blesses the oil of the sick, or, if it is already blessed, says a prayer of thanksgiving over it. Then he anoints the sick person with the oil. First he anoints the forehead saying: *Through this holy anointing, may the Lord in his love and mercy help you, with the grace of the Hoy Spirit.* Then he anoints the sick person's hands saying: *May the Lord who frees you from sin save you and raise you up.* After the anointing the priest prays in words like this: *Father in heaven, through this holy anointing, grant (person's name) comfort in his/her suffering. When he/she is afraid, given him/her courage, when afflicted give him/her patience, when dejected, afford him/her hope, and when alone assure him/her of the support of your holy people. We ask this through Christ our Lord.* The gathered family and friends recite the Lord's Prayer.

Communion: The sick person and others receive Communion.

Blessing: The priest blesses the sick person and the others present with words such as these:

May the Lord be with you to protect you.
May he guide you and give you strength.
May he watch over you, keep you in his care, and bless you with his peace.
May almighty God bless you, the Father, the Son and the Holy Spirit.

The Sacrament of marriage

Marriage was recognized as one of the seven sacraments of the Church in the thirteenth century. The Catholic Code of Canon Law (#1055) describes it as a "covenant by which a man and a woman establish between themselves a partnership of their whole life, and which of its own very nature is ordered to the well-being of the spouses and to the procreation and up bringing of children." The term covenant, meaning *steadfast love and faithfulness*, is drawn from the relationship between God and the people of Israel, and the relationship between Christ and his Church.

In Catholic marriage, the spouses themselves minister the sacrament to each other, and the priest or deacon is there only as a witness on behalf of the Church. The free consent of the partners is required for the marriage to be valid, and the moment that free consent is expressed in the marriage ceremony the marriage is sealed. The Church teaches that marriage has two purposes which are equal in importance. First is the emotional and spiritual happiness and well-being of the partners, and second is the procreation and parenting of children. Catholic marriage, when all necessary conditions have been met, is considered to be exclusive, permanent and indissoluble.

> Marriage therefore is a loving partnership of the whole of life, established by the free consent of the spouses and ordered equally to the mutual well-being of the spouses and to the procreation ad birth of children. When such a marriage is between two believers it is both covenant and sacrament. (Laeler, 1995, p. 826).

Structure of the ritual

Catholic marriage involves the partners making vows to each other in front of the community witnessed by the priest or deacon. The ceremony may be conducted within a Mass, in which case it is called a Nuptial Mass, or there may be a shorter ceremony, with readings from Scripture, intercessory prayers and the making of vows and exchanging of rings, but without the Eucharist.

Holy Orders

History of the Sacrament

In the earliest years of the Church the apostles entrusted the leadership of the community and also leadership in prayer and Eucharist, to an overseer who was later called a bishop (Greek: episcopos). The bishop had a council of advisers called elders or presbyters (source of the word priest). Deacons assisted the bishop in the practical tasks of leading the community and in worship. However, as Christianity spread, especially to rural areas, by the end of the first century leadership of the communities and presiding at the Eucharist fell more to the presbyters, and this lessened their role as advisers to the bishops. Bishops gradually became less involved with the liturgical life of the small communities. As presbyters became more important, the role of deacon became less so, until gradually it became the main step on the way to becoming a presbyter.

The ordered or ordained ministry of the priesthood was derived from the Apostles, who passed it on to those who came after them through the laying on of hands and prayer. This was the original way in which men were set apart for ministry in the faith community (cf 1 Timothy 1:6). Those who are ordained enter an unbroken line of authority and teaching from the Apostles, and this is called apostolic succession. Only those who are ordained within this succession are recognised as true bishops, priests and deacons in the Catholic Church.

From the early centuries, the ordination of priests was seen as giving the power to consecrate the bread and wine in Mass. Eucharistic ministry was emphasised in the medieval era. The sacrificing priest was seen as acting in the person of Christ at the altar. Both bishop and priest share this sacramental power. By the twelfth century, Holy Orders was listed as one of the seven sacraments of the Church. Two Councils have influenced the way that Catholics think about the ordained ministry, especially the priesthood. The Council of Trent upheld the priesthood as an essential ministry in the Church. This Council taught that Holy Orders is one of the seven sacraments of the Church, that through this sacrament priests receive the power to consecrate the bread and wine at Mass and to absolve from sin. The Council repeated the teaching that bishops have authority over priests in the leadership of the Church.

The Second Vatican Council placed the ordained ministry in the broader context of the priesthood of the faithful, which members of the Church share through baptism. Even though the ministries of priest and lay person are distinct and different, the two callings are related, and both are needed for the building up of the body of Christ, the Church.

The ministry of the priest is centred on the **word,** the **sacraments** and on **pastoral ministry.** This means that his duties are to teach and help people to become familiar with the gospel of Jesus Christ and the teachings of the Church; to lead the people in the celebration of the sacraments, especially the sacrament of the Eucharist; and to be a guide, and leader within the Catholic community. The priest carries out these duties in collaboration with the bishop or archbishop, and with his fellow priests who together form the *college of priests* of which the bishop is head.

The celibacy of the priesthood

In the western Catholic Church, priests take a vow of celibacy, which means that they sacrifice marriage and having a family for the sake of being available to the whole People of God. From the earliest years of the Church celibacy was seen as a preparation for, and a witness to, the coming Kingdom of God. Jesus himself taught this by his words (Matthew

19:10-12) and by the example of his own celibate life. In the first century some Christians took on celibacy, but it was optional. The Apostle Paul praised celibacy and practised it himself, but he recognised that it was not a gift given to all. He advised that those who could not live the life of celibacy should marry (1 Corinthians 7:1-9). Although celibacy became more popular among those who wanted to dedicate themselves to the Kingdom of God, there was no universal rule about celibacy for bishops, priests and deacons in the first three centuries, although there was an attempt to make it universal Church law as early as the Council of Nicea in 325 AD. Celibacy grew in favour as monastic life spread throughout the Church. In the east it was required of all bishops, but not of priests and deacons who had married before ordination. In the west, Popes, Councils and local synods promoted celibacy for all the clergy, especially as a way of reforming the life and ministry of parish priests. Finally the Council of Trent (1545-1564) upheld that celibacy should be a requirement of the priesthood as a witness to the Kingdom of God. However, aware of different practices among eastern Christians, the Council recognised that celibacy was a Church law, rather than an unchanging divine law. Celibacy was proposed as a lifestyle that witnessed to the Kingdom of God, not as a rejection of the goodness of marriage. This teaching was repeated by the Second Vatican Council (1962-1965). Within the Church in recent years, there has been much discussion of celibacy. Some Catholics ask if the rule could be modified in regions where celibacy is not part of the local culture, or in the case of priests who do not find a celibate lifestyle helpful. They also point to permitted exceptions to the rule, and to Eastern practice. Other Catholics defend the positive values of celibate commitment and service, which Pope Paul VI described as *love without reservations*. While the discussion continues, celibacy remains part of the life of a priest, a commitment to the Church and a sign of the coming Kingdom of God.

Structure of the Sacrament

The ordination of a priest is celebrated during a special Mass. The candidate is first recognised and welcomed by the community. Then he makes a vow of obedience to the bishop. After the litany has been sung, the bishop lays his hands on the head of the candidate, and other priests present then come forward to lay their hands on him. Then the bishop says the prayer of consecration, which imparts the sacrament of Holy Orders. After the newly ordained has been vested in the stole and chasuble, the bishop anoints his hands with Chrism and hands him a paten with bread and a chalice of wine as a sign of his power to offer the Mass with and for God's people. Finally the bishop and other priests present exchange a sign of peace and brotherhood to welcome the new priest, who then concelebrates Mass with them for the first time.

The **stole** and **chasuble** are vestments (garments) worn by a priest when he celebrates Mass. The **paten** and **chalice** are used in the Mass to hold the bread and wine, which Catholics believe become the body and blood of Christ.

References and Further Reading

Fink, P. (ed) (1990), *A New Dictionary of Sacramental Theology*. Collegeville, MN: The Liturgical Press.

Jones, C., Wainwright, G., Yarnold, E., Bradshaw, P. (eds). (1992). *The Study of Liturgy*, rev.ed. New York: Oxford University Press.

Lawler, M. (1995). Marriage. In McBrien, R. (Gen.Ed). *The Harper Collins Encyclopaedia of Catholicism*. San Francisco: Harper Collins.

Martos, J. (1991). *Doors to the Sacred: A Historical Introduction to Sacraments in the Catholic Church*, rev. ed. Tarrytown, NY: Triumph Books.

Rahner, K. (1963).*The Church and the Sacraments*, Quaestiones disputae 9. New York: Herder & Herder.

Schillebeeckx, E. (1963).*Christ the Sacrament of the Encounter with God*, trans. Paul Barrett. New York: Sheed & Ward.

White, J. (1995) *Roman Catholic Worship: Trent to Today*. New York: Paulist Press.

CHAPTER 19

Catholic Moral Theology

Richard Wade

Introduction

Catholic moral theology offers a moral program to nurture the life of individuals and communities, and to motivate and assist people in the transformation of the world during their life time. The foundation of Catholic morality is faith. Faith is an act of commitment to the person of Jesus in a relationship of loving kindness, and it also involves an intellectual assent to the truths of Christian revelation. If we are to live as committed Christians in the Catholic tradition, there is an expectation that our behaviour, values and attitudes will conform to the will of God, as expressed in Church teaching. The Church invites Christians to live decently, and stands in solidarity with them to sustain their practices of the love of God and neighbour. To treat people with decency indicates that there are limits and constraints to our moral choices and behaviour. This is because we appreciate the God-given dignity and preciousness of the individual person, made in the image and likeness of God. To behave indecently is to undermine the dignity of the human person.

This chapter presents one insight into Catholic moral theology, by focusing on a foundation stone in its moral program, namely respect for the dignity of the human person. It offers, perhaps, one of many useful ways of explaining human dignity. I have developed what I call five interrelated senses of human dignity. Each of these senses helps to throw light on the meaning of the dignity of the person. Each sense stands alone but is connected to the others. These five senses are evocative of our five physical senses. We see, hear, smell, taste and touch God's world. To have a sense of something is to be rationally and emotionally aware of it, and to be willing to act out of this faith awareness in our lives. The five senses of human dignity are:

- A Sense of the Divine.
- A Sense of Freedom/Autonomy.
- A Sense of Community.
- A Sense of Conscience.
- A Sense of Embodiment.

A Sense of the Divine

People want to be happy and they often experiment in the search for happiness. Under–pinning the notion of happiness is a commitment to particular values and goods such as God, truth, love, family, nature and so on. The search and discovery of happiness takes place in the reality of our lives, which involves many and varied experiences and relationships (success, failure, oppression, tragedy, love, evil, hardship, struggle, inspiration, ordinariness and celebration). One of the important re-discoveries of people today is that the human person lives as part of nature and not apart from nature. This is an important context in which the person tries to live happily and decently. To contemplate the human person and nature, and to sense nature's cycles (e.g. the seasons) can be a path to the Divine and a means of strength to enable us to transcend ourselves in honouring and rejoicing in the creation. The aesthetic enjoyment of nature also inspires in us wonder, joy and peace. St. Francis of Assisi danced in a spirit of delight under the glory of the stars, while St. Ignatius of Loyola wept with joy at the sight of the stars. For them, a real presence of the Divine was in the stars, and their dancing and weeping was prayer or communion with God.

For Christians, the answer to the search for meaning and happiness is not simply in nature. It is found in the person of Jesus and the Triune God. Through wise and loving choices, Jesus created a new humanity, a new cosmic community (Col l:18-24; Eph 2:15), Col 3:1-4:6) and established right relationships with the Triune God and others. Jesus, though tempted like Adam, did not try to become like Nietzsche's "superman" grasping power and challenging God. The wisdom of Jesus does not dominate or exercise power and condescension over people in their relationships. The essence of Jesus' wisdom ethic is loving service in the name of the reign of God (Mk 10:42-45, Jn 13; 15:12-18).

We rediscover our own humanity by our awareness of our Christianity; in other words by following the example of Jesus. The reign of God is a *kairos* (here and now) time of opportunity to choose to accept the transforming love of the Divine into our lives (Eph 5:14-16).

To have a sense of the Divine is to hear the call to conversion and faith and to act lovingly in our relationships with God, other persons and non-human creation. A key part of this conversion experience is an environmental conversion that makes us aware of the harm we have caused to God's creation. This is the experience of a dignified and decent human person who is a Christian. The inspiration to treat people with common human decency is found in the grace and love which comes from the risen Jesus, who is our life giving Spirit (Rev 21:5). Jesus in his person made present the unconditional love of the Divine. All of us who are baptised "in Christ" (Rom 8:1) witness to the wisdom and love of Jesus. This sense of the Divine stirs us to reach out in hospitality, particularly to the stranger, the poor, the sick, the persecuted and the lonely (Lk 6: 20; Mt 14: 14). Part of this wisdom involves the gathering of all things in Christ (Ephesians 1:10). Not only has humanity been set free from the universal experience of alienation (Rom 1:21-25; 7:13-25) but the whole of creation has also been reconciled and given new life (Rev 21:5, Col l:19-20, Rom 8: 18-25), (Byrne, 1996).

When we look at another person we see that person as a symbol of the Divine presence. We are reminded that the human person is a spiritual being whose origins, depths and destiny are divine. This reminder helps us to appreciate that human lives are sacred, precious and inviolable. Catholic morality summons forth a sense of the Divine in all our relationships. This is the motivation, stimulus and context for treating people and the non-human world with respect, decency and courtesy. The Sabbath and the celebration of the Eucharist is a time to pause with God, to contemplate the presence and providence of the Divine in our humanity and in the created world. In the light of this contemplation, we are called to ensure that our faith does justice to the God's earth.

Comment on one point that was made in the foregoing section of the chapter.

A Sense of Freedom /Autonomy

The word freedom/autonomy is a code-word for talking about the human person as a subject. To describe the human person as a subject is to say that the individual has an enduring sense of self and makes autonomous choices. It is through our free self-conscious choices that we forge a personal identity and take control of our lives. We choose to marry and have children, to work to reduce carbon emissions, and so on. Freedom, is not merely the absence of external coercion or non-interference. It is the power to choose rationally and calmly. It is also the power over the laws of instinct (urges and desires) and the laws of nature. Within the subjectivity of the person, it is possible to reflect on the question: what is God asking me to do and what kind of person is God asking me to be in the many situations of my life? Through reflection and the right exercise of freedom, the human subject discovers the answer to this question. Love, justice, wisdom, the Church's teaching and greater accountability guide our ethical use of freedom.

Autonomy (self-determination) enables the human creature to say yes or no to God. In saying yes to God, the human person opts for a particular moral attitude in the process of becoming like Jesus (Lk 9: 23, 18; 5;30-32; 6:20-49). Basically, it is God's gift of grace in the Spirit that makes it possible to walk in the "way" of Jesus (Rom 6: 4; 8: 4f, Gal 5: 16-25; Eph 4:1-3). This "moral walk" in love finds expression in our relationships. It is through these relationships that I gradually shape my personal identity as I draw towards the Triune God. Through morally right actions, we praise and worship God and are slowly transformed in Christ (Rom 12:2-20). However, it is possible to say no to God's grace and to opt for a life of sin in my relationships (Eph 2:1-10). Sinful actions are those whereby a person knowingly and willingly chooses actions that are undermining of human dignity. When we say we have committed sinful actions, what we mean is that we have done wrong and caused unjustified harm to persons. Gradually, through dehumanising actions, I become committed to attitudes (condescension, discourtesy), actions (violence and rejection) and an outlook (untruthfulness, injustice and exclusion) that reflects the dark side of human nature. In this sense, sin is a failure to love and leads to unhappiness. It is these unloving choices that detract from our humanity and are irreverent towards God (Kelly, 1992). Evidence of other peoples' sinful or evil choices are found in the world (e.g. ecological destruction, cruelty to animals, brutality, racism and sexism) and unfortunately for us they make our choices painful and difficult. However, the gift of freedom enables us through faith and God's grace to repent and convert to the vision (conversion-faith), values (love of neighbour, God and enemy, forgiveness, non-violence etc.) and virtues (compassion, justice, care, generosity, hospitality, hope) of the reign of God (Mk 1: 15; Lk 4:43).

A sense of autonomy consists in the right use of free will and the exercise of judgement. To the extent that we are free, self-aware and responsible we transcend the material world, its causes and explanations but are interconnected with it. This excludes the view that our moral choices are determined by previous choices. Some sociobiologists seem to suggest that our behaviour, our actions and omissions, are totally determined by our genes (Dawkins, 1999). If this were the case then our choices would not be voluntary. Consequently, actions would not be blameworthy or praiseworthy and hence people would not be considered responsible for particular actions. We would not be moral persons as all our moral behaviour would be pre-determined. For example, some men have been socially conditioned to believe that women are inferior to men.

Some people have been conditioned in the belief that the environment and animals are simply there for human benefit. This type of attitude has been a contributing factor to the environmental crisis. Through education and compassionate correction it is possible to change peoples' attitudes. Moral action assumes that the acting subject is not totally determined by external circumstances and internal tensions. Despite genetic, biological, psychological, cultural and sociological influences the moral subject is morally responsible for what is freely done. Personal dignity is undermined if the capacity for the ethical use of autonomy is unfulfilled. To have a sense of autonomy is also about empowering others in their choices. This involves being honest and truthful in our personal and professional relationships. It also involves correcting imbalances, such as listening to the voices of women, including their experience and expression of that in language.

Summarise the Catholic view of freedom and autonomy as discussed in the foregoing section.

Cornerstones of Catholic Secondary Religious Education

A Sense of Community

The human person is not only an individual but also a person in community. To an extent western society is characterised by a disintegration of extended family relationships and belonging to a local community. However, at the same time, contemporary society is characterised by its networking among people, structures, civic and state institutions, associations and community groups. Through these networks, people participate and co-operate in a relationship of solidarity, inter-dependence and service for the public good (education, health, law and order, supplying of amenities and services). Responsible participation in the community ensures the basic needs of people are met. This networking of people, institutions and groups is another way of talking about the common good, which is the sum total of social conditions, which allow people, either as groups or as individuals, to reach their fulfilment more fully and more easily. (Flannery, 1996, 927 #26)

The inspiration and driving force of the common good is love of neighbour (Jn 13:34; Mt 5:43-48). To function well, society must be built on love, justice, peace, equality and respect for the dignity of the person, and genuine dialogue to seek the right practical solution to every problem. The right ordering of relationships between people in a modern democratic society is guided by the social norm and virtue of justice. The implementation of justice is shaped and guided by love and prudence. Justice is analytically identified as of three types - distributive, commutative and social justice (Finnis,1980). Distributive justice in a democratic society is concerned with the just distribution of benefits and burdens, resources and profits on a proportional basis. It also focuses upon needs and the rightful claims made by individuals and groups (especially the poor and the vulnerable) to access and participate in public funds (Hollenbach,1979). Commutative justice focuses upon the transactions between individuals and groups. Contracts are expected to be honoured. Breaches constitute fraud, theft and unjust damage. Restitution for the harm done is a significant duty since it safeguards the public peace and is an exercise of mutual good will and freedom. Social and ecological justice is concerned with personal responsibility for the community and its members and that civil laws and structures do not impose unnecessary burdens and suffering on its citizens. It oversees the instruments of governmental power to ensure they are compassionate to its citizens and respectful of the environment (Hollenbach, 1992). These three dimensions of justice protect the environment and the equality of people in society.

Society and its structures will flourish if they serve the person justly and also respect non-human creation. It is within the web of social duties that our responsibilities to non-human creation and to other people arise. As a consequence, society must respect individual human rights and recognise its duties to the wider environment. Human rights are claims made on others and society to respect the needs of persons (food, clothing, education, culture, health, information etc.). Human beings are endowed by the Creator with natural gifts of freedom, rationality and will. Through these gifts, people seek truth, beauty, and goodness. These gifts of God are the basis for the natural rights to which humans lay claim to what they are due (e.g. right to life, right not to be sexually abused). These rights or claims are expressed personally (life, freedom, religion), socially (food, housing, just wages) and instrumentally (unemployment benefits, migration, political participation). (Hollenbach, 1992). Rights are like a net which protect our God-given human dignity (Cronin, 1992). The theology of human dignity recognises that, because of baptism and faith in Christ, believers are raised to a new life of equality and unity as members of the people of God (Jn 1:12).

While we have rights, we also have duties to others and to non-human creation. Christians are motivated to act out of a sense of duty because of the love command of Jesus (Mt 22: 34-40; Lk 10: 9-37) and because the Divine is present in all created reality. While Christian love is the basic motivation for our duties, this does not mean that we end up morally exhausted. There are limits to our duties. Time, location, circumstances, complexity, proximity of kinship, and the proportionality of the needs of each being constitute the frame for determining our ethics of duty (Spohn, 1992). However, duties also exist at times when no rights are claimed. For example, the Christian love command obliges us to love our enemies. Our enemies and those who have hurt us, however, have no right or entitlement to our forgiveness.

While the common or public good is an important good, there is a tendency for some to merge the needs of the person into the anonymous collective (dictatorships). A healthy attitude of suspicion towards such interpretations of the common good is important because some of them have been oppressive. There is also a tendency in our modern democratic societies to consider individuals as moral strangers separated from communities and traditions. This overemphasis on the individual can have a destabilising effect on the good of the community. In our pluralist societies, which are also multi-faith and multicultural, we are called to be open to new forms of community. This calls for toleration, co-operation and compromise. There is also an obligation to be hospitable and welcoming to groups that have been marginalised, like the homosexual and lesbian communities. Any notion of the common good which does not permit people to develop (physically, mentally, culturally and spiritually) and fulfil their true potential is contrary to the dignity of the human person. The common good includes persons, personal relationships, political structures, cultural expression and the non-human world to which we relate. It is a complex and inclusive notion of the common good which will involve a nuanced and prudent evaluation of competing needs and interests.

> Draw from the foregoing section some principles of Catholic social justice thought.

A Sense of Conscience

Conscience describes the individual person striving out of love for the truth, and a judgement of what is morally right in the circumstances (Aquinas, in Suttor, 1974). The practical role of conscience is concerned with taking responsibility before God for choices freely made. Many demands are made on our conscience today. For example, while people are dying of hunger and lack basic necessities, we in the west are well off and comfortable. Given the Church's option for the poor, the question is how we should behave in a way that is decent, humane and Christian? Should I spend that hard earned money on gifts or on a holiday at the beach or donate it to a charity to help ease the burden and suffering of others? (Hallett, 1998).

Conscience, is not a Jiminy Cricket voice that keeps us right, or rings the alarm bells when something is wrong. Nor is conscience simply a matter of feelings, or a subjective hunch motivated by love. The horizon of the Christian conscience is a call to live out the truth in love and wisdom, as was done by Christ. Hence, we turn to the Church and its teaching to sustain us in our judgements.

Another way of talking about conscience is to refer to the "heart" of the person. Sometimes we say a person's heart is "hardened." In this sense people become insensitive to others (family hardships, bullying, sickness, unemployment and so on) and to the will of God in their lives. It is within our "hearts" that we know we have wronged others, and it is also within our hearts that we listen to God's voice in order to do what is right. However, we have to be attentive to the voice of our own prejudices and assumptions (e.g. attitudes to other religions and races). It is the "heart" of the person (Jer 31: 31-33; Ez 36: 26-27; Rom 2: 14-15) that is converted and renewed by the grace of the Spirit. This renewal of our "hearts" is characterised by the call to love God and our neighbour (Mt 22:39; Mk 12: 28f; Jn 13:34; Rom 13: 1-11). From this perspective the moral life is viewed as a journey towards the good or as a journey of love. The pain of remorse which follows failure to love is an acknowledgement that we have failed to appreciate the preciousness and dignity of the human person. We realise we have committed moral evil. This is the experience of a bad conscience. The Church, aware of the reality of evil and of the ambiguity of the human condition places itself at the service of conscience in the search for the good and on the journey of conversion (John Paul II, 1993). As Catholic Christians, we are obliged to listen to the Church's teaching as we search for what is true and right (Miller, 1996).

Conscience also needs the intellectual and moral virtue of prudence/ practical wisdom (Greek *phronesis*, Latin *prudentia*) to ensure that the act of conscience makes the morally right decision in practice (Aquinas, in Gilby, 1974). Prudence or right judgement is shaped by love and the life of grace and it gives direction to reason. A prudent judgement deliberates on what practically ought to be done in a particular situation. For example, should we permit supervised drug injection rooms? To assist this deliberation, prudence/practical wisdom also looks for good advice, consults widely and develops self-corrective reflection. This involves both caution and risk (Aquinas, *Summa Theologiae: Prudence.* 2a2ae. 51, 1-4, 95-131). The caution is involved in making careful and reflective judgements, and the accompanying risk - to varying degrees- is upon all human action in a complex and unpredictable world. Basically, prudence is a skill that comes through seasoned practice.

Try to come up with a definition of conscience from the material provided here.

A Sense of Embodiment

The human person is a multi-dimensional being and the bodily dimension is basic. Bodiliness includes, matter, DNA, the biological, the chemical, physical, psychological, vegetative, sentient, emotional, spiritual and rational dimensions. It is through our bodies that we relate to God, other people, animals and the world. The human person is an embodied subject in time and culture who is also part of the wider created reality. Through the physical body of the human person, the material world of matter reaches personal self-awareness and is transformed into the praise of the creator.

This person-centred vision respects the created world and other living beings such as animals. Animals are intrinsically valuable in themselves and because of their experiences and purposes. Rocks and mountains, however, have an intrinsic value for others. This intrinsic value lies in the fact that rocks, and mountains provide the objective foundation of value for others. The beautiful red colour of Ayres rock, for example, is valuable for humans and possibly animals.

The task given by God to humans is to develop a rational and emotional awareness of the needs of the embodied self within the context of the wider created reality. The physical body as the exterior is inseparably linked to the interior. In other words, the human person is a psychosomatic unity of mind, spirit and body. In the past, one extreme spirituality was to exaggerate the spiritual over the physical, as if the spirit was locked inside the body as in a cage. This form of spirituality emerged from a dualism which saw the body as inferior to the soul and culture separate from nature. In this view, the body was seen as simply an instrument of very little value. This often justified torture and slavery and the exploitation of non-human creation. This double aspect of the dignity of the human person derives from the body-soul unity. New forms of genetic manipulation such as cloning raise new ethical challenges to what it means to be an embodied human person. The transfer of genes between animals and humans and other species also raises new ethical concerns about the manipulation of nature. Biotechnologists promise us a land of "milk and honey." However, the environmental catastrophe has made us cautious about the hype of unfulfilled promises. The tools of biotechnology may make a profit for business corporations but it may leave the planet and the human person undermined in the process.

Personhood is based on the being of human nature and this includes the biological which is integral to human nature (Ford, 1998). This is a non-dualist perspective, which recognises the unity and diversity between body and soul. The human foetus in the womb is ontologically a person already, but it does not have the maturity it will acquire in the years ahead. It is the same person as the adult but what changes is the physical size, development and the personality. The human person is dependent on creation, God, others and society to achieve this. Every individual with a rational nature, and this includes new-born infants who are brain-damaged or physically impaired, is a person (Ford, 1998). Human nature enables newborn infants to grow into rationally self-conscious beings, when they can express themselves in free and loving responsible actions. They are the same individuals before the age of reason as they are at their commencement. This also applies to people who suffer from forms of dementia, such as Alzheimer's disease. Persons are autonomous, communicate their inner life to another, engage in meaningful and insightful conversation about the truth, have a lasting sense of self, make choices and express these in language. The human person has specific needs, character and attributes embodied in a rational and spiritual nature. Through our bodies it is acknowledged that humans have arisen from the earth and share many dimensions with the animal, vegetative and material world. These five senses give a blue print for living life with dignity and with decency. They are one way of looking at what constitutes a foundation stone of Catholic moral theology.

References and further reading

Aquinas, T. *Summa Theologiae: Prudence. 2a2ae. 47, 3, 5, 8; 48, 1-8.* ed., Thomas Gilby (1974). Vol. 36. London: Blackfriars.

Aquinas, T. *Summa Theologiae: Man 1a.79, 13.* ed., Timothy Suttor, (1974) Vol. 18. London: Blackfriars.

Byrne, B. (1996). *Romans.* Collegeville, Minn: Liturgical Press.

Cronin, K. (1992). *Rights and Christian Ethics.* Cambridge, [England]; New York: Cambridge University Press), Pp. 131-133, 163, 250-253.

Dawkins, R. (1989).*The Selfish Gene.* revised ed. Oxford: University Press .Pp, 2-4, 18-19, 44-45, 60, 112, 192, 267-268.

Finnis, J. (1980) *Natural Law and Natural Rights.* Oxford: Clarendon Press. Pp 163, 166.

Flannery, A. ed., (1996). *Vatican Council II. Vol 1, The Conciliar and Postconciliar Documents,* new rev ed, Dublin: Dominican Publications.

Ford, N. (1988). When did I Begin? Conception of the Human Individual in History, *Philosophy and Science.* Cambridge: Cambridge University Press, Pp. 77-78, 82.

Gula, R. (1989). *Reason Informed by Faith: Foundations of Catholic Morality.* New York: Paulist Press. Pp. 130-135.

Hallet, G. (1998). *Priorities and Christian Ethics.* Cambridge: Cambridge University Press.

Hollenbach D. (1979). *Claims in Conflict.* New York: Paulist Press. Pp. 144-148.

Kelly, K. (1992). *New Directions in Moral Theology: The Challenge of Being Human.* New York: G. Chapman.

Mafico, T. (1992).Just, Justice, In David Noel. Freedman, ed., *The Anchor Bible Dictionary Vol. 3.* London: Doubleday.

Miller, M. (1996). *The Encyclicals of John Paul II.* Huntington; Indiana: Our Sunday Visitor.

O'Connell, T. (1990) *Principles for a Catholic Morality.* revised edition San Francisco: Harper and Row.

Pope John Paul II, (1993). *Veritatis Splendor: On Certain Fundamental Questions of the Church's Moral Teaching.* Homebush: St. Pauls.

Scullion, J. 'Righteousness: Old Testament,' 724-736 In D. Freedman, ed., *The Anchor Bible Dictionary,* Vol 5.London: Doubleday.

Spohn, W. (1992) The Return of Virtue Ethics. *Theological Studies,* 53, 74.

CHAPTER 20

Developing a Catholic Spirituality

Kath Engebretson

Introduction

Everyone has a spiritual dimension to their lives, just as they have physical, social, intellectual, emotional, and psychological dimensions. For some the spiritual dimension is fundamental to all others, and contributes in a special way to the person's identity. Spirituality is concerned with the meaning of life, with whether and how God can be known, with the questions of why we are here, why life is as it is, the mystery of suffering and evil, how we should live and what we hope for. All religions of the world confront these questions and respond to them in their different ways. Pope John Paul II wrote that these are: *questions that have their common source in the quest for meaning that has always compelled the human heart. In fact, the answer given to these questions decides the direction which people seek to give to their lives (Fides et Ratio [FR] #1).*

Religions put a shape and form on spirituality and gives it expression. In the responses they give to the fundamental questions of life they propose a Buddhist spirituality, a Hindu spirituality, a Jewish spirituality, a Muslim spirituality or a Christianity spirituality. Within Christianity then there are spiritualities that emerge from the different Churches such as Anglican spirituality, or Lutheran spirituality. There is a specific Christian spirituality that has a Catholic shape and form. It has a great deal in common with the spiritualities of other Christian Churches, and indeed with other religions, but it has a particular Catholic character. Many people construct the expression of their spirituality from a range of different sources, but here we consider the specific hallmarks of Catholic spirituality, the development of which is central to the vocation of the baptised Catholic, and is of interest to all who work in Catholic schools.

What is Catholic spirituality?

Within Catholicism there are many traditions of spirituality. For example, each of the religious orders has developed a spirituality of its own with particular emphases. In this chapter we reflect on the particular aspects of lay spirituality within the contemporary Catholic Church. It is not an exhaustive list of aspects, for each person will bring to their Catholic spirituality their own emphases, but the list of aspects that follows helps us to begin to define what we mean by Catholic spirituality.

A God–centred spirituality. Catholic spirituality affirms that God exists, and that God is personal and in a loving relationship with the human community and each individual. God gives life and is present and active in the lives of individuals and communities. God's providence, that is the divine plan for the human community and each individual in it, can be trusted. God wills the best for each person and invites them to a life of love now and beyond death.

A Trinitarian spirituality. Catholic spirituality affirms that God is one in three persons, Father, Son and Holy Spirit. This Trinitarian belief in God is revealed through the New Testament, and was given specific shape by the Councils of the Church up to the fifth century. In the Trinity Catholics acknowledge God the Father, the one God who invited Israel into covenant and whom Jesus of Nazareth worshipped. They acknowledge God the Son, the pre-existent Word of God made flesh in Jesus Christ. Finally they acknowledge God the Holy Spirit, the advocate, teacher and counsellor sent by the Father to guide and teach the Christian community. These are not three Gods but one God revealing three different persons.

A spirituality of revelation. Catholic spirituality is based on the belief that God can be known, for God is revealed in the Scriptures, in the history and tradition of the Church, in creation, in human life, human events and human history, both at community and individual levels. Most of all God can be known in Jesus Christ, God's Word made flesh.

A gospel spirituality. Catholic spirituality is based on the life and teachings of Jesus of Nazareth, who is recognised as God the Son the second person of the Trinity. The four gospels contain his teaching and vision of life, and they are fundamental to Catholic spirituality. Along with the gospels are the other apostolic writings. These are also contained in the New Testament and they amplify the teachings of Christ in the gospels, spelling out the way of life of a Christian and of a Christian community.

A Eucharistic spirituality. Fundamental to Catholic spirituality is the celebration of the Eucharist. In the Eucharist Christ is encountered in his life, death and resurrection, and the mystery of God's love and the salvation he offers in Christ are made present. Under the forms of bread and wine Christ comes among his people, and effects for them the salvation won by his love and obedience. In this sacramental presence of Christ and his salvation, all of human life is transformed and graced.

A sacramental spirituality. Just as human life is marked by a number of stages from birth to death, the Catholic life is marked by sacramental celebrations that deepen the individual's belonging within the Catholic community. In this pattern of celebrations are the sacraments of initiation, Baptism, Confirmation and Eucharistic, the sacraments of healing, Reconciliation and Anointing of the Sick, and the sacraments of commitment, Marriage and Holy Orders.

A spirituality of grace. Grace refers to all that God gives, the gift of Christ, the gift of the Holy Spirit, and the gift of God's life, which allows people to share in the life of God. Christians are assured that God's grace in their lives is constant. Grace also refers to the many small and large gifts that God gives throughout life. It may be given in the strength to follow a particular right action, the strength to remain faithful to conscience; the strength to do the right thing in a relationship. It may be a sense of the presence of God, or a sense of confidence in God's help. Through grace the person is assisted by God in the challenges of living daily life.

A spirituality of conscience. The moral life is an important aspect of Catholic spirituality. It is formed by the ten commandments and the teachings of Christ, by the later teachings of the Church about the moral life, and by the body of Catholic social teaching. Fundamental to the Catholic moral life is the importance of an informed conscience, which helps the Catholic to make decisions about moral issues and to have an informed perspective on the ethical issues of the day.

A spirituality of justice and peace. Catholic spirituality is informed by a rich body of social teaching, which emphasises the principles of human dignity; community and the common good, social justice and human rights; an option for the poor and the vulnerable, participation, the dignity of work and the rights of workers, stewardship of creation, human solidarity, subsidiarity and peace.

A spirituality of hope. Catholic spirituality is full of hope. This hope comes from a belief that the reign of God, already present within life, will ultimately come in its fullness. In a Catholic way of life, hope for the full coming of God' reign is combined with action to bring it about. Hope is centred on the final coming of Christ's kingdom of justice love and peace, and so the Catholic seeks these things in daily life and works for their increase.

A spirituality of love. In Catholic spirituality, love is central. This does not necessarily refer to the emotions. Christian love is decision, a responsible choice or commitment that one makes. It refers to the goodwill, compassion, kindness and justice that the Catholic offers to others, and to the human community.

A communal spirituality. Catholic spirituality is not individualistic, but is lived out constantly in the in the community of the Church. This community includes all those in the local and Australian Church as well as those who belong to the universal Catholic Church. It includes all who have gone before in previous generations, the saints and martyrs, and those who have died in the Catholic community. Catholic spirituality then has past, present and future dimensions.

A spirituality open to others. Work for Christian unity is enjoined upon every Christian, and inter-religious dialogue is part of the Church's evangelizing mission. Catholic spirituality involves a respectful, open invitation and listening to other denominations and religions, from the firm ground of our own tradition. In this dialogue we come to know our own Catholicism more deeply, and also enter with empathy into the world of the other.

A Marian spirituality. Catholic spirituality includes the ancient tradition of honouring Mary the mother of Jesus, who has been pronounced *theotokos* or Mother of God by the Church. Many Catholics have a special devotion to Mary calling upon her to intercede for them before God.

A spirituality of prayer. Catholic spirituality involves a commitment to prayer, both personal and public. Prayer can be formal, as in liturgy or paraliturgy, or it may be a private lifting of the heart and mind to God. Prayer involves praise of God, asking God for help, thanking God for his gifts, and seeking God's forgiveness. The many traditional prayers of the Church can help Catholics to pray. "Pray any way you like, so long as you do pray." advised Pope John Paul II.

- What, for you, are the differences between spirituality and religion?
- Do you agree that religion can be one way of expressing spirituality?
- What are important aspects of your own spirituality?
- How much is your spirituality expressed through Catholicism?
- From the list of aspects of Catholic spirituality above, which ones are most important to you and why?

References and Further Reading

Dreyer, E. (1995). Christian Spirituality. In R.McBrien (Gen Ed). *The Harper Collins Encyclopedia of Catholicism*. San Francisco: Harper Collins.

Hughes, P. (2007). *Putting Life Together. Findings from Australian Youth Spirituality Research*. Nunawading, Victoria: Christian Research Association.

Rausch, T. (2006). *Being Catholic in a Culture of Choice*. Collegeville, Minnesota: Liturgical Press.

CHAPTER 21

The Role and Vocation of the Religious Educator

Michael T. Buchanan

Introduction

The Catholic school is a privileged environment where Christian education is carried out. The schools are places of evangelization, of complete formation of the human person (Congregation for Catholic Education, 1998) and they participate in the Church's mission to "tell the truth of Jesus Christ" (Pope John Paul II, 2001). Teachers of religious education undertake an important role within the Church. The extent to which a school is able to realise its aims and participate in the mission of the Church depends primarily on the teachers (Congregation for Catholic Education, 1982). The role of the religious education teacher is perceived as both a vocation as well as a profession. (Ryan, Brennan & Willmet, 1996). Therefore teachers of religious education are in a privilege position because they are able to support the whole school community in its articulation a Catholic view and way of relating in the world.

Vocation

In some Church documents, teaching in a Catholic school is described as a vocation within the Christian tradition. Teaching is understood as a vocation in situations where teachers see their role as one that serves the Church. Helping the Church to fulfil its mission is central to any act of service to the Church. Teachers of religious education serve the Church by providing opportunities for students to be formed in the life of the Church, as well as preparing them for service in the Church and the world. This understanding of teaching as a vocation is portrayed by the Congregation for Catholic Education.

The vocation of every Catholic educator includes the work of ongoing social development: to form men and women who will be ready to take their place in society, preparing them in such a way that they will make the kind of social commitment which will enable them to work for the improvement of social structures, making these structures more conformed to the principles of the Gospel. Thus, they will form human beings who will make human society more peaceful, fraternal, and communitarian. (Congregation for Catholic Education, 1982).

Pope John Paul II (2001) considered the formation of students to be an integral role of a person committed to the vocation of teaching. "For lay people involved, teaching is more than a profession; it is a vocation to form students, a widespread and indispensable lay service to the Church." Lay teachers who perceive teaching as a vocation are able to provide a model of the role of a lay person within the Church. The Sacred Congregation for Catholic Education emphasises the importance of this role modelling within the Church.

> Lay educators must bring the experience of their own lives to this social development and social awareness, so that students can be prepared to take their place in society with an appreciation of the specific role of the lay person - for this is the life that nearly all of the students will be called to live. (Congregation for Catholic Education, 1982, par 19)

Through their vocation teachers of religious education are able to assist students in engaging meaningfully in many aspects of school life which help to form them in the life of the Church. Some aspects of school life where a teacher's own witness to the faith tradition might inspire students are: prayerful participation in liturgical and prayer experiences, community service programs, social justice initiatives, retreats, and opportunities for students to nurture their faith.

The religious education teacher: A vocation and/or profession
Discuss whether the role of the religious education teacher is a vocation or profession or both?

Profession

Teachers of religious education hold not only an important role within the Church but also within Catholic education. They are subject to the same professional expectations as any other educators. One distinguishing feature of teaching as a profession is the expectation that teachers have undergone formation and formalised training in their area of expertise as an educator. Professionals are also appointed to the role or task of teaching and are paid a salary to perform a high quality service. The teaching profession has a clear career path and teachers are committed to ongoing professional development (Ryan, Brennan & Willmet, 1996). Within the context of Catholic education the complementary nature of the bi-dimensional role of the religious education teacher in terms of vocation and profession contribute to the formation of the student in the life of the Church.

Buchanan and Hyde (2006) reported on the perceptions that Religious Education Coordinators (RECs) in Catholic secondary schools held about the role of teachers of religious education. The RECs revealed five areas pertinent to the role of the religious education teacher, and they did not distinguish between the vocational and professional dimensions of the role. They perceived the role as requiring qualified professionals who were also committed to ongoing formation in the Catholic tradition, as well as witnesses and portrayers of the image of a Catholic school. The role of the religious education teacher was also perceived as one responsible for delivering high quality religious education curriculum. Buchanan and Hyde (2006) found that the REC's perceptions of the role of religious education teachers were consistent with perceptions portrayed within Church documents.

Qualified professionals

The RECs perceived qualifications in religious education as a very important factor. They felt that teachers who were not qualified and did not have a strong background in the knowledge content associated with the discipline, were not able to dialogue with students in a way that linked knowledge and faith. The Congregation for Catholic Education (1977) alluded to the importance of religious qualifications for teacher of religion. The Congregation suggested that the school has a responsibility to support teachers in attaining relevant qualifications. "The school must do everything in its power to aid the Church to fulfil its catechetical mission and so must have the best possible qualified teachers of religion" (Congregation for Catholic Education, 1977). In 1982 the Congregation encouraged bishops to promote and provide opportunities for lay teachers within Catholic schools to gain qualifications in religious education thus emphasising the importance of qualification for lay teachers of religion in contributing to the formation of students.

With appropriate degrees, and with an adequate preparation in religious pedagogy, they will have the basic training, both for teachers of religion and for catechist; at the same time, they will not neglect the kind of dialogue with the corps of teachers being formed that can be mutually enlightening. (Congregation for Catholic Education, 1982, par 66)

A commitment to ongoing formation

The RECs believed that it was important that teachers of religious education pay ongoing attention to their own personal and faith formation. This was viewed as very important in enabling the teacher to further engage in the Catholic faith tradition as well as reflect an ability and willingness to dialogue with the faith tradition. Buchanan and Hyde (2006) report one REC's contention which expressed a shared responsibility on the part of the school to provide opportunities for teachers to attend to their own formation.

Opportunities for spiritual formation are vital, particularly for young adults. But it is also important for adults who for whatever reason have become disconnected from their tradition, and for those who are neither aggressive towards it, nor dismissive of it, but where the tradition has failed to find a place to be nurtured in their lives. I think we are responsible for that. We talk about ourselves as the Church, and so I think we have to take responsibility for that. (Buchanan & Hyde, 2006)

Central to the mission of the Church is the formation of the whole person and Catholic schools form part of the saving mission of the Church, especially for education in the faith (Congregation for Catholic Education, 1977). This issue was explored further within the context of Catholic schools in *Lay Catholics in Schools: Witnesses to Faith* (Congregation for Catholic Education, 1982). It emphasised a need for continuous and ongoing religious formation for lay Catholic religious educators and acknowledge that it was not only a personal responsibility of the teacher but a responsibility of the Catholic community.

Lay Catholic educators also have a right to expect that, within the ecclesial community, bishops, priests, and Religious, especially those dedicated to the apostolate of education, and also various groups and associations of lay Catholic educators, will help to awaken them to their personal needs in the area of formation, and will find means to stimulate them so that they can give themselves more totally to the social commitment that such a formation requires (Congregation for Catholic Education, 1982)

Opportunities to engage in ongoing personal and faith formation
Make a list of possible opportunities a teacher might have to engage in ongoing personal and faith formation in the Catholic school.

A witness

A teacher's ability to give witness to the Catholic faith tradition was perceived as vitally important for the school to make a significant contribution to the formation of young people. Some RECs suggested that without authentic witness to the Catholic faith by the teacher, students would not perceive religious education as meaningful. Buchanan and Hyde (2006) report the following reflection from one REC:

> We have large numbers of staff who don't practice their faith in terms of Mass attendance and so forth. I think this has an enormous bearing on their ability to teach RE given that the primary gift of the RE teacher is to be a witness. I would much rather have someone who was whole heartedly convinced of the Catholic faith teaching RE, than someone who simply has a qualification. The kids see straight through it. If a teacher is teaching math, and feels that math is meaningless, the kids pick up on it, even if the teacher is teaching well. A large role of the RE teacher is to be an evangelist.

Pope John VI emphasised this point succinctly stressing that, "Modern man [*sic*] listens more willingly to witnesses than to teachers, and if he does listen to teachers, it is because they are witnesses" (1975). The faith witness of the lay educator provides students with a living and believable example of what it means to live as a lay Christian in the world. This witness of the teacher provides an opportunity for the students to realise that Christian behaviour is not an impossible ideal.

> Conduct is always much more important than speech; this fact becomes especially important in the formation period of students. The more completely an educator can give concrete witness to the model of the ideal person that is being presented to the students, the more this ideal will be believed and imitated. For it will then be seen as something reasonable and worthy of being lived, something concrete and realizable. It is in this context that the faith witness of the lay teacher becomes especially important. Students should see in their teachers the Christian attitude and behaviour that is often so conspicuously absent from the secular atmosphere in which they live. Without this witness, living in such an atmosphere, they may begin to regard Christian behaviour as an impossible ideal. (Congregation for Catholic Education, 1982, pat 32)

Portrays the image of a Catholic school

The RECs perceived the role of the religious education teacher as one that freely and willingly mirrors the image of the Catholic tradition. Teachers fulfil a significant role in portraying the culture and image of a Catholic school. "By their witness and their behaviour teachers are the first importance to impart a distinctive character to Catholic schools" (Congregation for Catholic Education, 1977, par 78). The image of a Catholic school portrayed by the teacher can be viewed from an internal and external perspective. A lay teacher has a tremendous responsibility to portray and a particular image of the school and that is presumably a Catholic image. Church documents acknowledge the significant responsibility lay teachers in Catholic schools have inherited.

> Catholic Teachers who freely accept posts in schools, which have a distinctive character, are obliged to respect that character and give their active support to it under the direction of those responsible. (Congregation for Catholic Education, 1977, par 80)

The Second Vatican Council's *Decree on the Apostolate of the Laity* states that, "the layman [sic] is at the same time a believer and a citizen and should be constantly led by Christian conscience alone" (Apostolicam Actuositatem, 1965, par 5). From this perspective it is arguable that the role of a lay teacher in a Catholic school extends beyond a professional role to a holistic way of life and living.

Challenges faced by teachers

What challenges might the above excerpt from the *Decree on the Apostolate of the Laity* pose for teachers in a Catholic school?

High quality curriculum

The RECs also perceived the role of the religion teacher to be one responsible for delivering a high quality curriculum. This was understood by the RECs to mean that a teacher was able to help students to gain an adequate understanding of Church doctrine and an ability to converse with that doctrine in a manner that enabled them to reflect on the place of that doctrine within their own lives (Buchanan & Hyde, 2006). It was acknowledged that religious education involved much more than the passing on of religious knowledge. In addition, to this religious education teachers are also concerned with the contribution that learning and teaching in religious education makes to the personal and faith formation of the student. As such the religious education teacher is called to be a deliverer of high quality curriculum.

> Without entering into the problem of teaching in schools, it must be emphasised that, while such teaching is not merely confined to "religious classes" within the school curriculum, it must nevertheless explicitly and in a systematic manner to prevent distortion in the child's mind between general and religious culture. The fundamental difference between religious and other forms of education is that its aim is not simply intellectual assent to religious truths but also a total commitment of one's whole being to the Person of Christ. (Congregation for Catholic Education, 1997, par 50)

The nexus between religious education and other aspects of Catholic education find expression in the development of a student's whole being in Christ. To this end the emphasis Catholic schools place on a high quality curriculum and its delivery is very important. The ability to deliver a high quality curriculum in religious education and other curriculum areas is essential in any educational context that aims to develop the whole person (Buchanan & Hyde, 2006). The Congregation for the Clergy (1998) has stressed the requirement that religious education in Catholic schools as equally important as any other discipline area with in the school curriculum and teachers play a very important role in this.

> It is necessary, therefore that religious instruction in schools appear as a scholastic discipline with the same systematic demands and the same rigour as other disciplines. It must present the Christian message and the Christian event with the same seriousness and the same depth with which other disciplines present their knowledge. (Congregation for the Clergy, 1998, par 73)

Employment in a Catholic school

When seeking employment in a Catholic school, potential employees are asked to consider their commitment to a Catholic education philosophy. It is expected that teachers will have an adequate understanding of Catholic teaching relevant to their discipline area and other aspects of their work. It is also expected that teachers will model behaviour that reflects an appreciation of Catholic values and teachings. Some employment teaching contracts contain expectations similar to those listed in the table below.

An example of employment expectations for teachers in Catholic schools

Your acceptance of this offer of employment will be taken to mean that you have accepted basic requirements of the school as conditional to your employment in that you

i.   Accept the Catholic educational philosophy of the school;
ii. Develop and maintain adequate understanding of those aspects of the Catholic teaching that touch upon your work;
iii. By your work and personal example strive to help students to understand, accept and appreciate Catholic teaching and values; avoid, whether by word, action or known life-style, influence upon students that is contrary to teaching and values in the Church community in whose name you act;...

Discuss each of the above employment expectations.

- Is it appropriate for employers of teachers in Catholic schools to require such expectations?
- Should these expectations be required of personnel employed in a Catholic school or teachers only?
- Should employment expectations of religious education teachers differ to those of other classroom teacher in a Catholic school? If so in what way? If not why not?

References and Further Reading

Buchanan, M. T. & Hyde, B. (2006). The role of the religion teacher: Ecclesial and pedagogical perceptions. *Journal of Christian Education, 49* (2), 23-34.

Congregation for Catholic Education (1977). *The Catholic School.* Homebush, NSW: St Paul's Publications.

Congregation for Catholic Education. (1982). *Lay Catholics in schools: Witnesses to faith.* Sydney: St Paul's Publications.

Congregation for Catholic Education. (1998). *The Catholic school on the threshold of the third millennium.* Boston: Pauline Books and Media.

Congregation for the Clergy. (1998). *General directory for catechesis.* Australia: St Paul's.

Paul VI. (1975). *Evangelii nuntiandi.*
*http://www.vatican.va/holy_father/paul_vi/apost_exhortations/documents/hf-vi_*
exh_19751208_evangelii-nuntiandi_en.html

John Paul II. (2001). *Ecclesia in Oceania: The Church in Oceania.* NSW: St Paul's Publications.

Ryan, M., Brennan, D. & Willmet, T. (1996). *Catholic schools Australian landscapes: Resources for creating distinctive Catholic schools.* Australia: Social Science Press.

Second Vatican Council, (1965). Decree on the Apostolate of the Laity "Apostolicam Actuositatem" In A. Flannery, (Ed.). (1981) *Vatican Council II: The concilliar and post con*